A Ligurian Odyssey

ISBN (Print): 978-1-7336161-1-9

Interior design by Booknook.biz.

A Ligurian Odyssey

Alan R. Fridkin

*Dedicated to the Mantellassi and Viglietti
Families who have shared their friendship,
knowledge and love of Alassio with us*

Preface

One of our bookcases is full of memoirs of folks who upped stakes and bought one-way tickets to a foreign country. This journal celebrates a place we consider a second home. But we have only gone half native in Liguria. We have grown to love, and to some measure understand and contribute to this patch of territory. There are no illusions about its long-term problems and our inability to solve them. This is a different form of ex-pat behavior, caught between two cultures and countries. Maybe tomorrow we will buy those one-way tickets. Maybe not.

One president of the insurance company I worked for over many decades said: "you can never be too careful in picking your parents." He was thinking of health and insurability. That luck of the draw also impacts your direction in life. My father was a professional musician and wanderer. My mother preferred to stay at home. In that respect, I have more of his genes.

Perhaps it's a genetic flaw or a character defect. Often, I would rather be somewhere else. Each trip, to new or familiar territory, is planned with exhilaration. An appetite for being on the road has not diminished now that I have mostly gray hair. Away from home, there are the perennial questions: why have people chosen to live here? Are they content? What would it be like to call this place home? Of thousands of places, most viewed fleetingly, several dozen evoke deep affection. A few are very hard to leave.

Like a good piece of music or a fine meal, they stay with and in you. They enliven the senses and spirit. Only Paris and Alassio have tempted us to move. The many lures of Paris are obvious; that of Alassio less so. Life seems better when we are in either place. Both sing for my wife and me. They are lovely venues filled with many singular and appealing people.

With an affinity for saltwater, we have traveled almost every mile of the European and North American coastlines and many ports and shores elsewhere. Sea, sand, sun, transients and locals intersect in myriad places. The difference between commodity and community lies in the inhabitants. With more than sixty years of travel under the belt, it's a question of where do we hear the siren song and want to be when it stops.

Bear with me, while I speed through the first half of my life.

Table of Contents

01

Before and On Station

The first time I entered paradise, I was 24. It was probably the second most important day of my life and remembered as clearly as if it were yesterday. Five decades on, I close my eyes and am there once again. But let's go back a few frames.

There was a war going on. While Vietnam wasn't the most popular or noble one, I had long considered a military career. When you are in your twenties, brought up on Conrad and Melville and have spent six years in college, it seemed long past time to enter the real world. I had broken up hard with a girl and no longer enjoyed law school. The French Foreign Legion was not an option. A sixth winter in Ithaca was taking its toll. My father had worked his way around the world with a band in his twenties. I was still in the library. He continued to sail on passenger ships until a few months before he died when I was nine. I had made two trips to South America with him before becoming a teenager. It was time to jump ship, or more accurately, on to one.

Memories of those early trips were part of my DNA. There was the smell of coffee off the coastline of Santos, Brazil wafting from long conveyor belts on the piers. Watching enthusiastic passengers dancing for hours while my dad's band played rumbas, sambas and tangoes in a warmly lit floating ballroom. Nights filled with thousands of stars as we coursed through the South Atlantic. Rio was eye poppingly beautiful and Buenos Aires had a European elegance even for a very young boy. After gut wrenching foghorn blasts, I could still see our ship gliding to or from some foreign pier.

After my dad was gone, my mother went back to work. Women had fewer career options then. She was an executive secretary, an interior decorator, a small hotel manager and always willing to sacrifice too much for my benefit.

I knew she worked very long hours, but was blissfly ignorant that we were only slightly better off than poor. As an only child, I both appreciated and resented her singular focus on my future. The missing male influence was replaced through scouting and summer camps in Maine and Cape Cod. Her perserverance earned an Eagle Scout badge as much as I did.

I missed my dad, but then I had a lot of practice. He had spent more time at sea than on dry land. Once, in a week between cruises, he tried to make it up to us. We saw two Broadway shows in a day, with a Chinese dinner in between. When I asked if we could go to a western movie afterwards, he agreed. When off the ships, he worked nightclubs and hotels. His day job was preparing for his night job. Ebbets Field was three blocks from our apartment. Just once, together, we saw our beloved Dodgers. I often played sandlot ball in their parking lot.

He had no time or inclination to give an eight-year old career counseling, although he taught me how to tie a Windsor tie knot. I wasn't allowed to study piano until after his passing. He had started violin at 5. Once I had a birthday call from him in Buenos Aires. It sounded like he was 5,000 miles away.

There were a handful of indelible memories after his death. Like a jigsaw puzzle, the rest was put together from sporadic conversations with my mother, short visits from the guys in his band who kept in touch, some recordings, and a few boxes of old photographs. Our apartment bookshelves were filled with his sheet music and travel books. I was shielded from the pain of his last illness, and the joy of knowing him more.

A first effort to chart my own course involved joining the Sea Explorers. It entailed more than an hour's journey by bus to the flat outer reaches of Brooklyn. At the end of the bus line, where the city ends and the sea begins, the adult leaders took us by car to Floyd Bennett Naval Air Station or to a reconditioned World War II LCVP landing craft. We cruised on weekends into Long Island Sound or up along the Connecticut Shore Line. It was invigorating stuff for a 14-year-old city kid who didn't even have his own bike.

We bought real Navy uniforms outside the old Brooklyn Naval Shipyard. A gangly 6 foot two, I hid my bell bottom trousers, jumper and Cracker Jack hat under a civilian coat until near the end of the bus line. On cold fall and winter nights, the crowded city streets gradually slipped away until what was left was marshland barely above water. Nothing stopped the wind. The sky was surprisingly dark and cold on the outskirts of the city. At the base gym, we practiced close order drill, learned seamanship skills and planned for our next trip into coastal waters.

For four years, I rode the subway into lower Manhattan to attend the then all boys Stuyvesant High School. It was renowned for its science and math training. Fortunately for me, I also had an off-Broadway actor as an English teacher and a Greenwich Village sculptor for art. In the private recesses of my mind, the career path changed from astronomer, to airline pilot, merchant marine captain and by graduation, potential English professor.

In spare hours, I walked the piers along the Hudson and East Rivers daydreaming of distant lands. When I could, I boarded vessels to meet Deck Officers. I never fancied myself in the Engine Room. The Seamen's Church Institute had an incredible ship model collection, original Conrad manuscripts and enough old salts hanging around to fill the air with tales' stranger than fiction. With an appointment to the U.S. Merchant Marine Academy, I was heading to sea until spooked by a national strike by the Masters, Mates and Pilots Union. Who wants to be out of work half way around the world?

There are moments in life when the next step sneaks up on you. In a few minutes you need to make a major decision and not look back. Tom Carson was an odd duck, a tall, thin and uncommonly friendly Assistant Admission Officer at Cornell. He had a habit of visiting high schools and walking the halls. While he looked at academic records, as with a divining rod, or by instinct, he zeroed in on a few students he met face to face. I had a part-time job in the Guidance Office filing college catalogs. Suddenly, a cheerful stranger was encouraging me to apply to a college I hadn't considered. That was quite a contrast from some of the prestigious schools I visited that seemed to be doing us a favor granting an interview.

After researching their English Department, and a trip to Ithaca, the College of Arts and Sciences was my next destination. Cornell and Ithaca are places I deeply love to this day. My fraternity, the college radio station, where I did jazz and news announcing, and the English Department were places of belonging in a big school. My fraternity brothers were the brothers I didn't otherwise have. You felt the exertion of thousands of young and bright people trying to make their mark.

Yet there was little pretension in the "cow college" of the Ivy League.

With a Bachelor's Degree in English, I wasn't sure what was next. My faculty advisor was 4,000 miles away in Italy my senior year. With only a vague notion of the profession, I stayed on for Law School. But after six years at the books, I was burned out.

My politics were slightly to the right of Genghis Khan. While Cornell had a traditional liberal bent, I was a member of the Conservative Club. I'm not quite sure where it came from, other than a contrarian view, but I was prepared to argue many of our problems would be solved if we adopted King Juan Carlos as our king. More seriously, I detested communism and fascism.

I wonder what my dad would have thought about my working for Bill Buckley when he made a somewhat theatrical run for Mayor of Manhattan. Dad was a charter member of the musician's union, and a supporter of Roosevelt and Truman.

The war in Vietnam was ramping up. Even without a high draft number, it was time for me to sign up. The legal career was placed on hold. In H.M. Tomlinson's *"The Sea and the Jungle"* an unhappy bank clerk is urged by a friend to go on a sea voyage with him. They make a wager standing on a London street. If the next man walking across the street gets on a bus, Tomlinson would quit his job and sign on. He was soon sailing up the Amazon.

It didn't occur to me at the time, but both of my parents were tough loners. While they took care of their immediate family, they charted their own course. I was beginning to do the same, even to my mother's consternation.

After a Navy aptitude test, there was a wintery bus ride to Buffalo for a physical and swearing in. At the end of the semester, I took a leave of absence from law school and was headed to Navy OCS in Newport, RI. But I could choose the reporting date. With the help of the Law School Dean, I made some good contacts in New Orleans. I wanted some day to practice Admiralty Law, no surprise, and what better place to do so? A summer clerkship with the largest law firm in the city meant real world experience after two years of tediously grappling with law books and case law. The Navy could wait until mid-August.

From my first visit for interviews with a half dozen firms, the Crescent City had a powerful and pungent allure. The near tropical climate, smells of Creole and Cajun cooking, a laid-back pace and vestiges of Deep South music, latent corruption and segregation didn't fit into my New York matrix but it was intriguing. I had relatives in Georgia and Florida. But this was a different country.

On arrival, I planned to stay at the Y for a week. Then find an apartment for the rest of the summer. After the first night, I wanted that apartment by sundown. I had lived in an open fraternity dorm, but there was nothing collegial at the Y. A block or two from the local skid row, it was an uneasy address.

I had worked four summers at a sailing camp on Cape Cod owned by two school teachers from Baton Rouge. It was an interesting cultural mix of kids and counselors from New York, New England, Louisiana and Mississippi. But I knew no one in this city. With a copy of the *Times-Picayune* and a small amount of cash in my pocket, I rode the cable car out to the Garden District and looked at two dark and dreary apartments listed in the classified. Back in the French Quarter, I wandered somewhat aimlessly around Jackson Square and Saint Louis Cathedral.

Walking down Saint Anne Street away from the Cathedral, there was a small handwritten sign attached to a door: "Apartment for Rent. Inquire Within". The listing wasn't in the paper, but the location was great. It was a 15-minute walk to the law offices; two blocks to Preservation Hall; and on one of the prettiest streets in the Quarter.

I was wearing a suit and tie and had a briefcase. I rang the bell. After a short time, a slightly overweight lady in curlers and a house coat came to the door. She looked at me intently and suspiciously. I made my sales pitch. I was down in New

Orleans for the summer to clerk at Jones, Walker and needed a place to stay; I didn't smoke and could I see the apartment?

She knew I wasn't from the South, nor was she. She was from Michigan or Wisconsin and asked where I was going to school. I told her Cornell. She mentioned that the daughter of a good friend was a junior there. "Her name is Holly Huntley.". Do you know her? My reply: "she is in my church group." The door opened, and I was shown the apartment.

The lady's husband was an architect and, on the Vieux Carre' Commission. You couldn't change the color of a shutter or do anything to the outside of a building in the Quarter without their approval. The couple had been in the city and under its spell for almost twenty years.

It was an interesting apartment, the size and shape of a squash court. Extremely tall ceilings, with narrow shuttered windows looking out on the street. There was a small bathroom and kitchen in the back. The style was called a shotgun house, long and narrow and raised three or four feet above the low ground. At one time, it had been part of the nun's quarters for the order associated with the Cathedral. There was the distinct background smell of insecticide. Down there they had bugs large enough to put a leash on and train as pets.

The rent ate up most of my limited budget, but I sensed I had gotten a deal. It was a delicate dance that summer, being friendly, but not too friendly with my short-term landlords.

While I played piano a bit, I didn't have my father's talent or intensity. I fancied myself a jazz buff and had been in charge of my college radio station's Jazz Department. That summer gave me an exposure to and appreciation of Dixieland, Blues and Zydeco; three strains that I had previously felt were too raw. Listening to the old guys at Preservation Hall, and Pete Fountain and Al Hirt in their own clubs, made me realize how true and visceral the music could be. There was sweat, smoke, pain and joy. Unlike the more introspective and intellectual music that I had admired, these sounds still had one foot in the bayous, shanty towns and Deep South. Chicago and New York were a different planet. I walked some of the streets in Storyville where Louis Armstrong had gotten his start. The Red-Light District was gone, or at least no longer visible. North and west of North Rampart Street the neighborhood was run down, depressing and unsafe.

New Orleans was a majority black city. Just walking around and into stores, gave me more exposure to a mixed-race culture than I had ever experienced in the North.

Louisiana took cooking very seriously. You didn't need an expense account to sample ethereal food. I was shocked at how casual my fellow law clerks were about muffaleta sandwiches, Oyster PoBoys, fried crawfish, gumbo and beignets at Café du Monde or the Morning Call. Alone, more often than not, I would have my big meal at Morrison's Cafeteria. The variety and quality were amazing and cheap. But I never did get used to the intense and detached black waiters who brought your tray to a table for a modest tip.

All the other second year summer law clerks were from Louisiana. They didn't know what to make of me, but they were cordial. One fellow and I made small talk about sailing. After a few weeks, he said he had to go away for the weekend, but some friends were taking their boat across Lake Pontchatrain and through the Intercoastal. It would stay in Biloxi for the summer. Would I like to crew in his stead?

"Sure!" I envisioned a bunch of twenty and thirty-year olds, a few cases of beer and a primer on Louisiana culture. To discuss the logistics, the boat owner's wife called and asked if I might like to come over to their house for dinner on a Wednesday night. She apologized in advance; they were only having red beans and rice. I told her that was something I had always wanted to try and would be honored to be included.

That was the beginning of a forty-year friendship with the Bagots. Mike and Betty had six children, then ranging from 6 to 17. The plan was for the youngest and oldest to go by car to Mississippi with their mom, and the four middle kids, Mike and I would take their 30-foot sailboat out from the New Orleans Yacht Club. Most of the time, we used the engine. Mike was a superb and well regarded Real Esate lawyer. He was also a veteran Naval Intelligence Officer. They lived in a beautiful old house in the Garden District with a wonderful jet-black Hungarian Puli, Lambie, a living shag rug with the sweetest disposition. The Bagots were from Cajun country to the north-west, but they had lived in New Orleans for decades.

At dinner, Mike expected a report from each child as to what they had learned at school that day. If they couldn't remember, out came the encyclopedia, and some instant knowledge was imparted.

On Saturday afternoon, I set out with this trusty crew. Everything was fine until about five or six the next morning when I managed to ground the boat in soft mud on one bank of the Intercoastal. This was not to be my *Lord Jim* moment. No one was hurt. After about an hour, the tide came in. Putting all of our weight in the bow, we broke free and moved on. I was embarrassed as hell, but Mike bit his tongue and never said a word.

We arrived in Biloxi late Sunday morning. Betty gave me a ride to the Bus Station where I was only too happy to use the dirtiest rest room I had ever seen.

The summer went quickly. I researched cases involving accidents on off shore oil rigs, river barges running amuck, obscure questions on telephone line right of ways and delivered briefs to a lawyer working on a discrimination case at a paper plant in Bogalusa. For lunch, I had my first catfish. On the radio, on the way back, I learned of pollution in the Pearl River, where it swam.

After a few days home in Manhattan, it was time to report to Newport with a short list of clothing and belongings. I had been there once before, to a white tie and tails debutante ball courtesy of a fraternity brother from a very wealthy family. A few of us felt like imposters then, or movie extras, watching a dozen or so beautiful young ladies come down the spiral stairway at the Elms. I had one dance with the prettiest girl in the room, and never saw her again.

This was a different Newport, no chartered busses or fancy hors d'ouevres enroute. From Port Authority, it was one bus to Providence and another to Newport. I took a taxi out to the Base Motel, a rather basic wooden structure in long walking distance to the Main Gate. We drove past tattoo parlors and pawn shops along a not yet gentrified Thames Street. The disheveled taxi driver told me he had almost joined the Navy. He lived in Jamestown, across the bridge, and was once on his way to the Navy Recruiting Station in Newport. But, he needed a smoke. He stopped at an Army Recruiting Office in his hometown to bum a cigarette. He wound up in the Army. I looked at him from the back seat of the cab and was grateful for his career choice.

In wartime, all the services needed more officers than the Service Academies and the ROTC programs turn out. OCS, at least the Navy's, took a select group of college graduates and put them through a 16-week, 6 day a week, 17 hour a day program. It supposedly made qualified officers out of the raw material. At the peak of the war, they graduated classes of roughly 600 junior officers a month.

On an August morning, I set out on foot with a suitcase and a large manila envelope containing my orders. Minutes later, there was a long line of similarly burdened young men straining to follow the commands of a growling Navy Chief just outside the Main Gate. There were a lot of lines that day: to sign forms, get close cropped haircuts, hypodermic shots, pick up sets of uniforms and boots, towels and sheets, laundry bags, stencil kits, name tags, and an M-1 rifle.

We were ordered to form into groups of 30 and assigned to different Companies. I had struck up a conversation outside the base with a couple of guys from Penn State. Their fraternity brothers were already upperclassmen at OCS. They maneuvered themselves into Delta Company and I tagged along. Then we were ordered to quick march across the equivalent of a football field distance towards King and Nimitz Halls, the two OC barracks. Awkwardly, we carried our old and new belongings.

Our days were programmed from six in the morning to eleven at night. I fit right in with my company, Delta 802. We were first in academics in the Regiment, second in athletics, and next to last in military comportment. I once made it through a dress inspection and Saturday Parade with my leggings on backwards. Three quarters of my company had at least a year of graduate school under our belts. None of us wanted to walk

14

through a jungle with a backpack on where the natives were distinctly unfriendly.

Because of our college degrees, we were sworn in as E-5s, "Officer Candidates under Instruction". In the fine print, if we flunked out or chose to leave the program, we still had a three or four-year commitment to serve as enlisted men. While the course was not as physically demanding as that for the Marines or Army, some did leave, for failing a Navigation Exam, refusing to jump off a high diving board in an abandon ship drill, or being unable to stay afloat for 40 minutes in a pool in survival at sea training.

Roughly six weeks before graduation we filled out "dream sheets", our three preferences for assignments. The scuttlebutt was that the career enhancing move was to a destroyer, the workhorse greyhounds of the fleet. They were small enough that a junior officer would have to carry his weight and big enough to be the training ground for command at sea. Influenced by my affection for the Merchant Marine, I picked Oiler (Tanker) or Auxiliary Ship, East Coast Ports. Those ships would more likely deploy to the Mediterranean rather than Southeast Asia. I wasn't afraid of the war. But I preferred transiting the part of the world I wanted to know.

A year later, I was on a gray hull auxiliary ship on the Mediterranean. A newly minted Ensign, they had turned me into a fledgling Engineering Officer. English Majors have to be flexible. I first saw my ship, covered with rust, sitting out of water in a Virginia dry dock. It was not a pretty sight. But a month later, covered in liberal layers of grey paint, and back in the sea, she had the appeal of a worldly lady. There were several rows of combat ribbons on the bridge. She had been around the block a few times.

It was mid-October and a moonlit night. After the mid-watch, just past 4 A.M., I left the bridge slowly and shambled towards my stateroom. My whole body was crying out for sleep. A new work day was only hours away with little chance to recharge. *Aucilla*, a World War II vintage tanker, steamed along slowly a mile or so off and parallel to the French coast. Shuffling down an outside ladder, the cool air was bracing, but not quite enough to give a second wind. Beyond the rail on the 01 deck, the sea was a wintry gun metal gray.

The ocean was fairly calm, with only sporadic and frothy whitecaps. But there was a damp chill and the scattered dark clouds overhead were weakly backlit by the moon. To the North, there was a haze of distant coastal lights and the shadowy deeper darkness of steep hills. It was the vaguest of outlines. The French Riviera was out there, a place I had never been, except in reading F. Scott Fitzgerald, Hemingway and the like. In the morning we would anchor in the harbor of Villefranche-sur-Mer.

It was 1968. Many of my Navy OCS classmates, refugees from myriad college campuses and one step ahead of the draft, were half a world away. They warily coped with the random monotony and mayhem of a war of attrition. With the luck of the draw, I was on a World War II rust bucket, a throw back to the "*Mr. Roberts*" Navy. This time the backwaters of conflict were in the Mediterranean.

Assigned to the Sixth Fleet, our ship was a bit player in a quiet game of cat and mouse between NATO and the Soviet Navy. The game played out in shifting watery venues between Gibraltar and the Bosporus. Russian ships often showed up and shadowed us when a carrier conducted flight ops. Most likely, American submarines had them in their crosshairs. The cold war was lukewarm, at least, in this sector. We had dubious friends: Franco in Spain, Salazar in Portugal and a cluster of unpopular Greek Generals. DeGaulle and France went their own way for awhile.

Perhaps, rust bucket was an unkind cut. The old gray lady had served with honor in both the Med and Pacific in the 40s and 50s. With a fresh coat of paint and a young crew, even in her twilight years, she could still deliver the goods. The ship's motto was: "Anytime, Anywhere", and there was hardly a corner of the world where *Aucilla* had not been. But with engines, pumps and other equipment more than 25 years old, unpredictable breakdowns and jury-rigged repairs were needed every week or two. It was well out of warranty. She steamed alongside sleek men of war, nearly always winded.

Round the clock for many weeks, we refueled aircraft carriers, cruisers, destroyers; ammunition and supply ships in the

Western Med. Frequently, there would be a ship close and parallel on both sides as we pumped tens of thousands of gallons of fuel through five or six elephant trunk hoses, a giant moving filling station at sea. When one ship left, another took its place. These sessions could go on for many hours.

As Liquid Cargo Officer and Damage Control Assistant, I was usually on the "jungle deck", an open rabbit warren of pipes and risers. Theoretically, I supervised my team as they opened and closed large valves sending thousands of gallons of black oil and JP-5 coursing through hoses and nozzles. That equipment was streamed across on wires to refuel thirsty ships as we sailed on parallel course. I tried not to think much about sleeping on top of 146,000 barrels of flammable fuel every night or the consequences if one ship or another swerved.

The repetition of bridge watches and shipboard routine had made me too tired to focus for long on the shoreline that night. It was time to catch a few hours of sleep. Soon there would be some respite. In a few hours, I would be in France for the first time and at our first liberty port.

I opened and shut the weather door and walked down a narrow dimly lit linoleum lined passageway. The thin metal door to my stateroom opened without a squeak. No need to turn on the light and disturb my roommate in the small steel compartment we called home. My khakis went on a hook; shoes on the deck. I had the lower rack. In seconds, I slid into my berth and quickly fell into a deep sleep.

OOO

02

Getting There

Transiting the Atlantic from Norfolk, we refueled the same four destroyers every other day for a week as we steamed at 16.1 knots (about 19 miles per hour) across an agitated ocean. Even a moderate sea in the North Atlantic reminds you that the ocean is a living thing with a temper. The routine and rituals of shipboard life follow an inflexible sequence: reveille, breakfast, quarters, changing of the watches around the clock. We worked during normal business hours and often beyond. Bridge and other watches were 24/7. Carriers liked to refuel late at night and into the wee small hours minimizing interference with flight operations. This was no problem for a crew of thousands on the carrier. There was much more wear and tear on the small contingent on an oiler. Unlike a tanker, going from port to port, our primary mission was to refuel other ships at sea.

During each watch, hand written entries were made in the ship's logs on the Bridge, in Navigation, in "Communications" and in the Engineering watches below. Maintenance logs were kept for each piece of equipment; radio messages were read or sent, classified communications coded and decoded in "crypto", in those days this was a tedious mechanical process. A small toaster size device of interlocking plastic wheels with letters and numbers around their rims had to be configured to conform to the day's sheet of codes or the results would be gibberish. Peeling paint on outdoor surfaces was chipped off, sanded and repainted. Supplies were disbursed.

The contour of military life followed the Plan of the Day, a brief written outline chronicling daily events. On deck, day or night, windy gray skies and gray sea surrounded us in all directions. The wide V of our wake marked our passage then disappeared. The distant rumble of 30,000 horsepower turned the screws. Long, low and broad, we cruised along like an aging Cadillac. The destroyer squadron fanned out front or circled us on our way to join the Sixth Fleet.

Above and below decks, almost every surface was painted gray, with some red, black and yellow contrast for valves, electrical connections and other mechanical junctures; the exceptions were some living and working quarters done in an ugly color sometimes referred to as seasick green. With the crew in dungarees and the officers and chiefs in working khakis, we moved about in a sepia tinged monastic world. It was an all male Navy at sea then, and that explained some of the more exuberant behavior when sailors came ashore.

Most days we were alone on the ocean, slowly trudging eastward. The destroyers would often jump over the horizon, considerably faster and intent on their own exercises and preparations. Occasionally, we would see another ship or two in the distance crossing on a tangent. Just behind the bridge, in the chart room, the navigator plotted our course in pencil on yard square empty mid-ocean charts.

At the start of each watch, the relieving officer of the deck was briefed by his predecessor as to our location, equipment problems, and any specific orders from the Captain. After verbally assuming the watch, he went to the Ship's Log. In a few terse words, he noted the time he assumed the watch, our geographical position, and the course and speed. Sextants, gyrocompass and dead reckoning were our only tools in mid-ocean. GPS had not been invented. We were well past the reach of Loran radio navigation. We knew in which direction we were going, but not exactly where we were. On a clear night, there was a sea of stars above.

Every course and speed change were recorded in the large and thin green log. There were no erasures. If you made a mistake you lined through it and started again. Such records are maintained by every Navy ship for posterity and hopefully, obscurity. After a collision, military engagement or other unpleasant incidents at sea, the log would be critical evidence.

After a year, the logs leave the ship and eventually find their way to the National Archives.

On calmer days, there were four to six-foot waves for as far as the eye could see. Often the waves were twice as tall, a bubbling and angry cauldron. At 553 feet long and weighed down nearly to the gunnels with black oil and JP-5, we rode down to the Plimsoll lines, deep in the water. The narrow and bobbing destroyers had a much rougher ride. Standing amidst the pipes and valves on the jungle deck, at refueling stations, white water sluiced alongside. A few feet of thin metal frame and a chain stood between us and the grasping and churning ocean. On the windier days, we wore life jackets. The water could surge across the deck, knee or armpit high. A metal stanchion or a door jamb became a life line as you found yourself suddenly in the horizontal.

Refueling destroyers came alongside, parallel, 60 to 100 feet away. A shot line was fired across their bow and then quickly grabbed by a deck hand. The rope line, attached to metal cables, was pulled across. Within minutes, steel wires with thick rubber hoses and couplings below would stretch across the sluicing waters between the ships. With hoses safely clamped and valves opened on the receiving ship, we started pumping under high pressure. Three thousand gallons a minute of fuel would course through each 4-inch hose. These were small meals, compared to the larger hoses and higher volumes pumped for hours on length to an aircraft carrier or cruiser.

My duty station was a little hatchway in the middle of the jungle deck. From there, my division sailors fanned out opening and closing valves, turning pumps on and off and sending tens of thousands of gallons of fuel to the hoses stretched like dangling rubber bands across to the ships alongside.

We stood on top of a giant steel egg crate. The 30-foot-deep tanks had to be tapped in a sequence and manner that would not subject the ship to too much stress and strain. Done wrong, in heavy seas, the ship's hull could splinter like green wood. I relied on an ancient operating manual, a metal bob on a metal tape measure lowered into each tank to verify the ullage, the empty space, and a mechanical levered device which estimated the weight of the fuel in each tank. My Division Master Chief, a savvy E-9, was not shy about giving advice. It was a long way from highlighting law school textbooks and fledgling arguments over legal precedent.

We traveled east nearly as fast as the old girl could go. It took nine days to sail from Norfolk, Virginia to Rota, Spain. South of the Azores, late one afternoon, there was a strange sound, or more properly no sound. We lost our generators, and experienced the eerie silence of a ship whose heart had stopped. Except for a few emergency lights, the ship went dark and quiet. The myriad and incessant hums of motors and equipment ceased. We drifted lifelessly in the splattering waves. The Chief Engineer and Captain, both frustrated and animated, were on the bridge. They conferred under the pitiful beam of a battery lantern.

At that time, I was Junior Officer of the Deck and instinctively stayed on the periphery of the debacle. We had lost steerage and began to drift. From a chart, I calculated the bearing and range to the nearest land, one of the Azores Islands. It was more than a hundred miles away. If we sent a radio message for help, it would take at least eight to ten hours for an ocean tug or someone else to come and help us, if we were lucky. Our "four striper" Captain was increasingly gloomy, no doubt taking in the embarrassment of our predicament and the implications for his career.

For more than an hour we bobbed up and down like a mammoth row boat, with the destroyers impatiently circling in a half mile perimeter. Eventually, a crusty engineering Chief got an emergency diesel running with shots of compressed air. Slowly, other systems kicked back on. Then all power came back and the ship returned to life. The familiar hums and noises throughout the ship signaled we were ok. The prospect of a long motor boat ride, a lifeboat paddling towards the islands, or a degrading towing operation receded from mental view. Impatient, the destroyers left us, and sped onward towards Gibraltar. We reset our course for Rota, Spain.

With a compliment of 18 officers and 190 in the crew, we were a small town, and eventually you knew everyone to some extent. The older officers were career Navy, some having spent twenty or more years in uniform. The XO was a former aviator, and the rumors were that he had once frozen and was unable to land on a carrier. Sometimes he was caring and warm, but could turn into a rage like a lowering barometer. Our Navigator had been in the Cuban Navy befor fleeing to the U.S. He was in the Bay of Pigs operation, but was now separated from family and friends. He was a gentle and caring man that had lost his country. The Supply and Engineering Officers were Mustangs, starting their careers as enlisted men and working their way up to Limited Duty Officers, tough, but knowing their stuff.

The Operations Officer had seen combat duty in Vietnam. He was brusque and smart, with a hard edge. After I left, he had a PTSD flashback that took him off the ship. My first roommate was a junior Deck Officer. A restless jock, he volunteered to become a SEAL and left us during deployment. The second was the new junior Supply Officer. Despite the fact that he was a Dartmouth grad, we became friends, so much so that he later was my best man.

Every officer and sailor had a story, or more than one. A deck seaman had been a commercial artist in New York. The Navy had a painting job for him too, but it involved large expanses of metal. When he was done scraping rust and painting bulkheads, he created handsome ship's plaques out of dental cement. A potential playwright found himself in the radio shack. Several of my Ship Fitters were avoiding West Virginia coal mines and my best Damage Controlman left and returned to the Seattle Fire Department.

Like doctor specialists, the different rates superficially favored different personality traits. The Deck crew did the grunt work and often had personalities to match. The engineering folks were usually covered in sweat and grease, like the people you would find down at your neighborhood gas station or truck depot. The storekeepers were the "operators". If you needed something, they would be able to get it, above or below the table. The radiomen and ops types, usually with some college, were the intellectuals of the crew.

OOO

03

In Chop

Rota is just West of Cadiz and Gibraltar. The U.S. Navy had been a permanent guest at this sprawling and austere Spanish Naval Base from the early fifties. A few miles offshore, a harbor pilot came on board from a tiny boat. A few minutes later a couple of tugs came alongside. With the maritime equivalent of training wheels near our bow and stern, we passed an array of gray ships at the docks and in early afternoon pulled up smoothly at a long deep-water pier just beyond another vintage Navy Oiler.

On our short port call, we wouldn't see much of the base or surroundings, only glimpses of the large expanses of concrete roads, piers and low-lying generic military buildings. This was an 18 hour overnight stop alongside the ship we would relieve. It was our turn to go to work with the Sixth Fleet and for them to go home; in-chop and out-chop in Navy parlance. After 7-8 months in theater, the *Caloosahatchie* would head back to

27

Virginia. Often, with Native American names, all Navy Oilers, at the time, were named after obscure rivers. Many years later, I passed briefly over the Aucilla River, a small stream starting in Georgia and emptying into the Florida Panhandle. At that point, it was considerably narrower than the bridge of our ship.

Within an hour, fresh provisions showed up on the pier in small trucks. The deck crew manned a conveyor belt stretched to the pier. Fresh milk, Italian Motta ice cream, vegetables and most important, mail, were hauled into the bowels of the ship. All of the wardroom officers, the XO and a couple of key chiefs scrambled down the accommodation ladder. We walked a few hundred yards down the pier and then up the ladder to our sister ship's quarterdeck.

A third of the crew was granted brief base liberty: a chance to go to the PX, the enlisted club and/or just stretch their legs on land.

A petty officer escorted us down to their wardroom and we met our counterparts. The ship was much the mirror image of ours, although it had been stretched in the middle. At one point it had gone into a shipyard, was cut in half and a hundred feet of additional tank sections were put in place. Then they were welded together.

For a few hours we sat around a large rectangular gray metal table. We drank coffee and heard about their tour and what we might expect in sea operations. For now, they were the experts and veterans. After the ice was broken, each department head, and some chiefs, in turn described their successes and headaches in servicing the fleet. There were a few diplomatic comments about what the Task Force Commander, a two-star Admiral, expected of his service force ships. Then, we broke up into smaller groups with our specific counterparts to talk shop. We asked all the nitty gritty questions we could think of.

I was especially concerned with how we would cope with the dangers of loading and unloading fuel with civilian and military people speaking a host of different languages: Spanish, Italian, Greek, Maltese and Arabic. How would we be sure we weren't getting contaminated fuel? Could we trust a remote fuel depot to stop pumping in an emergency? How much pump pressure would we get and how long would it take to on load fuel in various ports?

The LCO from the other ship was unperturbed: "no problem", "just use your hands a lot like the Italians". He went through a pantomime of some universal gestures, rotating his hands to speed things up and pushing down towards the deck to slow them down. Most importantly, he said, to make them stop, he put his hand against his throat in a choking motion. We all soaked up as much transient experience as we could. The meeting was cordial and open. Our being there meant they were heading home.

In the six months before, with our ship barely out of a ship-yard for major repairs, we had sailed up and down the Atlantic Coast refueling destroyers and carriers practicing our craft. Then there was a grueling three weeks at Guantanamo Bay, Cuba going through "Reftra" (refresher training) with myriad fire, damage control and simulated warfare drills upwards of 16 hours a day.

Of course, now that we were in Europe, nearly everyone was looking forward to the various pleasures of foreign ports of call: churches, museums and shopping for some, bars and women for others. The afternoon waned, and when business was done, we headed off together to the officer's and ohief's clubs. The other ship had a few jeeps and station wagons at their disposal, and we piled in. We savored our first libations in a couple of weeks. As with sailors from time immemorial, truth and fiction merged in swapped tales of liberty ports past and to come.

Only pretzels and chips softened the gin, whiskey and beer, more or less discretely consumed despite the highly subsidized prices. It would have to last for several weeks to come. The XO prescribed an early night. High tide and sea and anchor detail were well before dawn. We would be back at sea before daylight. A naval task force operating just east of Gibraltar was expecting us.

Early the next morning, we were through the Straits, heading for a thirsty carrier battle group. There wasn't much time to reflect on being in the Mediterranean. Planes were swarming, landing and taking off from the *Independence*. They needed lots of fuel for the carrier, its planes and the protective screen of destroyers. Fuel was the life blood of this military operation and we were there to supply it.

We had refueled carriers before, but it was always an awesome sight to see a gray blob on the horizon gradually turn into a looming 81,000-ton cliff city stretching over and under a 1,000 feet long flight deck. With some 5,000 souls aboard and 90 aircraft, it was a floating town. In contrast, our tanker was made up mostly of fuel tanks, with a small bridge attached, a comparative village.

For over two weeks, we patrolled the Western Mediterranean at the beck and call of two aircraft carriers, the *Independence* and the *Shangri-La*, a dozen destroyers, destroyer escorts and the odd light cruiser. Other oilers ferried fuel out to us, transferring at sea, so we could stay close to the carrier operations. The blur of daytime duties, fire drills, bridge watches, and refueling stations at any hour, too much coffee and not enough sleep began to wear. My blood was brown and caffeinated.

Most people who earn their living at sea are happy to come back ashore, at least for awhile. Whether heading home or into a new port of call, getting off the ship is the objective. For a supply ship, often it is a gritty fuel depot or a remote industrial pier. Once in a while, for "rest and recreation" you visit an idyllic harbor or an ancient city.

Unlike (war) ships of the line, tankers are not fashionable maritime ambassadors. They don't project their country's power or grace. More often they are viewed as an accident waiting to happen. They are rarely welcome near tony resorts or prosperous cruise ports. Even if we weren't taking on fuel, we still needed a deep channel and a long pier. Alternatively, we were forced to anchor well off in the harbor, at a distance. In peace time, few attractive towns would risk their pristine beaches and promenades to host a working-class ship.

The abundance of colors and amenities of life we take for granted on land were washed out of our daily existence. Returning to shore for some rest and recreation was like switching from a black and white to a color movie.

Fortunately for us, our Captain was quite senior. A deep-water draft tanker was often a stepping stone to command of a Cruiser or Aircraft Carrier. We were destined for some very pleasant liberty ports.

04

Through the Looking Glass

S parkling morning light danced on the water and seeped through the port hole. The view could have been a Dufy painting; only it was a real sea and village landscape. Our tanker gently pivoted on its anchor tether. We were a half mile from a palm tree lined crescent promenade. In the foreground, the azure water in the harbor was a brilliant pastel hue. A hauntingly beautiful and gentrified fishing village with gelati colored houses filled my sight. Reaching high above, lovely wooded hills with perched villas added a pleasing vertical dimension. Overhead there was a deep blue sky with some high cirrus clouds. This was Villefranche-sur-Mer, the most beautiful place I had ever seen. It was also our first liberty port in the Mediterranean and ultimately the prettiest.

That day routine chores on board ship passed slowly. First a quick breakfast in the wardroom. All hands on deck at 0800. We raised the colors. On the bridge, the captain whispered a few words to the executive officer and department heads, and returned to his stateroom. The chief engineer scooted down a couple of outside ladders and quickly passed some now long forgotten information along to his division officers, each of us standing a few yards in front of our men. We saluted, pivoted 180 degrees and marched a few feet to stand eyeball to eyeball with our chiefs.

Key points were reiterated. Then, in turn, we ordered the chiefs to put the men at ease. I outlined, to my dozen and a half sailors, a few things that had to be done before sundown. On the most important subject, there would be liberty while we were in port, subject to meeting our obligations under a watch bill to be prepared by the chiefs for my approval.

The crew was dismissed from formation, and we all went to work. In less than fifteen minutes, my senior chief came into my tiny office with a handwritten watch bill in hand. Four or five guys would stand all the watches, and everyone else would go ashore. I wondered what deals had been done. The watch standers would get their turn in the next liberty port.

My two divisions had plenty of equipment to service, repair or test, records to keep, and fire drills to spring on the less than appreciative crew. We were also in charge of maintaining the fiberglass and the brass boat beading along the length and breadth of the ship's launches and the captain's gig. Most importantly, we were responsible for fire safety and keeping the ship afloat if there was any flooding or explosion damage. That included three damage control lockers and teams, fore, mid and aft. At sea, and at the pier, we were the local fire department. I had fought fires and smoke at DCA School in Philadelphia and swam in flooded compartments to shore up shattered doors and walls. In the Caribbean, we put out an electrical fire at sea before it got out of hand.

In fueling ports, everyone in our two divisions was needed until cargo operations were complete. But in this fishing, yachting and leisure town, we anchored out in the harbor.

By mid-morning, the captain's gig and two motor boats were lowered to the water. There were quick runs to the landing half a mile away. Soon fresh provisions were brought on board. Milk and ice cream, vegetables, meat and poultry, and everything else needed by 200+ hungry sailors and officers. For the first time in two weeks, we would have mail.

The disbursing officer went ashore to purchase french francs, italian lira and spanish pesetas, and trade some of our 16 mm movies with those from other ships. Movies on the mess decks on an occasional quiet night, was a tradition going back to World War II. The captain left to pay his respects to local dignitaries. I went about my work on board, frequently glancing at the lovely harbor, impatient to leave the ship, gathering glimpses of a place of dreams. I thought of my dad

35

putting his violin in its case and going ashore. Most of what I know about him was snippets from other people. I knew he had been to Nice, and had sailed along this coast.

As the most junior ensign, I was assigned shore patrol duty for two of the three nights we were in port. There would be no free-range wandering. The first night, five or six more senior members of the ward room took a little pity on me. I could join them for a shoreside dinner before starting my beat.

Our ad hoc shore patrol would keep the peace, or at least intervene before any of our sailors got into too much trouble in town. As the only naval ship in the harbor, we set our own portable and temporary buffer of law and order. A Status of Forces Agreement gave us the responsibility for the conduct and discipline of our men. Only a very serious crime would warrant intervention by the local police. They didn't want to see us and we didn't want to see them.

By the late sixties, the French had pulled out of the military accords of NATO, remaining a theoretical ally, but a wary and prickly one. Only a few years before, the Sixth Fleet flagship called this harbor its home port.

As temporary policemen, we made a discrete presence in dress whites, with black and gold SP armbands, symbols of our temporal authority. We hoped neither we nor our charges would meet the french gendarmes. We had no firearms and no special police training. My detachment of three petty officers carried billy clubs to use as a last resort.

Before they crossed the gang plank, I asked my sailors to keep their revelries down to a dull roar and not to cause any international incidents. They were required to go ashore in dress whites, and were as visible as walking lighthouses. They wouldn't have blended in to local life anyway. Several local bars welcomed the trade, some more respectable than others. The least choosy and most thirsty sailors headed for the first few watering establishments, the seedier the better. Others knew enough to head further a field.

The officers could and did don civilian clothes. Most headed for the more sophisticated pleasures of Nice and Monte Carlo.

What I most remember from that early fall night was a convivial table at a lovely and homey restaurant. Especially the UPS brown soupe de poisson redolent with the essences of myriad varieties of crustaceans I had never tasted; a garlicky aioli mayonnaise slathered on chunks of baguette croutons, and mineral water with gas (no wine for the lad on duty). The sight, smell, taste and texture of that soup are permanently imbedded in my brain. This is what French food was all about! If I had to order my last meal today, it would be a comparable fish soup, but pared with a crisp white French wine.

A charming and ageless hostess appeared and disappeared with glasses and wine, hefty soup tureens, luxurious salads bathed in premium olive oil and ultimately picture-perfect fruit tarts. The old timers swapped tales of good times in exotic ports, and the mood was the most jovial since I reported aboard. I didn't realize, at the time, but I was at the U.S. Navy's home away from home on the Cote d'Azur: La Mere Germaine.

Germaine Halap Brau and her husband Louis opened their wonderful restaurant in 1938. Long after her husband died, Madame Germaine continued to open her heart and kitchen to the sailors and officers of the American Navy. Family members continue the tradition today, although the restaurant has certainly gone more upscale and the presence of U.S. sailors is now rare. Today, on the outside wall of this fine and increasingly snooty establishment, there is a brass plaque, a gift from the U.S. Navy, in tribute to Ma Germaine.

After dinner, most of the wardroom took a cab or bus into Nice, just a few miles down the shoreline. That night, for the first time, I wandered the ancient, quiet and winding alley ways of this pungent seaside village. In October, most of the tourists were gone. With roots dating back to the Greeks, perhaps Ulysses really did come here as local legends tell. How do you fully understand and fathom a port inhabited continuously for more than 2,500 years?

On duty, the four of us broke up into patrols of two. With three quarters of our sailors on dry land for the first time in six weeks, and in full party mode, things would get interesting. We kept a vigilant but passive eye on sailors with money burning holes in their pockets. Many were bound and determined to make up for lost time in one night. Most were well behaved, but a few would push the limits when lubricated by their favorite form of alcohol.

We had the authority to keep the peace, at least as far as the Navy was concerned. The french authorities were conspicuous by their absence. So too were most of the respectable civilians. The town seemed almost deserted. My authority came from a single gold stripe, an officer's cap, a black felt arm band with the initials: "SP" and no powerful reservoir of brawn or experience.

With a ship's company this small, we all knew each other. While our shipmates kept a low profile, we kept our distance. We hoped for no serious trouble, no arrests and nothing we would have to read about in the local papers. Every hour or so, we left our impromptu post at "fleet landing", next to the small customs building, and walked the town. Behind us, as the evening moved on, a ship's launch would come and go every hour or so, a taxi service, traversing the distance out to our ship in a little over ten minutes.

Most of our crew behaved as well as they would in their home towns. Even those that hankered for demon rum were still pretty good natured. Still, a handful had a tendency to seek or find trouble. We spent much of the evening quietly walking into bars. If our people were there, we gauged the tone and temperature and usually backed out.

The Navy's *Mediterranean Port Guide*, kept on the bridge or in the chart room, contained a fascinating mix of useful and sometimes obscure information. From phone numbers and procedures for obtaining tugs, harbor master rules, quarantine procedures, where to obtain potable water and lighterage, to an abbreviated and plagiarized history of the environs.

The *Guide*, and updated messages, continued with a short list of recommended restaurants, and a longer summary of bars and marginal hotels that were "off limits". They were the source of prior episodes of rip-offs, petty crime, drugs, venereal disease and/or general trouble. Any known local health problems were summarized in some unsettling detail.

We had duly posted the "off limits" warnings on a ship bulletin board. For some it became their insider's guide of where they wanted to begin, or perhaps end, their evening. To my surprise, everyone made it back to the harbor under their own power. The shore patrol took the last boat back to the ship, with the most incoherent sailors.

On my "night off", as with most junior officers, I was short of funds. I stayed on board ship for dinner and then went ashore. It was roughly a 15 minute bus ride into the heart of Nice. Walking for a few hours, I got a little sense of this much larger and more cosmopolitan city. The famous Promenade d'Anglais was fairly deserted. It showcased blocks upon blocks of tony apartment houses and a few large hotels all with a mostly elderly clientele. Not much appeal for a young bachelor officer. Nor did the residential quarter a few blocks back from the waterfront seem any more welcoming.

I walked over to the old town. It was livelier than Villefranche, even after the outdoor market had closed for the day. But it was not as pretty. There were some signs of decay, seedier and possibly more dangerous bars. Without any special destination, and no desire to settle into a ratty watering hole, I circled alone around the inner harbor. It was filled with boats and yachts of all sizes. My legs began to ache. At the outer end of the horseshoe harbor there were large ferry boats, almost as big as our ship, waiting their turn to sail to Corsica and Sardinia. All the shops and reputable businesses, other than a few bars and restaurants, were closed for the night. I headed for a bus stop and back to the ship.

Sailors don't have many places to spend money on board ship. When they reach port, the extra cash seems perishable. As an alternative to spending it all on booze and babes, the Navy Supply Corps had arranged discounts with a number of vendors. On the second afternoon in port, my roommate, the disbursing officer, had arranged mess tables on the fantail. Different "representatives" were there, with samples of their wares: high end cameras and stereo equipment, Noritake china, Mikimoto pearls, even a guy who took measurements and orders for a "Hong Kong tailor". Rumor was that he had gone AWOL from a ship more than a decade before; married a French girl and laid low until the service stopped looking for him. A good story, whether or not it was true.

Our last night in port was much like the first. Other than extricating a few sailors from places where they had over-stayed their welcome, they were quiet tours. But I couldn't get over the spell of this singular town, so ancient, beautiful and relatively clean. There were people already living there when the Greeks and Romans came to trade. The massive pastel colored houses on the waterfront were easily four to six hundred years old. I had never seen the likes of the cobble stoned rabbit warren of narrow alleys and inner courtyards, buildings out of plumb with small rough-hewn wooden doors. When a door was open, narrow ladder like stairs disappeared upwards into darkness. Steep alleyways were often covered, like tunnels, and the buildings leaned into each other for support.

In the heart of town, somewhat better lit, lay a narrow crescent shaped street roughly parallel to the water, scarcely eight feet wide, with small one room shops and bars interspersed along its length. Ancient and irregular shaped stone dwellings with tiny doors, shuttered windows and fortress like thickness stood side by side. A few lampposts barely pierced the dark night.

Down steep paths, with many uneven stone steps, the water front area was peaceful and inviting, bathed in lantern light. At the harbor, the outdoor cafes were closed, out of season. Their presence suggested more convivial times and the cordial mixing of visitors and locals. Vividly painted small fishing boats were pulled up on the narrow beach and heavy black fishing nets were piled beside them ready for pre-dawn departures.

The locals didn't come out in earnest until after many of the sailors had finished their rounds and had settled firmly into some of the seedier bars. These lay in shadows, in less prime locations, catering primarily to seamen and other dubious itinerants. With names like California and Florida, they were cheap, basic and sometimes raw. The female clientele were mostly of the commercial variety, transient and often known to follow the fleet from port to port. Some of these ladies of the night knew more about our operating schedule than we did.

Just before one AM, the shore patrol caught the last liberty boat back to the ship. With us were two dozen mostly mellow, deeply inebriated enlisted men reluctantly ready to pour themselves back on board. It is a good thing that none of them had to drive home.

I stood, in the back of the boat, next to the coxswain. We were both in dress whites. With two to three-foot waves in the inner harbor, it was a rocky ride, even for those sober. One incoherent and unbalanced sailor proceeded to barf on the deck and splatter one of my shoes. One of my boat crew shook his head in disgust and hosed the area down with a bucket of seawater. He then pulled in the mooring lines, and we were underway.

By default, with no other officers on board, I was the officer in charge of the boat. My chief concern was to get folks back to and on the ship without having anyone fall overboard. With the lines taken in, the coxswain skirted a few large yachts and carefully brought us bobbing alongside the ship's lee side accommodation ladder.

Tires were attached to the aluminum rig hanging over the side of our ship, and styrofoam buffers hung along the boat's side. With bigger waves, we moved up and down as on a seesaw, first above and then below the relatively stationary ladder. We were a tinker toy alongside the vertical wall of the tanker. Each sailor gauged their leap on to the platform, like catching the fourth or fifth step of an escalator erratically moving up and down with varying pitch. Despite a few close calls for those furthest gone, each mastered the unpredictable rocking motion; and no one wound up in the drink.

With passengers delivered, I stood as the boat crew attached cables to stanchions. The wires became taut and we were lifted out of the water and on to the deck like any cargo. When level with the rail, we clambered down before the boat was hoisted into its chock. *Aucilla* would head back to sea at dawn.

After a quick salute on the quarterdeck, I looked back at the sparkling lights of the town gleaming half a mile away. I knew I would be coming back. It was a long way from home, but it felt good to be here. Life was a work in progress and the journey felt truly begun.

In 1925-26, my father had sailed around the world on the *S.S.Belgenland*, a British ship. He kept a journal, which my mother gave to me after this trip. He was about my age back then, but leader of a band. They sailed from east to west chasing the sun. After Asia, India, Ceylon and Egypt, they threaded their way into the Mediterranean. During a port call in Monte Carlo, he took a bus over to Nice along the corniche, describing the views and houses down to the sea the most beautiful he had ever seen. Now I agreed.

OOO

05

Rapallo; South, East, West and Homeward Bound

F our months later, after much time at sea and the occasional liberty port along the way, our ship was anchored in another beautiful Mediterranean harbor: Rapallo, Italy, our first stop on the Italian Riviera. We had refueled several hundred ships at sea, and managed to spend a few days ashore in many fascinating places: Cartagena, Spain, Palma de Mallorca, La Spezia, Gaeta, Napoli, Augusta Bay, Sicily, Souda Bay, Crete, Piraeus, Greece and two stops in Valletta, Malta. On the way home, we would also spend four days in Tangier, Morocco. Each place was saturated with history and afforded unique experiences. Like most first time transients, only a sliver of their character registered in my mind. Their beauty, culture and complexity would only fill in years later on subsequent trips. A walk in a park, a fine meal, a souvenir bought for someone at home, a glimpse of a pretty woman, a chance encounter with some locals. Even now, I could tell some tales. But they would be postcards from the past.

Back then, I had little mental baggage and savored the chance to sample this pungent coastline. Life at sea could be tiring, tedious, and sometimes dangerous. A lot was encompassed in that word "liberty". On your own in a foreign land, anything was possible.

We all looked forward to this port call. But in a fit of pique, the captain cancelled liberty. To make matters even more galling, our boats would ferry sailors from a couple of destroyers to the landing. Before, relations between the captain and crew were formal but cordial. We knew he was an "airdale". He needed deep draft ship experience as a candidate for an Aircraft Carrier or Cruiser assignment down the line. His seniority got us better liberty ports and some minor courtesies between ships at sea. He was an old-fashioned naval officer, quiet and aloof.

Clearly, he wanted our ship to excel. As a fighter pilot in WWII, he had been shot down by a Japanese merchant ship. He took our ancient array of 3"50 and twin 40 mm AA gun mounts seriously. Seriously enough to schedule a couple of additional days at sea for target practice. The boatswains were tasked with painting an empty oil barrel taxi cab yellow. It was cast astern and the gunnery crews aimed at their target from various angles and distances.

Much of the crew was skeptical that our antique, 1940s era weaponry would be a match for any modern enemy. Sitting on top of 146,000 barrels of fuel didn't give us much comfort either. The first day's target practice had gone badly, with guns and crew far off the mark. The Captain ordered another day of drills, postponing and shortening our port call.

That night the yellow barrel mysteriously disappeared. Word went out from an angry captain that whoever was responsible for the loss of the barrel would be punished. He demanded that anyone who knew about the incident should advise their division officer. Whether it was a solitary sailor or a group didn't become known. No one was about to rat on a shipmate.

We anchored over a mile out in Rapallo's beautiful hill crested bay, the shallower draft destroyers closer to the harbor. The executive officer announced that all liberty was cancelled until the perpetrator was found. The atmosphere on board ship turned sour. Many eyes were trained on our boats ferrying other sailors to the beach.

On the second day, the routine call of "muster all restricted men on deck" was passed on the 1MC loudspeaker. A handful of men were serving extra duty for minor transgressions, nominal punishment 'awarded" at recent captain's masts. They took their place on deck to be assigned additional cleaning and painting chores. But then, more than a dozen other sailors lined up behind them, and then more. Almost everyone was there who was not on watch.

Someone in the impromptu gathering starting singing softly: "Roll out the Barrel". You could almost see the captain, who was on the bridge wing, turn red. Word was passed to have the executive officer come to the bridge. That afternoon, without explanation, liberty was reinstated. We never did find out who threw the barrel overboard.

The skipper was a good man. With the collateral duty of legal officer, I saw how he treated the men at captain's mast, stern but fair, and never with anger. Every couple of months the captain would join us for dinner in the wardroom. At all other times, he ate alone. When we were in port, he either entertained the local dignitaries, or went off on his own. He never did get his carrier, but after that became apparent, he seemed to relax. One quiet afternoon, in port, and at a side rail of a cafe, he told me a little about being stationed in Peru, our first casual conversation.

I didn't really understand why he was so arms length, until I became a commander and then a captain twenty odd years later. You couldn't be equally friendly with everyone, and friendship undermined the need for unswerving discipline. It's not easy being the "old man". The privileges of rank come with responsibility and a price.

The captain's night orders, written on the bridge, tell you when he should be called; for example, when another ship is expected to pass within half a mile, when a major piece of equipment malfunctions or an urgent radio message is received. Any whiff of danger, he needed to know.

On the promenade just after sunset, Rapallo's pastel colored houses were softly lit and appealing. Stately palms and tall pine trees added elegance. Street lamps cast splatters of light on the water. Though bigger than Villefranche, it was more faded and less welcoming, at least to foreign sailors. Clusters of the crew headed directly to the train station and on to the more raffish attractions of Genoa. The boulevard of old and stately stone houses wasn't a place for young, single and lonely men four thousand miles from home.

I knew that Ezra Pound had spent the war years in exile here. He was another displaced American far from home, getting in plenty of trouble of a different kind; but someone with a powerful gift for poetry and a sense of history.

After a short walk through the buttoned-up town, I too opted for Genoa, joining four shipmates at the train station. Our tour guide was an older sailor who had made many Med cruises. When one of his former ships was home ported in Italy, he purportedly lived, part time, with a woman of easy virtue in "the gut" or sailor quarter of the ancient city.

In about an hour, the local train deposited us at Brignole Station in the heart of the more modern sector of the city. We were surrounded by stolid and monumental buildings from Mussolini's day. We walked down the arcades of busy Via XX Settembre, the main shopping street, to Piazza De Ferrari. The Piazza center piece was a giant and theatrical statuary fountain. All around the square were massive and ornate edifices: banks, governmental agencies and Carlo Felice Opera House, dating from the 1820s, rebuilt after substantial damage in World War II. Then we turned into the old heart of the city. The giant palaces on Via Garibaldi were especially imposing and somber at night, dimly outlined by streetlights. Only decades later would I begin to understand their full significance and prior grandeur.

Christopher Columbus set sail from this ancient seaport, and up until a short time before our visit, the harbor was teeming with ocean liners. Cargo ships, tankers and ferries still crowded the several harbors, but the city had declined drastically, only to see something of a renaissance more than a decade later.

A few blocks from Principe Station, the main railroad terminal, we stopped for a couple of scotches at the up-scale Excelsior Hotel. The bar looked like a private English club. Fortified, a few of us wandered downhill towards the waterfront for a look at the most primal part of the city. Dark and potentially dangerous alleys meandered towards the harbor. Old buildings leaned inward, sometimes connected with horizontal buttresses to militate against earthquakes. Illicit goods and people were on display, and there was a sense that trouble was holstered but close at hand. This was not a place to wander alone at night.

In daytime, the alleyways were a scrappy Kasbah of shops and people from many countries. North Africans and Middle Easterners outnumbered Italians. Merchant sailors, fishermen, craftsmen, traders and shopkeepers mingled and did business above and below the table. At night, there were other kinds of trade. After an hour or so, walking on edge, too sober to want any trouble, we emerged unscathed on Via Providenzia. It was time to head back to the ship.

The sailor quarter is brought to vivid life in the keen and irreverent music of Fabrizio de Andre. As powerful a lyric poet as Georges Brassens or Jacques Brel in France, his personal story is even more colorful. He wrote and sang passionately in the dialects of Liguria and Sardinia and cared deeply about the poor and hard-working people who had no other champion. That continued even after he was kidnapped and held as a hostage.

Ahead, there were plenty of long, arduous and mostly routine days and weeks. Life centered on refueling ships at sea. Bridge watches, fire drills, completing maintenance logs, shipboard routine filled the hours. Gradually, winter and spring came.

There is a naval saying, mischievously and bogusly attributed to Thucydides: "A collision at sea can ruin your entire day." A collision would effectively end most naval careers, regardless of any measured analysis of fault.

We were scheduled to pass through the Straits of Messina just before dawn. The narrow gap between Mainland Italy and Sicily has strong currents and heavy ship traffic, including ferries going back and forth between two busy ports, Reggio and Messina. The natural whirlpool effect in the Straits gave rise to the legend of Scylla and Charybdis and occasional optical mirages.

I completed a mid-watch on the bridge perhaps an hour before we were due to transit that passage. By 4 AM I was back in my bunk dead to the world; so much so that I didn't hear the collision alarm around 0530. There was a tall cable laying barge anchored in the Straits. We didn't have the latest paperback Notice to Mariners that would have apprised us of that fact. The bridge watch saw a strange and hard to decipher array of lights as we steamed into the narrow channel at a good clip. You can't stop or even slow a large ship on a dime. When they figured out what was in our path, they made a sharp emergency turn. One of the cables scraped along roughly thirty feet of our bow. Some workers on the barge were so scared of a tanker looming above them that they jumped into the water.

Most of what I learned about the incident came from my doing a JAG Investigation afterwards. As legal officer on the ship, a collateral duty, I pulled together basic evidence from interviewing everyone on board who had witnessed the incident. I then submitted a report, counter-signed by the captain, to people somewhere else who would decide what responsibility the Navy had for any compensation. The damage to our ship was minimal, and that to the barge, not terribly significant. The impact on a few careers was more telling.

For ten days, over Christmas and New Year, we were scheduled to be in Beirut, a great liberty port and the Paris of the Middle East according to some of the old salts on board. We never got there. Things got too hot in that tinderbox. Instead, we sat alongside a pier in Piraeus, Greece. Shipboard operations dropped to their lowest ebb. It was cold and damp, but there was a little time to savor the ancient cities of Pireaus and Athens. But they were choked with low grade gasoline fumes. Surrounded by hills, the air quality was worse than Los Angeles. You could feel and see the gray haze eating into ancient stone, to say nothing of attacking your lungs.

Not far beyond the miles of piers, warehouses and ramshackle buildings at the heart of Piraeus lay Athens, the iconic city of the ancient Greeks. It was an uneasy mix of poorly built and ugly modern buildings intertwined with stunning ancient monuments and sites.

The Acropolis was especially poignant against a clear winter sky. Through the narrow and often steep alleys of the Plaka, the city's oldest neighborhood, we came face to face with what had once been small black and white pictures in dimly remembered school books.

This old residential quarter, often too narrow for cars, teemed with dining and bar customers in dozens of hole in the wall tabernas. The ancient hill itself was surprisingly empty. We could wander unsupervised right up to the rubble around the bases of the ancient temples. Vestiges of life some 2500 years ago were all around us.

Small restaurants in the Plaka and Piraeus introduced us to the staples of Greek cuisine. Ouzo, Retsina wine and Metaxa Brandy flowed freely. Despite the stench of hundreds of thousands of cars belching black smoke, and a greater sense of poverty than we had seen elsewhere, we fit in. We were just one ship out of hundreds in this maritime nation of islands and seafarers.

One night, a handful of officers hopped into two cabs and went to Vassilenas, the oldest and most famous taberna in Piraeus. The then owner spoke no English, and we only a few words of Greek. Some nine courses of seafood platters came one after the other, downed with liberal glasses of wine and ouzo. The food was extraordinary, an encyclopedia of the sea, simple but fresh and lovingly prepared. We didn't feel the cold when we headed back to the ship.

In the first full week of January, it was time to go back to sea and find more ships to fuel. We headed south through the Cyclades and took on fuel at Souda Bay, Crete, a few miles East of Chania.

Souda and later Augusta Bay, Sicily illustrated a point that took me some twenty-five years to learn. I never got beyond the piers. It took over 18 hours to load with primitive, gravity feed equipment. I was totally ignorant of the beautiful cities of Chania and Siracusa just a few miles away. Decades later I spent time in both those lovely venues. A short distance away from the path you choose, there may be a real gem you may easily miss.

Long weeks at sea were interspersed with short interludes in, for me, exotic ports. We replenished supplies and spirits in Valletta and Marsaxloxx, Malta; Augusta Bay, Sicily and Cagliari, Sardinia; Palma, Mallorca; and Tangier, Morocco. Each country, each city had a proud past and sleepy and hard to decipher present. My knowledge of geography and history were painfully deficient.

Malta, the island of the Knights Templar, after they were evicted from Rhodes, was hauntingly austere. The fortresses of the Knights, and the narrow protected harbor hid a cramped place that knew far too much about sieges. Arid, isolated and the scene of much carnage in the Middle Ages and World War II, the island people we encountered were especially re-silient, friendly, but reserved. The isolated fishing harbor of

Marsaxloxx, filled with dozens of small brightly painted fishing boats, seemed a timeless and remote Mediterranean cove. It was startling to know the Phoenicians were anchored here 3,000 years ago. Saint Paul was shipwrecked on the island, and lived and taught there.

Weeks later, we made our second stop in beautiful Palma, another refuge for the Knights as they were pushed further west by the Ottomans. Our return roughly coincided with a couple of promotions. My gold bar had turned to silver. A LTJG stripe was needed on my dress uniforms. Our Navigator had advanced to Full Lieutenant. We, and half a dozen wardroom well-wishers, set out for our "wetting down party", a night on the town, where we were expected to pick up the bar tab and all would share a meal. Someone chose an upscale restaurant. Most of the contingent was more interested in the booze than the food.

Meson Carlos I, in a narrow street near the massive Cathedral, offered the best meal I had experienced on the cruise. But the fine food began to fade somewhat in an alcoholic haze. The very careful and low-key Navigator didn't notice the shots being poured into his beer glass. By dessert, his behavior was a bit incoherent and loud. He thought the crust of his pie included the dish below. We paid our bill, and hastily left before being asked to go.

We all walked, somewhat erratically, through the mostly deserted medieval and gold hued stone streets of Palma. Down near the water, Le Seu, the city's magnificent cathedral stood guard like a Gothic aircraft carrier. Eventually we found our way back to the piers and our ship. It was transient, but being shipmates was a very special kind of friendship. We were tiny specks in a foreign land, looking out for each other, as ship's crews have done since ancient times.

Morning sea and anchor detail came all too soon. When faced with a short night, my dad used to say "you need to sleep fast." Plenty of extra cups of coffee were consumed and most of us left port not firing on all cylinders.

We spent a lot of time at sea, and it was good to be coursing the ocean with an important job to do and exotic places to visit. But we were removed from the rest of humanity, as seafarers always have been. I saw the kind of men who were "lifers". There was a price to pay in this career, and it was usually paid at the home end, as with my dad. I could easily do this work and enjoy it, but like the *Flying Dutchman*, where would it lead?

Tangier was probably our most intriguing and dangerous port of call. I admonished my sailors not to get in trouble there. If they did, we might never see them again. Even those who were apt to test the limits were not eager to see the inside of a Moroccan jail. A decade before "*Midnight Express*", the cockiest sailors knew that the local police would play by different rules.

The American Consulate arranged a good will project for us. With several dozen volunteers, we gladly spent a day building a playground for an orphanage in a poor neighborhood in the hills. The kids were very shy, but at the end of the day were testing our handiwork. They took to the slides, sand boxes and swings like old hands.

In port, activity on board ship was at a bare minimum. With skeleton watches manned, we walked around the old city for a few days. Several of us wandered through the kasbah, together for support and company, relying on pint sized amateur child guides. For a few dirhams, they steered us to craft merchants or extricated us from the white on white maze of the medina. If there were any street signs, they were in Arabic.

We bargained for leather stools, slippers and small rugs. The lowest offer was achieved after walking out of the store, the merchant running after you and reluctantly offering his "best price".

At a semi-respectable bar, just beyond the souks, we met a Moroccan Army Officer who took us under his wing. None of us were astute enough to be puzzled by a Muslim drinking on the periphery of the old town, but he wasn't alone. There was a general sense of decay. The city had seen better times. None of us were interested or desperate enough for the drugs or commercial sex for which the place was notorious. The dangers outweighed any reward. After sharing some tagines and couscous with our new friend, and perhaps minder, we headed back to the ship, glad to have our wallets and persons intact.

I didn't know at the time that Rick's Bar in *Casablanca* was really based on the watering hole at the El Minzah hotel in Tangier, a snakepit of spies and illicit business during the Second World War. To this day, it is an elegant and somewhat faded hotel with more of a past than a future.

Half a lifetime later I returned to Morocco. By then I had a far greater appreciation of the country, its history and people. If the secret police were not entirely gone, at least the standard of living had greatly improved. Under a younger and more liberal king, life was better for most. Morocco was the first country to recognize the young United States, and is still a friend in a turbulent part of the world.

Our projected return to Virginia changed several times. In late May we finally had orders. Without a stop in Rota, we steamed west through the Straits of Gibraltar. The ship trudged alone across the Atlantic on the way home. Ten days later, we entered Hampton Roads. Transiting the ocean, there was rarely a blip on the radar screen. Now the monitor was full of buck shot; several dozen tiny dots. The bay was full of ships and myriad small boats. The bridge and navigation team tensely tracked range and bearing on anything that might get in our way. For a few long hours we crawled towards and then through the harbor. The smaller boats would just have to get out of the way. It took a half a mile or more to stop a tanker underway. The harbor pilot came on board. In an hour, we were tied up alongside a remote pier at Craney Island Fuel Terminal in Portsmouth, Virginia. Deployment was over. It would be ten years before I returned to the Mediterranean, in civilian clothes.

06

The Greatest Gift

*A*ucilla was scheduled for a few months of minor pier side maintenance and a few days at a time of sea operations off the "VA Capes". In mid-summer, we would return to Guantanamo Bay, Cuba for sea trials. The ship and crew prepared for another fall deployment. People come and go with some frequency on a Navy ship. Gradually, the ship's company changes. The wardroom atmosphere can switch from friendly to tense or vice versa with even a couple of substitutions.

For me, things were going in the wrong direction. Most people on board I liked and respected. But for a number of months I reported to someone who was hard to get along with. It was an unpleasant change. Would the chain of command see through or around this? I requested a transfer to another ship. When your path crosses someone who just doesn't like you, the feeling is usually mutual. Mistrust festers. In the close confines of a ship, when it's your immediate boss, the combination is toxic. A harsh and unfair fitness report could table a career. Fortunately, the XO had rewritten mine, but that hadn't changed the relationship.

While I waited for a transfer, the Navy had one more, and the greatest gift, to bestow upon me. I was in the right place at the right time. Most of the ship's bachelor junior officers were making up for lost time. We "went on the beach" almost every night, doing the rounds of officer's clubs and other hot spots. On the third night of one of those routines, I reluctantly joined the crowd. After a drink or two at Fort Story, an Army Officers Club, we headed down to the waterfront, bars and nightclubs of Virginia Beach.

That summer my wife to be was on a beach vacation with a girl friend. We met on the dance floor of a club and stayed late. It was an unlikely place for either of us to be. A tall, comely, thoughtful and gentle blonde, she made me forget everyone that came before. I walked her back to her motel and almost missed my ride back to the ship. After two more dates that week, she headed home to Ohio and we went back to sea. We exchanged lengthy daily letters for another month. There were no e-mails or texts in those days. Hers were delivered in batches when we returned to port.

Few people today understand the pleasure and pain of writing in long hand, or pecking at a typewriter. Neither method had an erase key. You write from the mind and heart and wait patiently or impatiently for a reply. Carrying on a conversation in slow motion makes you think long and hard on what you want to say. You carry a special letter around in your pocket, to be reread. Separation from someone you love is never easy. For some it strengthens bonds; in others, it shreds them.

We had the consolation prize of being busy as hell. Guantanamo Bay Refresher Training was often an 18 hour a day exercise in combat and fire drills, now in the heat of a Caribbean summer.

I had some leave time and suggested we meet in Ithaca, New York. After six years at Cornell, it was my second home. It was half way between Gayle's home in Ohio and the ship in Norfolk. After a few days in Ithaca, I would visit her hometown in Ohio. It was not planned. As she got off the plane and walked into my arms, I proposed marriage and she immediately accepted. Some 50 years later, it is still the best decision I ever made.

Orders came through for a transfer to the *John F. Kennedy*, a new carrier on its maiden voyage. It would mean at least a year at sea. At home in Manhattan on the last couple days of leave, I was excited about another Europe deployment. But how would this affect my future bride? We hadn't set a wedding date and I would soon be half way across the globe.

Then there was a call from an OCS classmate who had just returned from a tour in Vietnam. He mentioned a new "early out" program. The war was coming to an end. The Navy wanted volunteers to stand down as the service shrunk. I could call a number in Washington and get back to civilian life.

It was the end of August 1969. I enjoyed the service, but there was unfinished business. I wanted to do the best I could for the lady who would be my partner. I called the Cornell Law School Dean. The new term was less than two weeks away. Still, I would be welcomed back for my third year.

A few days later, I took a long last look at *Aucilla*. She was alongside a pier at Craney Island, the outer reaches of Portsmouth, VA. My roommate, and future best man, would stay on board, now promoted to supply officer. I wished him well, and said good-bye to many shipmates. Then I carried my bags to my car and drove north. In a few more days, I would again be a civilian.

A lot happened quickly. The Navy issued orders transferring me to the reserves. I found an apartment in Ithaca. Clothes and belongings were shipped or carried from Virginia and Manhattan to upstate New York. In short order, I went back to the text books and Gayle started planning for a November wedding.

We had accepted each other on instinct and trust. I didn't even know if she could cook. Fortunately, she could magnificently. We shared a deep love of music. She had studied piano, organ and flute and I doodled at the keyboard. Both of us had a passion for travel which trumped any other pursuit.

Gayle grew up in a small town in Ohio, Apple Creek. It had fewer people than the city blocks I had lived on in Brooklyn and Manhattan. For many years, her parents ran a small grocery store that catered to the Amish and other farmers. With a 24/7 commitment, her dad had also been Chief of the Volunteer Fire Department for nearly 30 years. She had been an Executive Secretary at The Wooster Brush Company and then at the College of Wooster. Her UK ancestors went back to the Mayflower and well beyond, with relatives who fought in both the Revolutionary and Civil War. Not that I knew any of that at the time.

Perhaps her parents were a little apprehensive about a New Yorker whose ancestors left what is now Belarus in a hurry in the 1880s. But they never showed it. They knew we were in love and accepted me as a son.

Wooster County wasn't quite Norman Rockwell country. But the rolling hills, incredibly rich black soil, multiple churches, hard working people and sense of community were genuine. On the outskirts were Amish farms. Black horse drawn buggies carried the faithful when they left their homesteads. It was pastoral and pretty. Still, neither of us wanted to stay there.

We were married in Ohio, and spent a long and snowy winter in Ithaca. My wife gave up a job she loved and took a temporary one, the best she could find in a college town, until the end of the school year. We couldn't afford, in time or money, much of a honeymoon. But I have tried to make it up to her ever since. Our dreams of exploring Europe had to wait.

How do you pay tribute to a happy marriage that stretches to a half century? We still enjoy being together through the silences as much as the conversations. There is much that is complimentary: I am a man of sometimes too many words; she few and well chosen. She is a better judge of character, a better listener. Perhaps I have the better imagination and empathy. We remember the same things-differently. Together they form a better whole. She can get pretty angry. But it blows away quickly. I almost never lose my temper. My optimism is sometimes unfounded. Her occasional pessimism equally unwarranted. She remembers our neighbors, cousins and acquaintances children's names and birthdays, and I don't. At the end of the day, and every day, we give each other strength, meaning and merriment.

Winter began its annual upstate siege. Together, we headed out on job interviews in New York and New England. By spring, we knew our new home would be near Springfield, Massachusetts. It was new territory for both of us.

Over the years, my wife has been the chief accountant, keeping us in financial equilibrium. She is pragmatic and self disciplined in regard to everything, except Italian shoes. I need her permission to buy another book, or a more expensive bottle of wine. She almost always makes reserves for an unexpected dental or car expense. She is a fine cook and as hard a worker as I know. While mostly practical and skeptical, sometimes a romantic strain wins out. She is probably a better judge of character than I am. We are always on the same page when it comes to a fine restaurant, a show or the open road. We have never had a profound argument, and I suspect we never will. We are growing old, but it doesn't really matter.

07

Looking Back; Looking Forward

The next May, we packed our few belongings into our Dodge sedan and the front third of a commercial moving van. It was 300 miles east to Springfield. I had accepted a post as an attorney with a large life insurance company. Gayle soon found secretarial work with a paper and packaging manufacturer.

Neither of us had any family ties in the area. We would try living in New England for awhile. Our only prior experience there was her family's driving vacations and my summers as a camper and counselor in Maine and at a sailing camp on Cape Cod. The Pioneer Valley was then merely a place on the map. Nearly 50 years later, we are still here.

We both worked long hours and started low on the respective corporate totem poles. In the early years, there were driving vacations. With modest incomes, limited time off and fledgling careers, we were grateful to head out for a few weeks of budget motels, scenic roads and the American and Canadian country-side.

Starting with sandwiches and salads from our favorite deli in a cooler, we drove on various trips to the Blue Ridge Parkway, the Great Smokies, Florida, New Orleans, the flat expanses of Texas, and over the border to Nova Scotia and the Gaspe Peninsula of Quebec. Eventually, we drove cross country twice.

Frugally, we bought juice and Danish at a local supermarket for breakfast in motel rooms. Sometimes we would picnic at lunch or dine in a cafeteria in a shopping center. We splurged on an elegant or at least interesting dinner, if one could be found.

They were few and far between outside large cities, especially in the Deep South, the Plains and Atlantic Canada. In Winnemucca, NV, the best recommendation was to the Husky Truck Stop. At least we were going someplace new and together. We relished the freedom of the road, our company and a glimpse of a totally different life. But we were just passing through.

Gayle's parents continued to live in Apple Creek, Ohio. My mother and favorite aunt called a tiny apartment in Manhattan home. We visited dutifully and alternately on holidays. Work weeks of 60-70 hours were routine. In my spare time, I stayed active in the Naval Reserve. For us, our time away was the highlight of each year, even visiting places we were in no hurry to see again.

My gypsy blood was from my father. Born in London, he came to the U.S. at the age of 2. Before World War II, he had sailed on more than a dozen ships as a musician. After the war, he returned to the sea, putting in five years or so with the Moore-McCormack Lines.

My mother and I made two 38-day cruises to South America with him when I was five and nine. We mostly stayed home and led a more conventional life. Not that it was my choice. I dreamed of careers that would take me a long way from our small apartment in Brooklyn. It was not a bad place to grow up, especially with the Dodgers three blocks away and the beautiful Botanic Gardens and Prospect Park nearby.

As a teenager, I read books about faraway lands, walked the piers in Manhattan, visited ships, and hung out in the library at the Seaman's Church Institute. I learned to sail on Cape Cod. It wasn't quite like *"Two Years before the Mast"*, *"The Sea and the Jungle"* or *"Mr. Roberts"*.

The Navy experience had been satisfying. I stayed in the Naval Reserve as a "ship driver" rather than as a legal officer. I liked the people, the strong fellowship and the potential to build a second career.

In the early years that meant driving to some WWII quonset huts in Springfield every tuesday night. Later it was a one weekend a month schedule at Westover Air Base or Sub Base New London. Spartan classrooms and a generic drill hall were a far cry from sea duty. The weekend warrior part was far removed from the regular Navy. I questioned whether I was doing much good for the Navy or myself.

Gradually, the Navy took the Reserves more seriously. We had specific mobilization assignments. Every year we did 14-17 days of training duty with the active Navy, at sea on various types of ships or at a stateside base. We were not always welcomed. The gap narrowed just before and during the Gulf War.

The naval commitment was rough on my wife and didn't help my legal career. But it paid big dividends in lasting friendships, travel, new skills and promotion in the service. Way down the road, it brought a nice little pension and health benefits.

In my last ten years of reserve duty I was assigned to Military Sealift Command, Europe. Exercises and operations in Washington, D.C., The Netherlands, Belgium and London were far better than drilling in a gym or classroom, or standing watches in New London or Norfolk.

By 1977, we could afford our first overseas trip: two weeks in England. I would see where my father was born. For a college English major, it was a great place to start. We might even understand some of the language. We booked a charter flight through work but made our own arrangements for car, hotels and exploring.

The first night, we stayed in a 16th century creaky inn in Rye, a very pretty and almost theatrical town. It was on a cobblestoned street. Steep roofed Tudor buildings leaned in on each other.

Pubs, thatched roofs and narrow lanes meandering into the ancient countryside kept us enchanted for 10 days, despite generally dreary food. London was intoxicating. I wish I could say we made lasting friendships or met some unforgettable characters. But we were just drifting tourists soaking up some atmosphere and history.

The three-story house on Beringer Street, where my father was born, was still standing. Gentrified, there was a Solicitor's Office on the first floor, perhaps a benign omen for my career. On the last night, I did what I had been doing for years. I looked in the phone book for Fridkins. One was listed. Soon I was talking to a cousin I didn't know that I had. He was a Solicitor too. I had called his elderly mother's number, and he was in the process of moving her out of the city. He mentioned that my dad had played his violin at his mother's wedding. There were still Fridkins scattered through England!

We were leaving the next morning, so we could only agree to stay in touch. He told me that my aunt Aileen, my father's only living sibling, had made a similar call a few months before on a trip to London. My mother had not stayed in touch with my father's family, nor had they with her. In a few months, we reconnected with my aunt and uncle. A piece of my past was restored.

In two years, we had saved for another transatlantic crossing. For our tenth wedding anniversary, we flew to Spain. On our anniversary day, we were heading to Marbella. In the early afternoon, we drove through a small town. A wedding procession was leaving a beautiful old church. We stopped the car, and I walked down the street taking pictures of the bride and groom. They were an extremely handsome couple and I got an extraordinary close up shot of them walking gracefully to a limousine. We don't know who they were, or even remember the town. I hope their marriage is as long and as fulfilling as ours. Someday, I hope to find them and give them that stunning picture.

That trip generated more intense images for us than England: a dirt road over the hills to Dali's charming fishing village of Cadaques; the silence and beauty of the hilltop Monastery of Montserrat; El Greco's exact view from our parador in Toledo; the graceful, nearly 2,000-year-old Roman Aqueduct in Segovia, still carrying water; a tiny father and daughter store in Madrid that sold just one thing: candied violets. There are intense culinary memories of angullas (baby eels), red mullet, and a dozen versions of paella in various coastal towns.

In the paradors and small hotels, we met and enjoyed other intrepid travelers. There was an expat couple, the husband worked for Aramco in Saudi Arabia. Living in that medieval kingdom was not easy, although amply rewarded. Their consolation prize: a month or so rambling through Europe each year. We could, and did, drink to that.

Before I reported for Navy duty, my ship had been homeported in Barcelona. We quickly knew why our sailors loved the city. Friendly, frenetic and attractive, it was a place to savor. We drove many miles, but felt most at home in languid coastal towns like Gerona and Sitges.

Two years later we headed to France. For good food and wine, what destination could be more enticing? It was possible to get a bad meal in France, but you would have to work very hard at it. Our very first lunch was at a formal restaurant in the little village of Senlis. An older gentleman and his son were at the next table conversingly quietly. Under the table was an obedient little poodle. We admired the dog, and the father asked us, in perfect English, where we were from. He mentioned that English had saved his life when the Americans liberated his town in WWII. He asked me to guess his age. I underestimated it by over 10 years. Sadly, he noted that his doctor had limited him to one cigar a day, and the wine he had at meals. He wished us a good journey.

That night, at a castle hotel in Picardy, we had the best and most elegant meal of our lives, to date. My wife told our host: "If the food is not this good in heaven, we are not going there."

No longer on an Ensign's budget, we navigated by the stars, those of the Michelin Red Guide. Back then the dollar was strong against the french franc. We tightened our money belt before and after, and celebrated in France.

Those who love french cooking regret the passing of earlier times of culinary grandeur. In the early 80s, there were still many legendary chefs in charge of time honored institutions. There were cadres of professional waiters, mostly male and in their fifties or older, vast sets of Limoges china, flowers and french silver on the tables and little guilt over butter and cream sauces. Dining was a very passionate and theatrical undertaking.

It was time for a brief dose of nostalgia. We drove down the coastal road past Nice. On the waterfront, I walked the harbor promenade of Villefranche, this time in mid-morning, and with the love of my life. The town was just as beautiful, a touch more modern and prosperous, and just as hard to leave. There were no Navy ships in sight. A cruise ship was anchored in the outer harbor. We soaked up the atmosphere, strolled medieval streets, and pledged to come back for a longer stay. But we had a long way to go that day.

In the south of France, the exact vistas captured by the great painters can be seen. A café in Arles still stands where Van Gogh painted a starry night. You can see the aspects that inspired Monet, Picasso, Cocteau, Matisse and Chagall.

Our love of travel has not abated. As only children, with no children, we have been able to go many places. There is little point in recording every trip and place. But some experiences stay with you.

At some point, being a tourist is not enough. Not if you want to know and care about a place at a deeper level. Staying put for awhile in a foreign land means that it and you become less foreign. The second, third and more times you set foot in a store, restaurant or house, you, the owners and employees are no longer ciphers. Conversation, courtesy, curiosity focus you on that place and time. There is the possibility of understanding, respect or even friendship. The full measure and charm of everyday life prevails.

08

Finding Our Second Home

In 1983, we made our first trip together to Northern Italy. Ancient cities, good food and wine were predictably entertaining. But I really wanted to show my wife the Italian Riviera, especially Rapallo and Genoa, favorite ports of call from the service. We felt very much at ease in a country where almost everyone has family ties to America.

Rapallo looked tired and even more faded. We stayed in Santa Margherita, a much cheerier town. It was livelier and prettier than Rapallo and less pretentious than Portofino. The latter was the iconic port depicted on millions of post cards. Its harbor was filled with fancy yachts, but it seemed too pretentious.

As our vacation time dwindled, we set off for Genoa, scarcely twenty miles away. We drove through a dozen or

more tunnels on the autostrada. Descending into the city it became an excruciating place to drive. Traffic was heavy and
street signs rare. Roads followed the contours of old hills and
the curvy harbor. Deep in the old city we approached gridlock.

Our hotel was on a traffic circle abutting a steep hill. We
saw it through the rear-view mirror. Unfortunately, we were
forced into a long one-way tunnel. In a few minutes we were
deposited within a few hundred yards of the main train station,
Principe, still in the midst of dense and unforgiving traffic.

I frantically studied my map, and my wife, always better at
the wheel, questioned why we thought we could drive in this
crazy city. Long before GPS, where streets change names every few blocks, finding where we were on a map was not easy.
By luck and instinct, we made it back to the hotel.

On foot, the city made more sense and was less stressful.
We have driven there many times since. Now we head for a
parking garage or lot near one of the two main train stations,
and then switch to bus, taxi or walking.

We spent the afternoon rambling through the old neighborhoods. The sailor's quarter was less threatening in daylight,
but still down at the heels. Asians, North and Central Africans
lived and worked side by side with the Genoese in tiny shops
and markets. A long period of gradual rehabilitation of the city
had not yet started.

Genoa is at the center of a boomerang shaped tiny province, Liguria. Once called La Superba, and The Proud, it was one of the wealthiest trading cities on the planet. Its power and self-confidence had declined, roughly parallel to the diminished importance of its port. By the seventies, there were few of the great transatlantic ocean liners. Only less glamorous ferries heading to Sardinia, Sicily and Tunisia, and an occasional cruise ship came in to berth.

Ancient palaces and churches are nestled along dark alleys. Almost anything, legal or not is for sale in the rabbit warren of passage ways. The grand old mansions are now museums, college buildings or bank offices. Like Matryoska, Russian nesting dolls, we find the more we dig into Genoa, the more we glean. Few other places envelop you with three thousand years of history and their memories. It was a big city, and totally oblivious to our meanderings. Being from New York, that didn't bother me a bit.

The next morning, on a splendid early fall day, we drove toward a planned overnight stop in San Remo just 70 miles away. San Remo was selected arbitrarily. Guide books said it was a pleasant and fashionable place, perhaps good for an afternoon and evening stroll.

Those books barely distinguished the coastal towns. From our map, there were dozens along the Riviera Del Fiori. Many might be worthy to explore if we had more time. On the outskirts of Genoa, we returned to the Autostrada. From La

Spezia to Nice and beyond it is an engineering marvel. With over a hundred tunnels carved in the cliffs, some are as short as fifty yards, and a few nearly a mile in length. It follows the coastline and is usually perched high above it. You catch glimpses of the ancient lands of Eastern and Western Liguria, the Riviera Levante and Riviera Ponente, as you rocket along between large trucks, camper vans and sedans.

We didn't have the slightest inkling that in a few hours our lives would take a serendipitous turn.

The Levante, east of Genoa is more dramatic. From a half mile or more up in the hills, you see tenacious signs of human life clinging to the slopes. There are hot houses on steep hillsides; small terraced plots of olive trees or vines, tiny primitive stone houses in the stone flecked and uneven fields. Small cemeteries and the occasional ugly land fill compete for limited ledges. Every inch of horizontal space is utilized. Nearly vertical slopes are terraced for agriculture.

West of Genoa, the hills are less severe. High rise tenement apartments wedge into narrow lots. Tiny balconies are filled with plants and plastic chairs. Further west, two to four story vacation condos, and some older stone houses, often cookie cutter designs, replicate like rabbits. Almost all are painted in seven or eight distinctive gelati colors associated with Genoa.

At, or near the water or beach, modest hotels, restaurants, cabanas are built close together. An old church or cathedral, town square, and cemetery anchor each town's core. In the countryside, the occasional wealthy villa and more frequent modest farmer's cabin are islands of shade under the powerful subtropical sun. As you get closer to France, there are glass hot houses filled with roses, orchids and other prized flowers.

Just west of Genoa are industrial suburbs with decaying hulks of heavy industries mostly abandoned, an Italian rust belt. The port continues almost unabated for more than ten miles. Waterfront warehouses, tankers and freighters sit alongside piers and staging areas. More ships are anchored off shore. Tankers discharge into thick pipes sitting above the sea and running out to anchorages. Towards the hills, elegant old apartment houses, mansions and public buildings, in various states of repair, hint of better times.

You can't see or savor much flying along at 75 miles an hour on a super highway. Large trucks carry goods from as far away as Romania, Greece and Spain to the opposite ends of Europe. You could cover 600 or 700 miles a day, but to what purpose?

From the bird's eye view of the Autostrada, many of the towns looked tired, even scruffy. But the Italians haven't ruined the charm of their seasides as much as the Spanish and Portuguese. Real estate developers haven't had the money or political license to bulldoze and build many high rises and package tour hotels. This happened in Rapallo to some extent and caused a backlash up and down the coast.

From a distance, a casual traveler might dismiss the boxy and plain mid-rise coastal apartment houses, and Spartan small hotels, as generic and depressing. Some streets and empty lots are more unkempt than dirty. But they were built mostly for the Italians and were an improvement over what was there before.

Brush fires in summer and mudslides in late fall can scar the pretty hillsides. Aside from cactus, umbrella pines and scrubby trees, anything else is intensely husbanded. Beyond a few wide beaches, spectacular private gardens and public parks, much of the scraggy sea shore is shared with railroad track, snack bars and gas stations. Steep hills almost dip into the sea, leaving little for people to latch onto. Absent a few upscale enclaves, access to the ocean is public.

Everyday life is focused at the water's edge and in hillside hamlets, with the concrete conveyor belt of a super highway thrust between. It was late morning when we started from Genoa. We needed to be in San Remo by early evening. With my priorities, the crucial question was: where to stop for Monday lunch?

Close to one, we were zipping through alternating tunnels and sunlight on the Autostrada. Gayle drove steadily on. I scanned the Michelin Red Guide. I am usually the navigator, and she the primary driver. The days are long gone when my vision was 20/15, but I can still spot or divine a good restaurant quicker than most.

With a mile or two to go, I said: "let's take the next exit." We were bound for Alassio for the first time. It was just a name in a guide book, but one that would be on our lips for the rest of our lives. We left the toll road dropping down to the farm patches of Albenga.

Albenga, a Roman market town, grows on you with increased exposure. But at first encounter, the commercial outskirts were homely, unzoned and unkempt. The old national road skirts the ancient walled city core. There are few hints of the interesting buildings, towers and squares within. The lush agricultural valley, for which it is famous, is on the horizon.

That valley, above and below the super highway, is filled with small fields of artichokes, olive trees, and tiny vineyards, some barely bigger than backyards. They compete with modest manufacturing plants, mini-warehouses and obscure discount stores on the outskirts of the city. They stretch out a few miles almost to the hills in the north. Along the non-descript road connecting the autostrada to the city, there are gas stations, a few new car dealers and car repair shops, small houses and tiny garden plots.

You pass some urban amenities, a small football stadium, a bicycle path, a little used promenade along a dry river bed. Later we learned that the course can quickly change from a trickling stream to a raging torrent. A pre-World War II Army casern on the eastern outskirts of the city was on its last laps. Later abandoned and even more forlorn, tall concrete fences ringed with barbed wire and empty guard posts, it is now used to house refugees from Africa and the Middle East. A homely and deteriorating downtown hospital served the town and neighboring villages for over a century. Some 25 years later, the town finally built a small modern facility a half mile away. There has been a halfhearted and unsuccessful attempt to turn the old hospital buildings into apartments and office space.

On the way to Alassio, the old national road makes an abrupt right angle turn parallel and close to the sea. Then it lines up with a stark 700-meter tunnel reinforced with a metal quonset hut cap. The cliff above from time to time rains falling rocks. Once through the massive hill, there is a single railroad track, a few tiny strip farms and a camper trailer park to the left edging towards the sea. The road ascends gently. Soon you look almost straight down on the sea a hundred feet below and just past a natural almost vertical rock wall. On the right is a mostly continuous stone cliff. Unseen, above is the path of an old Roman Road, now a popular hiking trail.

The winding road meanders up and down like the quieter end of a roller coaster. It hugs a thin ledge between rocky cliffs. Soon a narrow and wild beach lies below. Quickly you move from homeliness to beauty. We caught a few glimpses of comfortable, even elegant houses perched on minute patches of steep flat rock above or beside us. Some have a solitary parking space next to or on top of the home. As the road curves, there is a quick snapshot view of the resort town ahead and below. Then it disappears behind stone.

We entered Alassio, described blandly in guide books as a pleasant beach resort. It had a Michelin two knife and fork restaurant which was open on Monday. We hoped for a decent lunch, and intended to move on, taking in the sights of the coastal road until we reached San Remo late in the day. We hadn't anticipated falling in love with the town.

The cliffs pulled away from the road, allowing for a little level green space, an abundance of flowering shrubs, sidewalks and more distant hillside houses. Attractive mid-rise apartments, residences and small hotels hugged the road. It had turned into a busy city street. The buildings now formed a continuous urban strip. At intersections, there were glimpses of the beach to the left. It was two or three blocks away down narrow gradually descending streets. On the other side, past a railroad track, apartments and villas sat perched on the still steep green hillside.

With nearly a constant row of parked cars on either side, the highway was a luge run of two narrow lanes. Busses, trucks, cars, motorcycles and some intrepid bicyclists and pedestrians vied for position often edging over the center line. As we ran the gauntlet, I tried to determine where we needed to stop. The Red Guide's miniature map showed only a few tiny parking lots.

It was getting late for lunch. In France, they might turn us away so close to 2 PM. Would the Italians do the same? I glanced up and down, looking at buildings and palm trees, wrestling with the inadequate city map and the occasional street sign. Quiet, respectable, neat, and a little old fashioned, the town had a good vibe. The street changed names every three or four blocks. We continued to move forward, inches from the parked cars.

Fortunately, it was Monday and well past the high season. Traffic was bearable. Just as we came up to the municipal park, we saw a few open parking spaces and pulled in. Restaurant Palma was less than two blocks away, on the tiny but elegant Via Cavour, a small street flanked by tall palms. A lovely tan sand beach was scarcely a hundred feet ahead down a gentle slope.

The restaurant occupied the first floor of an old house across the street from a magnificent mansion; one we would later learn was perhaps the most opulent in the town. It belongs to a member of the Agnelli (Fiat) family. Just before the beach, there was a lovely piazzetta, ringed by a few more restaurants and a café.

Palma's door was locked. There was a brass button discreetly at its side. We looked quickly at a formal menu under a sparkling clean glass enclosure next to the door. I rang the door bell and heard a muted soft ring inside. In a few seconds, we were warmly and somewhat formally greeted by a smiling

Silvio Viglietti. He wore an immaculate white uniform and a little extra girth from years of cooking and enjoying excellent food. The smile was warm and engaging, and we were welcomed as if he was expecting us.

We instantly felt at ease. We were inside an elegant and beautifully furnished old house. His English was limited, but far better than our Italian. He radiated genuine hospitality and dignity. He seemed thoroughly pleased to have two unannounced American guests show up at the outer edges of the lunch hour. We apologized for not having made a reservation. The guide book indicated the restaurant was small, and recommended reserving. There were a few local customers, and the meal service was winding down.

I wish I could remember that first meal in exacting detail. It has blended into many memories of several dozen visits to this exceptional restaurant. We started with an exemplary fritto misto, lightly battered fried calamari, and other local crustaceans. The wine was either a local Pigato or Vermentino, the beautiful regional whites produced in limited quantities for local consumption. As we have frequently enjoyed for three decades, there were several little dishes, a tasting menu featuring the best local fish, produce and olive oil. All were intelligent riffs on traditional Ligurian cuisine.

Massimo, Silvio's son, was then merely the sommelier, but a passionate one. With his father's blessing, he had apprenticed in one- and two-star restaurants in France, and visited many innovative wine producers throughout Italy and France. Father and son alternated bringing courses, each one described and served with a combination of enthusiasm and modesty. Massimo's English was better than that of his Dad, but he kept a little distance, his Father clearly in charge. You could see the family resemblance in mannerisms and posture, although Massimo was taller and thinner.

Massimo responded thoughtfully to all my eccentric questions. It was the beginning of a friendship, an affection for this family, restaurant and town that has continued and grown for more than thirty years.

Over coffee and dessert, we learned a regular patron lived in our then hometown of Agawam, Massachusetts. This gentleman, once a renowned professional bicycle racer, had owned a bicycle shop in Alassio. He moved to America decades before and had an automobile service station in Springfield. Each summer he returned to Alassio where he was still a local hero.

We happily agreed to hand carry a restaurant post card in greetings to their friend. When we told Silvio that their restaurant deserved a Michelin Star, he beamed even brighter. As we left, he earnestly asked us to write to Michelin. Certainly, we would! Whether it had any impact, the next year they did get a star.

After a fine lunch, and the warm afterglow of the Viglietti family's hospitality, we reluctantly took leave. We drove back to Albenga and picked up the Autostrada west to San Remo.

San Remo was larger, and perhaps a wealthier town. But it was showing signs of faded or fading glory. We passed up its grandest Victorian hotels for a modern and generic one on the old national highway. A stroll around the town's extensive Marina was enjoyable. We walked up to the famous Casino and past the grand hotels on the west side of town. There was some window shopping and a fine meal. San Remo was an agreeable town, but Alassio was different. There was something about it that stayed with us.

OOO

09

Three Small Towns and Back to Alassio

After several driving trips, we rented a house in Europe for the first time in 1988. It was a fine country home in the tiny village of Campagnac, France. The southwest Languedoc region was rustic, had a tempestuous history and hearty food. Our landlords became long time friends. They knew France as well as their native Canada.

There are leaps of faith on both sides renting a house sight unseen to or from someone you don't know. Half way around the world, there is a tiny dot of a village. Before the internet, we scouted little ads in college magazines, international newspapers and magazines. A few cryptic sentences ended with an obscure area code.

On the phone with a stranger, you try to determine whether the house is charming or a clunker. They assess whether you will treasure or trash their place and if you are good for the rental payment. Fortunately, there are a lot of decent people out there who have staked their little corner of paradise. Most want to subsidize the expense of a remote second home.

We hit it off well, and our soon to be friends were impressed that we had stayed previously within five miles of their house, in the bastide village of Cordes. After being mailed some pictures of their home and an outline of suggestions on provisioning in neighboring and larger towns, we happily sent our deposit check and started dreaming of our fall 1988 vacation.

Armed with the best maps we could find, we set out for new territory. We were told the village was so small, 28 families, we might drive through it before finding their address, and so we did. On the second try, we saw their lovely farm house, across from a communal barn used for storing the vendange. A vineyard started thirty feet off their back porch. The house had five stone fireplaces, including one in the flagstone floored kitchen. Simply furnished, with airy and cheery bedrooms on the second floor, it was a place that had been loved and we were happy to settle in and savor the area.

Ten miles south down a provincial road, past rugged hills, was the small city of Gaillac. Known for its rough and ready red wine, it was also a little market town. We stopped at a large Leclerc supermarket. Back at our rental house, we put milk and juice in the refrigerator, left a bag of croissants on the kitchen table and went upstairs to unpack. An hour or so later, I came back down to the kitchen and found a mouse enjoying a gourmet lunch in our bread bag. The mouse meal was interrupted, the vagrant flung alive out the door, and the first croissants we had purchased were relegated to the garbage. Only then, I saw light streaming in through a tiny gap under the front wooden door. Lesson learned. Henceforth, all food provisions were immediately placed in cupboards. The oven became an interim bread box.

Going to the grocer, the baker, replacing propane tanks, and seeing local people regularly at the market placed us in the community. We were still tourists, but not just passing through. A few villagers politely said bonjour as we walked along the road, perhaps relieved that we weren't Parisians. With our primitive French and their rural reticence, regrettably there were few opportunities for longer conversations.

While delighted with our very comfortable digs, a little apprehension sets in when you realize you are deep in another country. There is no "front desk". If you have a problem, you are on your own to deal with the police, fire department, a physician's office or some other difficult situation. In an emergency, we would have to rely on the kindness of strangers.

Around Campagnac, there was much to see in all directions. We ventured west into foie gras and cognac country and east into the Gard. Just a few miles north was lovely Cordes, a fortified hilltop habitation since the 13th century, it is certified as one of France's most beautiful villages. An hour south, was the ancient river city of Toulouse and beyond that the Pyrenees.

It was rugged country. Think of men in camouflage, toting shotguns and hunting rifles, traipsing through the brush with their trusty dogs. There was game to be cornered. What is the French equivalent of "redneck"?

Theoretically, we could have done some very serious cooking with all the wonderful local markets. But we were on vacation. Other than some salads and fruit for respite at home, we were on the hunt for excellent restaurants. It was a region of myriad varieties of sausage, pate' and poultry, farmed and wild. Stony fields made life difficult, as they do in New England.

The next year, we found another intriguing rental, this time in Italy. The house was in Figline Val d'Arno, a few miles south of Florence. It was on the railroad line into that iconic city and an ideal place for exploring Tuscany.

Most European house and apartment rentals run Saturday to Saturday. With limited time, we planned a one-night stop in Alassio before heading on to this rental in Chianti country. We looked forward to returning to Restaurant Palma. It had retained its Michelin star for several years. Had our letter done any good, or had the anonymous Michelin inspectors just figured it out on their own?

The Diana Grande Hotel was our overnight stop. Rectangular and in an austere 1960's modern style, the hotel was rather sterile. It was right above the beach, had a large indoor pool and conference facilities, none of which were important to us. The few parking spaces out front were more useful. The likes of Kiwanis and Rotary Clubs met there regularly. It was a pleasant quarter mile stroll through a residential quarter to our much anticipated dinner. Reserving ahead, we had received a cordial letter from father Silvio. They were looking forward to our return visit.

We strolled through the budello, the mostly pedestrian alleyway a block inland and parallel to the beach. The town's ambiance and charm enveloped us. Budello means intestines in Italian. The sailors on my old ship talked about visiting "the gut" in some liberty ports, another name for these ancient passages. When you almost touch the walls on either side of the narrow street, the moniker made sense. The sidestreets, or vicos, were even narrower. Some buildings leaning in on each other, with stone braces overhead as some protection from earthquakes.

Unpretentious, the meandering and very clean walk way was lined with modest family run hotels and pensiones; small restaurants, bars and shops. Many catered more to natives than tourists. Even during the passeggiata, when half the town takes a stroll before dinner, the pace of life was slow and mellow.

Almost every small Ligurian town and many of the larger ones, have "caruggi" in dialect. It is another term for the narrow primarily pedestrian only alleyways. In the old days they might permit a mule or horse drawn cart or carriage to pass through. These long, often straight, market streets usually are parallel and just inland from the sea. They form the commercial heart of the community. In towns nestled along the hills, "crueza" narrow steps or ancient mule paths, climb and descend like ladders to or from the sea.

Approaching the dinner hour, we joined the leisurely throng inching its way through town. There were shoppers and window shoppers, whole families, young couples, old couples, solitary people, tourists. The natives often stopped abruptly to greet a friend, reason with a dog or a child, or light a cigarette.

The tourists were mostly Italian, with a smattering of Germans and Swiss, and a rare Brit. We felt we were the only Americans in town, although that probably wasn't true. Like gentle waves, people moved in both directions up and down the street, purposely or ambivalently, quickly or slowly. Surprisingly, there was minimal jostling or friction and no one seemed stressed or upset.

There were settlements here and nearby along the sea for thousands of years. Perhaps the earliest people came from beyond the hills and valleys down to the water's edge to fish. Some claim the town is named after Adelasia, daughter of

Emperor Otto the 1st, the ruler of the Holy Roman Empire in the 900s. No one is sure.

Unlike Albenga, Alassio was not a Roman colony. There is a small and crude Saracen Tower on a point not far from the modern marina. But the origins of the tower are unknown. Little Gallinara Island, closer to Albenga, but very visible from Alassio, was at one time a monastic retreat. Historians claim the town was under the alternating jurisdiction, for centuries, of the church, regional nobility and the larger community of Albenga.

The Regional Tourist Bureau calls this sub-region the Riviera delle Palme and sometimes the Baia del Sole. On lovely sunny days, the labels are justified. Even on a rainy day, it's a peaceful and pleasant place.

On Via Cavour, the familiar glass door was opened quickly by a smiling Silvio. His starched white uniform made him look vaguely like a prosperous doctor. The formal old-fashioned house foyer, with tile floors and oriental rugs, was unchanged. The Vigliettis, father and son, and Massimo's wife, all greeted us in a receiving line as if we were good friends, even though this was but our second visit and it had taken us six years to come back.

Silvio was a little greyer and plumper, Massimo, a little more assertive. Silvio's wife, responsible for many good things behind the scenes, remained in the kitchen.

101

For many meals to come, the dining ritual at Palma always began in that little mirror lined foyer, a truncated sitting room. You stood or sat briefly on tall upholstered chairs to study the menu and wine list They were oversized folios in beautiful script and thick folders. Silvio or Massimo made some tentative suggestions, and they leave you for a few quiet minutes of contemplation. Usually, there were only two tasting menus, one "traditional" the other "gastronomical". The latter had more courses and was perhaps a third more expensive.

Your host listened, made further suggestions, particularly from their unique wine list. Most were from small and obscure vineyards throughout Italy and France. Massimo knew nearly every producer personally.

With a few flourishes on a little white pad, the order is taken and you are ushered into the dining room and seated at one of nine small tables. Each is of a slightly different size, several seating just two. It is much like eating in a fine home, which it is. The senior and junior Vigliettis live in separate quarters above the restaurant. Flemish tapestries hang on the walls. There are exquisite chandeliers, candelabra, old silver and thick luxurious linens covering the tables. The restaurant dates back to 1922 and has an Italian-Victorian atmosphere. There are lots of little personalized touches. I love the silver dachshund knife holders; the faded gold tinted mirrored wall; the geometric patterned tile floor; a few old oriental rugs.

Over several decades, the cooking became more experimental, and to some eccentric. The baton was passed from father to son. Coffee, cinnamon, corn flakes and Coca Cola have shown up in some sauces. The Vigliettis passionately incorporate the finest local ingredients, herbs and spices, produce, and use only the freshest fish, meat and fowl. They never lose sight of Ligurian tradition. Little tasting courses come and go, presented artistically and often dramatically. Layers of flavor are unusual, some are emphatically successful, others less so. Nothing is routine.

Massimo's touch and direction evolves, influenced by cutting edge chefs in Spain and France. He admires Pierre Gagniare in Paris and Ferran Adria of El Bulli. But first and foremost, he is a Ligurian and proud of it. He pursues new insights but respects the terroir. It is a small restaurant with limited choices. All are thoughtful, often marvelous. There are few misfires.

After a quarter century, I can't remember all the dishes that night, but each was artistic and flavorful. Dinner ended with a spectacular dessert: a spun sugar bird's nest on top of home made gelati. Only two or three other tables were occupied that night. That is often the case.

At the end of the evening, we were alone with our hosts. The restaurant had transformed from a very good local establishment to a culinary destination. The transition from father to son was well under way too.

Over after dinner drinks, we told Silvio that next time, and much sooner, we wanted to stay in Alassio for a full vacation. All the other diners had left. We asked if he knew of any nice places we could rent. He nodded, quietly and seemingly with approval. He asked if we would like to see an apartment. Most certainly! He excused himself to make a phone call. When he returned, he motioned us to follow. After settling our bill, we walked toward the beach with Silvio, still in his starched white chef's apron, and turned right.

We strolled a short distance along the quiet ocean promenade. That is too grand a name for the cosy and quiet pedestrian lane between beach, cabanas and the solid row of pastel colored restaurants and hotels. It was scarcely a five-minute walk, past the town pier, beyond more informal restaurants, many with tables overflowing into the street. Behind some thick foliage, we saw the front entrance of Le Terrazze Residence. It was a brand-new establishment in an ancient building.

On the perimeter was a four-foot hedge wall of greenery, a small glassed in fitness room and a narrow tile path leading to thick glass doors and a small and elegant reception room. Silvio escorted us into the lobby and introduced us to the night clerk, a cheerful grandfatherly man, Senor Giuseppe, who we later grew to know and love. He was expecting us. Silvio waited below as we headed upstairs via a tiny elevator.

We were shown a second-floor apartment facing the sea. Clean white walls graced with a few simple sea gull paintings and sailing ship photographs; comfortable, but Spartan white and black furniture; a modern kitchenette with stove, microwave, small refrigerator and a modest supply of plates, pans and silverware. There were ample closets for storage. A small balcony, just yards away from and facing the beach and ocean was the crowning touch.

We looked at each other and smiled. Downstairs, we took a brochure, and told Silvio we would be back, perhaps next year, and all this was "tutto bene! He nodded, and with a little salute of the hand turned and headed home. There were many things I would have liked to ask Silvio, but it was past 11 PM, and his English was as limited as my Italian. I knew he was trained as an attorney. When his parents were ready to retire, it was between him and his brother as to who would continue with the restaurant. Did he choose the restaurant out of duty, passion or both?

We walked back to the Diana, and began making plans to return.

Just a few hours drive north, in the heart of Tuscany, the stay in Figline Val d'Arno was an enjoyable one. Our absentee hosts were a college professor and his wife. She was Italian, and had inherited the ruins of a small de-sanctified monastery church on the edge of the Chianti wine region. The monks had good taste, in wine and countryside. Just twenty minutes by train to downtown Firenze and close to all of what some British call Chiantishire, it was an ideal vacation location.

Our temporary landlords had turned the ancient building into three apartments, with the owners living in the apse of the old church. In the center was a garden full of fresh herbs. The furnishings were basic, but the setting was ideal. On a hill and down a little dirt road, just minutes from the town, we were deep in wine country. At night, you could see the flickering candles from a small neighboring walled cemetery. In daylight, vineyards and rolling hills filled the horizon.

With the owner's directions in hand, we first drove out a rural country road and without too much difficulty found the building. We knocked on the massive front door, but heard no signs of life. The owners' friend, "Giorgio", was to be available the afternoon of our arrival. He would give us the key. We waited. After half an hour it was getting dark and we were getting stressed.

We heard a rustling from behind the building, and then two fellows who looked like peasant throw backs to the Middle Ages came around and up to us. It was unclear who was more startled. We recited the name of the owners and that of Giorgio, and they seemed to relax. Their dialect was incomprehensible to us, and so was our English to them. We learned that they were tenant farmers tending the family's grapes along the back slope of the property. After a few awkward moments, they nodded and disappeared as quickly as they had come.

When we had almost given up, the smallest car I had ever seen noisily drove up. Giorgio got out, folding back the door as if he was taking off a coat. It was an Innocenti or Autobianchi, not much larger than a riding mower. He was a little dapper man, brimming with humor. Sitting next to him in the little contraption was a lovely young lady, perhaps in her twenties. Giorgio was a retired MIT professor, a nuclear scientist, and someone who lived in the neighborhood. With a bit of a British accent, he apologized for being a little late. He gave us the keys to the house, and a quick tour and tutorial of the building. He also left a phone number if we had any questions. In fact, we called several times with a temperamental washing machine, when the lights went out, and once when we smelled smoke around the fuse box.

The accommodations were comfortable, but basic. Daily, we left the house in the early morning, turned left through the vineyards, or right into town. Figline was austere, but right on the commuter railway line. The time flew by, bolstered by plenty of good regional food and wine.

On that trip, we had our leased Citroen serviced in a tiny village. The garage was so small that the office was in a matchbox building on one side of the street and directly across was the workshop, no bigger than a one car garage. We consigned our car to the proprietor and headed off for a nice lunch. When we returned, as we paid the bill we saw a prized possession; a photograph of our owner-mechanic, a man we didn't recognize, and in the middle, Luciano Pavarotti. His manager was from the town, and took him to the same gourmet restaurant we had enjoyed for a leisurely lunch. Getting the details was beyond our Italian, but it brought a smile to all of us as we admired the photo.

After Figline, in our last week we drove for one night stands in Verona, Mantua, and Sirmione on Lake Garda. All were good places to walk and soak up the local atmosphere. Two nights in Milano, one each in Torino and Nice and it was time to head home. It was all very pleasant. But Alassio was on our minds.

In 1990, we had another French rental opportunity, in a slightly larger village than Campagnac: Brissac. A former Sunday school teacher from my Brooklyn church owned a house in Herault province. Her husband had fallen in love with Paris on military assignment after World War II, so much so that they moved there for a couple of years. Paris proved too expensive and they found a place in the country.

For decades, they owned a lovely old house, once belonging to the town's mayor. The village was on a bluff overlooking a rural valley. It was a 15 minute drive to the regional market town of Ganges. Her husband had long since passed away. She and her adult niece rarely visited the house. Occasional rentals helped with the upkeep.

Montpellier was less than two hours away to the south. A little further, was the Mediterranean coast around Sete and

Aigues Mortes. The provincial Route 999, after a few dog legs, led straight and narrow to Nimes and the heart of Provence.

A little mobile van bread truck came up to the village several times a week. In Ganges there were a few supermarkets. It was not a pretty city. At the confluence of two small rivers, it had some strategic importance. In Louis XIV's time, it grew prosperous making silk stockings.

We were on the road by early morning. Often there was a long lunch stop somewhere. By dusk, we were back to the house for a quiet evening, a light supper, then reading and planning for the next day.

Many fine restaurants within a 50-mile radius of Avignon would keep any gourmet busy for weeks. But many years later, I most remember a simple farm homestead place half way to Nimes. The free-range poultry had a short walk or carry to the kitchen door. One felt like extended family in this cheerful unpretentious establishment.

On a longer drive south, we fell in love with Sete, a commercial fishing port. Broad canals ran through the heart of the city. Georges Brassens grew up there. To this day, there is a neighborhood bar where someone is always singing his poignant counter culture songs about sailors, fishermen and others living by hard labor. In local restaurants, fish traveled a few meters from the boat to the stove.

On the outskirts of Sete, on a hill with a commanding view of the Mediterranean is a remarkable cemetery. Pirates and shopkeepers are buried with a crow's nest view of the sea. Up the road along a narrow spit of beach is Cap Agde, a modern and sterile apartment and marina complex. The French, like anyone else, can ruin a pretty piece of coastline in the pursuit of leisure and real estate speculation. We will stick with Sete. The people who work the wharves and modest taverns reminded me of Gloucester.

Every corner of France brings new delights. Despite our language deficit, like a person with a disability the others senses are amplified. Brissac was plain and unremarkable. But inviting roads led off in all directions.

One day, we took a very long drive west to see the McPhersons, our hosts in Campagnac. We met them for the first time in a small town in the Gorge du Tarn area for lunch. It was roughly half way between the two locations. Our friendship has continued over the years, including several meals together in Paris and Ontario. A couple of years our senior, they are full of enthusiasm for travel and art. We enjoyed swapping experiences. Anne had published a book about the pilgrim churches on the road to Santiago de Compostela and organizes art exhibits near their home in Saint Catherines.

Deeply rural parts of France, as in America, are very hard places to earn a living. As we drove by the small Lycee between Brissac and Ganges, we wondered how many of the children would stay near home when they grew up. Would the brightest head for Montpellier, Paris and beyond?

We savored the countryside; and a glimpse of the France profonde. Closer to it than on a tour bus, we were still strangers and remained so.

OOO

10

An Apartment in Menton

It is 110 kilometers west by road from Alassio to Villefranche-sur-Mer my first French port of call. In photographs, they seem first cousins. The coastal region from Nice to Ventimiglia is very Italianate in architecture, food and culture. Nice, Nizza to our Italians friends, and this entire littoral were part of the Kingdom of Naples for a long time. After many wars and treaties, the area west of Ventimiglia came to rest as part of France in 1860. We have explored almost every kilometer of the French and Italian coast line. We love the now faded resort areas and their quieter hinterland.

The "beautiful people" have mostly decamped. There are still many pockets of extreme wealth behind private roads and elaborate gates. A few miles inland the pace has always been substantially slower. Half an hour's drive north, on many narrow mountain roads, visitors are rare. Each town along and above the coast has its own character and venerable history.

In 1991 we stayed in an apartment in Menton. A lawyer who knew our enthusiasm for French food told me about a colleague. The latter wrote restaurant reviews for several New England papers and had an apartment on the Riviera. After a few phone calls, we were renting his place. Menton was right alongside the Italian border, half way between Villefranche and Alassio. While we were unfamiliar with the town, we were happy to give it a try.

Menton, the most eastern town on the French Riviera, developed a British following in the 1800s. It claims the best micro-climate on the coast. Our prospective landlord enthused about a covered farmer's market two blocks from his apartment. He left a scrapbook full of restaurant and market recommendations from Nice to Genoa. The suggestions were from our host and various renters. Many have stood the test of time. La Capanna da Baci in Apricale and La Cambuse at the Soleya Market in Nice are perennial favorites.

It was a genteel old apartment building right along the beach road. There was a long and dimly lit hallways and a birdcage elevator. In contrast, the apartment itself was starkly white and modern. A recently redone kitchen confirmed a cook's passion. A second-floor loft was perfect for children, but we didn't have any. The tiny outdoor terrace, just big enough for a table and two chairs, became our breakfast nook. Lush and shaded landscaped grounds were many yards back from the beach promenade.

We have pleasant memories of that trip. But comparisons to Alassio were inevitable. Menton was bigger, with a wide and busy road in front of a stony beach. The promenade was lined with multi-family residences, small hotels, bars and shops, as in Alassio, but it felt more urban and brusque. We are not beachcombers, a good thing here as the strand was narrow and rocky. Why does anyone want to park their beach towels on stones and gravel?

Menton blends Italian and French architecture and food influences, but there was no question we were in France. The people were distinctly French, more reserved, even those with Italian names.

Unlike our prior rentals, we were in a small city, a fine walking town. Several miles long and nearly a mile wide, there were plenty of mini-neighborhoods to explore. We could stroll on sidewalks to the next town, Roquebrunne to the west and to the Italian border to the east. Garavan a modern evolving sector of mid-rise condos on the border was pleasant, but bland.

Back from the waterfront, there was a long and meandering pedestrian shopping street. It was wider and the stores more modern and prosperous than their Italian counterparts. There were more patisseries, shoe shops and art galleries, and fewer cafes, ice cream shops and jewelry stores than in a typical Ligurian town. Good, but not excellent, French and Provencal restaurants were readily at hand.

King Frite, a small stand owned by a young Belgian couple, attracted queues on the street most of the day. Their solitary item, steaming hot french fries served in a large paper cone. You chose from an array of condiments: curry, vinegar, sea salt, and yes, ketchup. Most of the day and evening, people were out walking, or sitting in outdoor cafes. But it wasn't the Italian passeggiata, just a busy streetscape.

Above the new town, and capped by a beautiful, well kept, small cemetery, were the ancient remnants of the original village. Narrow and steep winding streets, tall and thick stone walls on the perimeter, were a throwback to medieval times. The cemetery, on a half acre rocky promontory, has a breathtaking view of the sea. Along with a few natives, Russian aristocrats and poseurs, and a few English Anglicans rest permanently overlooking the town's small harbor. This quarter felt like the deep south of Italy or even Spain in architecture and mood. Life turned inward here, with little contact with outsiders.

In the hills behind the city there were substantial and once elegant apartment complexes. Some are in recycled Victorian era hotels. Others were abandoned. Retirees and others able to escape Northern Europe's winters thus had their own quarter north of the railroad track.

The covered farmer's market was a delight. We wandered through the stalls and sampled or gazed longingly at extraordinary cheeses, mushrooms, smoked meats, fresh fish, and exquisite fruit all beautifully displayed. After a few visits, the stall owners smiled a little more warmly when we stopped or walked by. Even with primitive french, we could point and choose. If we couldn't articulate how many grams or kilos we needed, we just said: "pour deux".

If we were too tired to cook and wanted a respite from the local restaurants, a few local traiteurs made gourmet meals for take out. Next door to the market was Lion d'Or, an atmospheric local bistro recommended highly by our landlord. Wonderful unpretentious meals were available: mussels, coq-a-vin, fish soup, all prepared competently for a mostly local crowd. The owner was a character, kind of heart, but with a mischievous streak. One night he was in formal wear, and walked around with a top hat turned down seeking contributions for a charity. Most customers were regulars. Thirty years later, I am sorry to say the restaurant is gone. In the ultimate blasphemy, there is a McDonald's on the site!

By the time of our stay, only one Anglican Church remained. At one time there were a dozen english churches in Menton. Russian and east european ex-pats, once in abundance, were rare, although a new generation of wealthy Russians would later return. Once again, it was a town mostly for the french.

By car, we took many day trips up and down the coast, returning to our quiet apartment in the evening. Still, we were mostly drawn east, back into Italy. Ventigmilia, Bordighera, Apricale, and Alassio were a short and tempting distance away.

We often passed a cheerful older American couple in the apartment house hallway. There were always a few words of greeting. We didn't want to impose on their holiday but were curious about them. They didn't have a car, but seemed adroit at using public transportation. After our first trip to the hilltop village of Apricale, and an especially satisfying meal, we thought about returning. The homemade zabaglione was reason enough. It was a pretty and in off-season, a relatively untouristed town. The next day we asked our neighbors if they cared to take a drive into Italy for lunch the following week. They readily agreed.

When the day came, we chatted in the car as we approached the border. The gentleman pulled out a thick brown passport, his wife a traditional blue one. He was a retired U.S. Ambassador to Switzerland and Bermuda! His wife had been a federal court reporter. They had plenty of stories to tell and the day whizzed by. Apricale didn't disappoint on the second visit.

They were an elegant and witty couple that thoroughly enjoyed each other's company. I mentioned that we had never been to Bermuda, but had heard many good things about it. If we were to plan a first trip there, I asked, how much time should we allow? The Ambassador said three weeks. His wife: five days.

We admired their accomplishments, but more so the example of a fine long-lasting marriage, a continued sense of adventure and an unquenched and discerning love of travel.

We had now spent more time in Menton than the few days in Alassio. But there was no question that our hearts were across the border. Comparisons may be odious but are inevitable. We felt more welcome in Liguria. Both were towns stocked with transients and some who have settled down. The people seemed gentler across the border. Still, we were grateful to have sampled someone else's dream.

11

A House in the Drome; an Apartment in Alassio

I n 1992 we returned to see if Alassio had stood the test of time. It had been a difficult year with major health problems for my father-in-law and my bittersweet accelerated retirement from the Navy due to force reductions. Desert Storm was over. They had enough Captains.

During the build up and that short war, I was executive officer of a reserve unit that supported Military Sealift Command Europe. My CO and I were both Navy captains; but the active force needed lieutenants and petty officers. We had to select our best young men and women and ship them off to London, Rotterdam and Bremerhaven right after Christmas Day. For half a year, they helped move massive amounts of equipment, ammunition and personnel by sea to the Middle East and did so with distinction. We had trained for this over a decade. Yet, we "old-timers" had missed the boat.

When the war was over, my active duty commodore was packing his things in London and getting ready to ship out for his "twilight tour" in Hawaii. I was invited to London to sit in his chair, for "the qualifications" and to have a few last pub lunches together. It would be an ideal "present" trip for my wife, for all she had put up with over the reserves; the many lost weekends and training duties when I was gone. Except that her dad had just had a major stroke, and she was needed in Ohio. I went with her to Ohio for a few days, and then, without her to England with a few of my sailors.

A few months later, a form letter from the Navy arrived after a long drill weekend. A selection board had met, and I was not selected for the rank of commodore (rear admiral, junior grade). No great surprise. The service was downsizing again. They thanked me for my service and asked that I pick a retirement date by the end of the fiscal year. At 48, I was piped ashore. Within a year, the unit was disbanded, my officers and crew scattered. Most were also forced to retire. My wife and I have kept in touch with many of our navy friends. Those friendships have endured.

*****

That year, we especially needed a vacation. We were looking for something more than just a change of scene.

We split our time, the first two weeks in another rental apartment. It was in Suze-la-Rousse in the heart of the Cote-du-Rhone wine country north of Avignon and Orange. Then we would head to Alassio. We flew to Lyons and picked up a lease car.

Suze, a small village clustered around a 14th Century castle is in the Drome region. It was a fine base. The castle was now a wine university and attracted students from most of Europe. There were a few thousand villagers outside the school; a Cathedral straddled by two bakeries. There was the inevitable Bar de Sports, the local hardware store, pizza restaurant, etc. The town was just north of the center of the Cote du Rhone. The emphasis on wine was not surprising. With fewer tourists than Provence, and even the Gard, we were within an hour's drive of more popular destinations such as Avignon, Vaison-la-Romaine, Nyons, Orange, Carpentras and L'Isle-sur-la-Sorgue.

Perhaps it was us, as much as the locals. We were outsiders, in the middle of a small courtyard and tiny town. We were treated courteously, but no one reached out to get to know us, or even more than nod as we passed by. French reserve again, perhaps. We were cocooned in our own language. Each morning we sightseed and our neighbors headed to work. In this rural area most were genuinely monolingual; of course, their right and their country. But I have also learned to never assume people don't understand your language.

Like us, these were private people who valued their space and yours. They didn't need to rush into superficial hospitality or friendship. If we ever improve our language skills, beside fluency in menus, we would go back and gently dig deeper into this quiet dignified area. Driving through the region a decade later confirmed the loveliness of the countryside.

Our landlord, who we had only spoken with by phone, was a classical musician from Germany. He lived in New York's Greenwich Village. After a few phone calls, we developed enough mutual trust to exchange a check for access to his second home. He had carefully renovated a small two-story house in the center of the village.

There wasn't much to do in Suze. The local bar was a little too local for us. The hardware store, patisseries, and gas station were handy, but not much more. A rustic pizza place wasn't bad, but nothing to write home about. We wandered farther afield in all directions. There were old villages to explore, vineyards, pleasing landscapes and superb restaurants, both modest and elegant. The two weeks went by quickly.

*****

Then it was time to turn south. The french A-toll roads made quick work of the distance down to the Mediterranean. Alassio was 250 miles away, an easy drive of around four hours on a high speed divided highway. The limited access road skirted the most congested parts of Nice, staying in the valleys between the northern hills and the coastal resorts.

For a more leisurely drive, the three old Corniche roads east of Nice, are closer to the sea. They provide exquisite scenery and a chance to stop and sample local life. On the AutoRoute, at the french-italian border, there were temporary looking one story government buildings on both sides. A few bored customs officials stood around. They approached every fifth or sixth car and most trucks, making cursory inspections. We held our passports up and out a rolled down window. From yards away, there was a slight nod, and we accelerated back up to speed, splicing through the hills on the Italian side. Since the Schengen Treaty, this border crossing was like going from Pennsylvania into Ohio. Of course, that changed a bit when southern Europe was inundated with migrants/refugees,

Above Diano Marina, we left the Autostrada and descended to the coast. Alassio has no direct access to the toll road. One arrives via Diano, Albenga or an inland route. Diano and Andora were mostly modern beach towns devoted almost exclusively to tourism. They were full of two- and three-star modest resorts, pensiones, hotels and seasonal apartments. Vague memories of the Jersey Shore and the less fashionable parts of Florida came to mind.

Years later, we learned that Diano had been largely destroyed by a devastating earthquake in 1887. Some 600 people were killed. The only good that came out of that tragedy was more careful attention to strengthening buildings along the coast against inevitable seismic tremors.

For the first time, we approached Alassio from the west. The shore road wove up and down over gentle hills. There were sheer drops to the sea and small harbors and coves. It descended into the lovely fishing village of Laigueglia. The Via Aurelia, once the old Roman Road, angled away from the beach, briefly becoming the main street in this neighboring town. Venetian style squares and a narrow budello parallel to the water lay hidden behind solid stone buildings. Most of the village was a pedestrian zone.

Then the road squeezed into a small flat strip between steep hills and the quiet ocean. In this narrow mile and a half long wedge, there were a handful of isolated houses, a railroad track, the road, a narrow pedestrian promenade and a long sandy beach. The road was just wide enough to provide a parking lane. It was entirely filled with small cars and camper vans.

The beginning section of Alassio is a dense mix of homely apartment houses and modest small boxy hotels. In less than a mile, we turned right into a block long outdoor public parking lot behind the post office. It was then the site of a weekday farmer's market, returning to its regular purpose by late afternoon.

After twenty-five plus years of visits to a favored place, reminiscences blur and overlap. The Saturday afternoon arrival in Alassio, by car or train, has become a pleasant ritual. Once bags are emptied and luggage stored, the minor anxieties of travel fade and one settles in.

Le Terrazze, like most European resort rental properties, does weekly rentals on a Saturday to Saturday cycle. Families leave in the morning. The cleaning staff gives an extra strenuous scrubbing. By late afternoon or early evening, the next wave of visitors moves in. Many are repeat clients of years or decades. Apprehensive newcomers soon settle in.

The town has one truly great advantage over several dozen other seaside resorts in the area. The city fathers did not build a conventional road or street along the beach front. Instead, there is a narrow-paved lane. It is for small service vehicles. Cars may drive cautiously one-way up to the front of a building to unload. It is primarily a pedestrian walk with encroaching outdoor bar and restaurant tables. Threading your way through the leisurely and dense throng on a weekend is always a nailbiter. You inch between people, strollers, bicycles, dogs, tables and potted plants. Pedestrians seem oblivious to approaching vehicles, but eventually give way.

After a quick unloading, contributing to the logjam, you must move your car to a distant parking lot or garage. This is a pain, but on foot you feel the logic and enjoyment of this anti-automobile bias. Even motor scooters and bicycles aren't welcome or happy on this narrow lane.

When on schedule, arriving by train is quite pleasant. The route from Nice traverses one of the most beautiful coastal regions in Europe. The track is often yards away and a few feet above the ocean. The two-and-a-half-hour trip chugs along at moderate speed through short and long tunnels, flits along backyards, hikes along hillsides, and peers into villas and tenements. In many places there is only one track. You stop until a train from the other direction moves on. Even the newer and fancier international trains can't pick up the pace because of the old track and narrow tunnels. Depending on what level of train, from Eurostar International down to the battered regional local, there are between 6 and 20 stops before you arrive in Alassio from Nice. It's a similar number of stations arriving from Genoa.

In the new century, there has been progress and decline. Some track has been doubled and/or improved, but moved inland or into tunnels. There are new train stations inland in San Remo and Arma-Taggia, Imperia and Diano. This frees up expensive seafront property. But longer stretches underground and behind drab factories diminishes the visual experience. Long distance international trains from Switzerland have disappeared. A new private line, Thello provides some service from Milan to Marseille. If you are not on that slightly more upscale train, from Nice, you must usually change trains in

Ventimiglia. It is a dowdy station with no elevators or escalators. Typically, you traipse down and up two set of stairs, with your luggage, to make a connection. Pickpockets have noticed.

While high speed trains have linked other Italian cities, the Genoa-Ventimiglia line is neglected. The trains got older and dirtier, and frequency had been reduced. In the last few years, Trenitalia is gradually renewing their fleet.

Befitting the Riviera dei Fiore, Alassio's station is partially covered in wisteria. Flower pots and planters on the platform, with hydrangea and other seasonal plants, add color and verve. While the station is plain and dated, it sits back on a pleasing little square, framing it in a way that gives it some importance. On the platform, disregard graffiti on the walls of outbuildings and savor the steep views into the hills.

The local lore is that the British Hanbury family donated land for the right of way and the train station with one condition. All passenger trains must stop in Alassio. To this day, the railroad, and the Italian government have kept that promise.

There is a small taxi stand in front, with four or five new and spotless white cars and vans. At street level a "left luggage room" is abandoned. A newsstand and a café with a terrace have doors opening on the square. Shrubs and ever changing flower beds add charm.

The café's hours are long and clientele fleeting. But regulars seem glued to their seats. Portable chairs on the sidewalk afford the business proprietors and taxi men with a good vantage point, especially on warm sunny days. The cafe makes a fine cup of espresso at half the price of the more touristy sector of town. The mostly elderly habitues read the paper, smoke, confer, observe, take in the fresh air, and stare.

The safest way to cross the busiest avenue in town is by underground passageway, the Galerie Charles Chaplin. Chaplin was one of many celebrities that frequented the town in its heyday. There are glass display cases featuring local clubs, cycling, mountain climbing, crafts and the like and card tables filled with used books offered for a small donation to a local charity.

There is a rotary at one end of the square, but no cross walk towards the sea for half a block in either direction. The intrepid or foolish run the gauntlet, climbing over or under an iron rope barrier. This is the SS1 as well as the local main street. It was the main national road before the autostrada. Since the town is only four or five blocks wide before you are up against the hills, nearly all traffic through town takes this road. A lovely park across the street borders city hall. At any time of year, there are fresh flower displays under tall palms, pines and besides shady benches. In one corner, there is playground furniture in primary colors.

It is six short blocks to Le Terrazze. With a pattern of one way and pedestrian streets, walking is as fast as the taxi. A few taxi drivers speak a little English, but all are cheerful, polite and honest.

We arrive as instructed: between four and six, hoping to avoid the growing intensity of the crowds as the day moves on. We enter the residence's lobby, usually behind large Italian or German families with enough bags and equipment to stay for a season. We wait our turn.

From that very first year, Dr. Egidio Mantellassi greeted everyone warmly and thoroughly at the front desk. Of lean, athletic and medium build, dark hair, a handsome moustache, his gaze is both sympathetic and intense. He has a calming influence on all who walk through the door. I have seen him agitated, but never angry. He switches effortlessly from Italian to German, French, Russian, English as makes his guests most comfortable. He is full of stories, observations and opinions that brim over with enthusiasm at the slightest encouragement. There is kindness, intelligence and warmth that radiate whenever we see him. No matter how busy, he always listens and makes you feel that what you want or have to say is important.

Having studied at both the Universities of Genoa and Heidelberg, he has worked for some fifty odd years in the hotel field. He is a man of many talents, good humor, intensity, hard work and integrity. Of course, it is nearly impossible to take the objective measure of a friend.

A second-generation hotelier, Egidio and his wife, Rita, have created two islands of serenity in a town with nearly a hundred hotels. The second property, Villa Firenze, is an elegant town house a few blocks further west and inland, a quiet enclave with a garden just behind the main street. For many years, he was also involved in a third city establishment, the larger Hotel Toscana, still run by another branch of his family. With Egidio, you can always tap into a deep well of nostalgia and information about the town's past. With some prodding, there might be a tactful comment on the politics and currents of the present. He also has a passion for the town's future. Perhaps that, and his diplomatic skills, explains why he was President of the town's Hotel Association for many years.

His father had been a poor farmer and coal miner in Tuscany before seeking his future in Alassio. As a teenager, or earlier, Egidio learned the ropes at the Hotel Toscana, cooking, cleaning and doing what ever had to be done on and behind the scenes.

After a hearty welcome, guests are provided with a big laminated cardboard folder. Inside are a dozen sheets. In four languages, they outline useful information on the facility and the town. There are a few restaurant suggestions, the operation of the appliances, parking advice, safety, a children's program are included. Two plastic key cards provide access to your apartment and the exterior doors.

There wasn't enough room in the small elevator for both of us and all our luggage. With two trips all of our bags were upstairs, and we unpacked. Pleasant cooking smells waft from other apartments. The neat white corridors, with black molding, are well lit. Black and white photos of the town from perhaps a hundred years before, add continuity and perspective. In 2009, a new and larger elevator was retrofitted.

We open the floor to ceiling glass doors and wood shutters in our apartment and step out on a little balcony. Ten meters ahead is an impeccably clean light beige sand beach, the best for hundreds of miles. Varying with the tide, it is a dozen meters more to the lapping waves.

On the small tiled porch, behind a waist tall iron railing, there are two folding chairs and a small table. Sideways, there is just room for two pairs of legs to stretch out. The metal fence is just a yard away. No complaints! We look down on the tables of a friendly neighborhood cafe, and watch a vast retinue of people in ones, twos and groups strolling on their own missions. There are large common terraces, sturdy metal tables and chairs on both the second and third floors with ample room to dine outside or just enjoy the surroundings. Below, pedestrian traffic flows intermittently in both directions, from early morning until the wee small hours.

The sofa/bed, with a simple grey blanket cover, is a convenient place to unpack. Long grey cushions fit on small black shelves above eye level. A trundle bed is beneath. There are plenty of dresser drawers and closet space. The bags are quickly emptied and stowed unobtrusively some eight feet up on top of coat closets. The studio apartment walls and furnishings are off-white with black chairs at a square table, with a crisp white table cloth. There are a few red pillows for contrast. The effect is simple and soothing.

It is time to find a proper parking place for the car, and some basic groceries. The Saturday early evening crowd is growing. We inch the car through leisurely walkers, and make it to the municipal lot some five blocks away and find a scarce empty space.

Back at the apartment, we scrambled down the back steps and through a glass door into the ancient budello behind the residence. Steady streams of people move in both directions.

It is now past six. We enter a small family grocery store, La Piazzetta. Everyday and gourmet brands are on the shelves. There is an agreeable bustle of customers, regulars and tourists, in the cramped aisles. We pass up the cheese, meat and takeout counter, and focus on basics. A small hand basket is quickly filled with: paper napkins, trash bags, dishwasher soap. A few edibles go in the basket: Illy Coffee, cereal, milk and Sicilian blood orange juice, a real favorite for breakfast. A bag of tall grissini, bread sticks with local olive oil, and some Ligurian flatbread go into our cart. Genuine Greek yogurt, Olympus, and some mountain honey from Piemonte make a wonderful breakfast treat.

Piled to the ceiling, there are all kinds of specialty items, bottarga, mustard fruits, dried porcini, cornichons, honey, and olive oil, all to be sampled another time. A small selection of wines is on one wall. On a table, next to the check out counter, is a cluster of fresh fruits and lettuces. The lady owner, or her daughter, always remember us and say "Grazie" and "Arrividerci", and an occasional: "thank you" as they put our purchases in bags. Each time we return, the reception becomes warmer. The all women business, with sometimes another two ladies behind the deli counter, is a throwback to the kind of stores I remember from Brooklyn in the '40s and '50s.

The mother behind the cash register stops and talks enthusiastically with each customer, a warmth and understanding not found in the big supermarket a few blocks away. Her daughter is a little more reserved, but has inherited her mother's smile. Good natured, a bit distant, perhaps she may not be as content trapped for long hours at the cash register. They are open from early morning to a mid-afternoon break. A little after 8 PM, the proprietress, who reminds me a bit of a more poised but equally kind and gracious Edith Bunker, closes the door and heads home on her motor scooter.

For many years, there was a small and cherished morning routine at Le Terrazze. At 8 AM you heard the rustle of a small plastic bag being placed on your door knob. Inside were a couple of freshly made cornettos, chewy croissant-like rolls, with or without a dollop of marmalade inside.

Also enclosed was your choice of newspaper, as long as it is Italian: The *Corriere Delle Sera* from Milano, *La Stampa* of Torino, *La Republica* from Roma or *Il Secolo XIX* from Genoa. The *Corriere* is considered the country's paper of record. We ordered it, even though we only understand 5-10% of its content. At least my wife enjoyed the fashion sections.

Thanks to the internet, we get a rough translation of online local papers and learn some of what is going on around us. We also made a beeline to our favorite news agent who ordered the *International Herald Tribune* (now the *International New York Times*) for the duration of our stay.

Local businesses have come and gone over the years. But ones from that trip stay indelibly in memory, even those that have disappeared or morphed into something else.

With our small cache of supplies put away, we head out for our first Saturday night meal in Alassio. With a recommendation from Le Terrazze and good vibes walking by, we tried Le Cave. It was a family owned restaurant where the seafood was always excellent, now sadly gone. With a folksy fishermen's tavern atmosphere, and no pretensions, there were more locals than tourists. It was a very happy place.

From that first tme, the proprietor family warmly welcomed us. On busy nights, such as Fridays and Saturdays, the chef/owner prepared Paella as good as any we have had in Spain. As each meal came to a close, he or his spanish wife made the rounds making sure that each guest felt appreciated. He seemed pleased, and a little surprised, that a few yanks had found their way to his place. We continued to head there often for another fourteen years. The seafood was always fresh. The owner made four roundtrips to Nice every week to get the best seafood. Advancing age and health issues intervened and brought that chapter to a close.

Many of our fondest memories are linked to restaurants. As a customer, you are part of the play. The owner, the cook, sometimes the same, the waiters are all actors relying on your patronage and approval for their living. Language and culture barriers fall in the universal ritual of service and dining. Besides the meal, you often take away much more understanding of the locale.

Another early mainstay for us was The Camel Club. Named after that high-octane American cigarette, it was an inexpensive spaghetteria where we had many enjoyable meals. There, for the first time, we had spaghetti with bottarga, the dried eggs of, in this case, tuna, but sometimes red mullet or sea bass. Like caviar, the flavor is intense, salty, and like no other. As a dry powder, it is pleasant. Made into thin strips, right out of the fish womb, it is a gutsy and intense taste you never forget. From scraps for poor fishermen, it has become a gourmet delicacy.

The two restaurants shared the same lovely beach view with more upscale places. We remember them, like old friends who are no longer with us.

We don't generally hang out in bars. In Alassio there are exceptions. Café Mozart, just down the beach from Restaurant Palma, was, for a long time, a classy and congenial place. The owners, a lovely and elegant middle-aged couple, had quiet and sophisticated music playing softly in the background. On Friday and some Saturday nights there were a fine singer and a piano player crooning Cole Porter, Gershwin and romantic Italian popular songs. Most of the year, you sat outside on rattan chairs with generous pillows basking in candlelight. Under an awning, you were close by the beach. When cool, gas lamps kept you comfortable.

When you ordered a long drink, the complimentary hors d'ouevres were a small sophisticated meal: a generous tray of caperberries, chunks of grand padano and asiago cheese, long peels of prosciutto, tiny and delicious local olives and focaccia bread slivers. These augmented the standard potato chips and peanuts that came out for every customer who ordered a beer, soft drink or glass of wine. A dinner jacket wasn't necessary but would fit in.

The long drink menu was a sophisticated range of cocktails, plus a remarkable choice of several dozen aged rums from all over the Caribbean and Central America. Further down the list were a good assortment of single malt scotches, and a cluster of cognacs, armagnacs and grappas. If you chose to damage your liver, at least you could do it in great style.

When it is time to turn in at night, we leave the windows or door to the patio ajar. We listen to the sound of the waves until we fall asleep. Sometimes, small fishing boats bob in the water. They use small lanterns to attract the fish. Half way to the horizon, or closer, cruise ships sail by lit up like Christmas trees. A few solitary figures might be outlined in lamplight at the end of the town pier. Mostly, they are crusty and taciturn old men fishing well into the night.

On Friday and Saturday nights, there might be a small band at Rudy's or other bars along the promenade. The electronic music often gets rather exuberant. The poorer the voice, the louder they sing. Computer/internet generated "music" is even worse. We close the doors until well past midnight. Then it is as quiet as a weekday night. We return to the soothing sound of the sea.

Half way around the world, we instantly felt at home, despite the language and cultural barriers. Of all the thousands of miles of coast line and places we have explored over the years, this suits us best. We still feel the urge to go new places. But this is where we always return.

We didn't know how much we would dine in on that first trip. My wife is a splendid cook and we were surrounded by tempting ingredients. Still, this was vacation and our kitchenette was basic: a two burner stove top, a microwave, a small refrigerator and no oven.

Beyond a light breakfast in the apartment, it was tempting, then routine, to set out for a cappuccino and maybe another roll. The stove top espresso maker worked well enough to get one's eyes open. Several nearby cafes make splendid spremuta, freshly squeezed orange or other juices. Breakfast, by local custom, is a very light meal.

For that cappuccino, we usually head for Rudy's next door. With brilliantly roasted Genovese brand café from Albenga, run through a professional grade multi-spout espresso machine, it is hard to surpass, especially with a sprinkle of cinnamon. A perfect view of the beach and sea is the clincher. Rudy, his wife Fiorella, and two sons are congenial hosts. Over the years they too have become friends. But everyone who goes to Rudy's more than twice becomes a friend.

Rudy is a bantam weight dynamo. Athletic and a passionate football fan, he moves around delivering coffees and drinks as if he is deflecting opponents and bringing the ball closer to the goalkeeper. Then he suddenly surprises you, stops to deliver a warm smile, a few moments banter or a sit down for an extended conversation. Then his eyes make a complete sweep of the premises, making sure everything is in order. He is fluent in German and passably so in French and English. When he is there, he does three times the work of his twenty/thirty something sons.

His wife is almost all business. But over the years, we have seen more smiles. She is not much for small talk except with a small circle of friends. Perhaps it is the language barrier. Her maiden name is La Guardia, the same family of New York fame.

The sons, in their 20s or 30s, charm many of the young lady customers. They work hard, but in a different way than their parents. They promote live music close to the weekends. Too bad it is usually too loud and not ready for prime time.

Now that the oldest son is the father of a very cute toddler, Eduardo, he seems to be acting more responsibly. Father, mother, and Eduardo in the Rolls Royce equivalent of a pram, arrive briefly in the morning--perhaps for a short meeting, and then usually disappear until the afternoon and evening shift.

When there is an important football match, the place fills with locals. They buy a beer and sit in rows watching a medium size flat screen. It is not a sports bar, except for an important game. Even then, others stop by for a drink, a sandwich, a snack oblivious of the transient fan club.

Outside, there are a handful of tables alongside the doors. Across the promenade, jutting onto the beach is a glass enclosed area. The ceiling and windows slide open when sun and temperatures permit. People sit there either mesmerized by the sea or ignoring it.

My city map lists 166 hotels and 19 residences in Alassio! There are holiday trailer parks too on the outskirts, and who knows how many rooms to let. Tourism is the primary industry, but the town isn't overwhelmed with tour buses; at least not when we have been there.

Most of the hotels have only 15-30 rooms. There are bigger ones on the main road through town, but none are over 100 rooms. With a population of 11,000, somehow the town isn't overrun outside of the high summer season. When 50,000 people descend in summer, we are somewhere else. I don't begrudge the merchants and hoteliers their livelihood, but even they must dread the summer hordes. Thousands of beach umbrellas and lounge chairs squeeze for miles on the sand. No thanks.

It's Sunday before dawn. With glass doors open, shutters closed, the sea sound surrounds us. The tossing and turning waves are like a giant's heavy breathing. The revelers are gone. If there is anyone out there, it's a solitary fisherman on the pier or someone walking a dog on the beach.

Gradually the sky lightens. Sky, ocean and sand meld and adjust their colors. I get up quietly and read for a time. Then I fill the simple aluminum espresso maker with good ground coffee and turn on the electric stove. Having seen hundreds of sunrises and sunsets here, I still marvel that each seems slightly different.

142

There is a slight rustle at the door. Our cornettos have arrived, still warm from the local bakery. Waiting for the water to boil, we try to make sense out of the stories in the Italian paper.

In the budello, several newsstands have a smattering of German and English papers. We look for the IHT. The back page has: "News for Travelers", often our first warning of transport strikes, unusual holidays or other deviations that can muck up plans. When jointly owned by the Washington Post and the New York Times, it had its own voice. Now, it's a Times-lite. Still, it is a link with home.

On that first trip, we had no English language television. Later, there was CNN International. When our hosts added Sky's cable service, Mr. Murdoch ditched CNN for Fox. Their international coverage is thin. But later, CNN reappeared.

Mostly, we watch the BBC, Sky, Deutsche Welle, France 24 and stations further afield. The French, Quatari, Russian, Chinese, Korean, Japanese and Israeli stations all have English language news broadcasts. They provide detail, perspective and bias we don't get at home.

Besides news and weather, the main Italian channels are a sorry mix of quiz shows, amateur talent programs, mediocre soap operas and dubbed American television, often vintage: Walker, Texas Ranger seems to be on perpetually. A few food, travel and design shows are a better bet.

The boardwalk to the east ends at the Marina on the outskirts of town. The narrow winding highway above to Albenga is not for pedestrians. Southwestward, the path stretches all the way to Laigueglia, a little fishing village two and a half miles away. In need of exercise, we head downstairs, and turn right. In less than a block, at the foot of Via Torino, there is a little Piazzetta. There is a small monument to local fishermen lost at sea over the years. Three stone benches set in a U are reserved with priority for fishermen, mostly the long-retired sort.

Just past the little park, we turn inland a short block, and left to the main caruggi, Vittorio Veneto, a commercial lane filled with tiny stores below ancient three to five story buildings. Narrow shops sell clothes, jewelry and groceries. There are a few bars and cafes. The narrow lane is parallel to and a block in from the beach. It meanders into a clearing dominated by the mid-rise Hotel Milano. Opposite is a fountain, a tall olive tree in a planter box and a snack stand. At night, the tree is bathed in yellow green light reminiscent of that under a swimming pool.

Then you proceed past the drab entrances to the main post office, the town library and a pharmacy. Now you are in another distinct neighborhood, Barusso. Egidio tells us when he was growing up there were five distinct dialects within Alassio. He could tell where his schoolmates were from by their accent!

A few ornate chapels in ancient stone churches sit cheek by jowl with the shops. Further along, the elevated boardwalk begins. A few larger hotels spread out back from the beach. Then the buildings recede and disappear. Along the sea and sand, the promenade stretches to Laigueglia.

The surface is smooth and about ten feet wide. Part of it is made of flagstone; other sections poured concrete or tile. Alongside are street lamps. At night they stretch like a beautiful pearl necklace viewed from the town molo or pier. Towards the water, a waist high braided steel rope railing is a reminder of the steep drop to the beach four or five meters below.

The walk begins in a neighborhood of larger and slightly posher hotels. A few snack bars intersect the promenade. Panini, beer, gelati and soft drinks are on offer. Some pedestrians stop for the view or a break from sunbathing, swimming or walking. Gradually, the hotels are replaced by small villa residences. The entire length of the walk is along a pristinely clean beach. Close to the town line, beach cabanas are farther apart.

The last is Scoglieri, or the cliffs. It is a windy and isolated beach enclave and restaurant once owned by Dr. Mantellassi with some friends as a youth. The city has now, wisely, put in a dog park next door. After some empty space, the Laigueglia cabanas begin.

At the Alassio boundary, the strip of flat land along the steep hills became narrower. At a walker's pace, we study the old highway and railroad track squeezed between the ocean and nearly vertical rock. Some sections of the hillside are trussed in wire mesh to cope with rock slides. Every thirty meters or so, there is an inviting park bench with or without some helpful tree shade.

The forty to fifty-minute stroll to the next town leaves plenty of time for reflection, conversation or just the good feeling of your limbs, heart and lungs in gear. A few joggers, bicyclists and dogs set a faster pace. On the hottest days you regret being there and yearn for the shaded budello that will eventually reward your efforts.

Flags on flagpoles or signs every few hundred meters advertise the private beach concessions. While ocean access is public, private cabanas, chairs, beach umbrellas, and impromptu cafes have been staked off for generations. In the off season, there are only scant traces. A few chairs and umbrellas are up, mostly vacant. In season, a full spectrum of different colored umbrellas and lounging chairs, green, orange, blue, red, gold, yellow, tan, black and white stretch out for as far as the eye can see, a gelati colored rainbow.

In summer, the noise level of all those families, couples and strutting teenagers and twenty somethings must be louder than the sea. Now, there is only the occasional squawking of seagulls arguing, laughing or signaling.

On an early Sunday morning in May, we stop a few times and look at the beautiful ocean. A couple of tankers and passenger ships are out towards the horizon. They sail tangents to or from Genoa, Savona, Livorno, Nice, Marseille or the North African Coast.

On the high hill slopes a few houses nest on flat patches of rock. Spider vein driveways connect with tiny access roads hidden in the brush. The coastal SS1 follows the old Roman Via Aurelia. The road and railroad are squeezed ever closer. Every fifteen minutes or so, a fast or slow train passes. They head West towards Imperia and the french frontier; or East towards Savona, Genoa and beyond. We see a sign, "Arrivederci Alassio". A few yards later, another: "Benvenuti a Laigueglia".

There are small hotels and pensiones a few meters up the hillside. Laigueglia is much smaller, once a simple fishing village. Perhaps it caters to a slightly more down-market clientele. The highway continues straight, while the beach "Ys" to the left, a fine strand of beige white sand. The boardwalk abruptly ends at an ancient mini-Saracen tower. Then a concrete surface walkway zigs and zags, an outer perimeter between town and beach. At the eastern end there is a small rustic square, Piazza di Pescatori. A stubby and massive stone pier and breakwater juts into the sea. It is usually teaming with amateur fishermen and when warm, a few elderly sunning themselves. The breakwater consists of large rocks thrown on top of each other, as if done by an ill-tempered giant.

Further west are two of the loveliest waterfront courtyards in Italy. Venetian in style, they are ideal places to while away an hour or two at an outdoor café or restaurant. The three- and four-story pastel colored buildings on the periphery date from the Middle Ages.

On the second square there was a favorite restaurant we enjoyed for more than a decade. Sadly, it has been dark ever since: Ristoranti Il Vascello Fantasma, the Ghost Ship, as in Wagner's *Flying Dutchman*. For a long time, the owner was the Norwegian explorer Thor Heyderhal. It was also then a member of the Assuricazioni Buon Ricordo, an energetic organization fostering the preservation of local dishes.

Member restaurants provide you with a commemorative plate when you order the house specialty. There are more than 300 of these restaurants, including a handful outside of Italy.

Heyderhal, the author of *Kon Tiki* and *Aku Aku*, lived in Laigueglia with his third wife, a French-American movie actress. For many years they were busy excavating an ancient village on the hillside above the town. The "frazioni", or neighboring village, Colla Micheri, has a stunningly beautiful setting. His vision was to both excavate the ancient site, and permit a limited number of new houses built with local materials and in harmony with the landscape and respectful of the spirit of the place. That project continues, slowly. A small modern vineyard is staked out in the upper reaches of the settlement and a trattoria is open to the public.

148

He was a charming and unobtrusive host. The town and time tempered his celebrity status. We enjoyed his hospitality without impinging on his privacy. His wanderlust must have again set in, and he moved to the Canary Islands. When he became terminally ill, he returned to Laigueglia and is buried at Colla Micheri. A voyager of every continent, honored in many countries, we take note of his choice of a final resting place.

The first owner/chef drew people from as far away as Rome and Milan. Heyderhal's turn added further cachet. After he sold it, the restaurant went down market, offering just simple Ligurian fare.

In good weather, the restaurant spilled out under an awning into the square. There were generous helpings of fried, broiled or grilled fish, and beautiful salads of arugula, fresh tomatoes and basil. Chilled bottles of the local white wines, Pigato and Vermentino, followed. Lemon sorbetto or fresh berries completed a satisfying meal. Sadly it became vacant. Fewer people are able or willing to spring for an upscale restaurant tab.

Here, and elsewhere, we often lament the loss of wonderful dining establishments. In 2018, surprisingly, the original family owners of Vascello reopened it with a very talented chef. As we returned in 2019, it was still afloat.

I tend to dwell on restaurants. As a stranger in a foreign country, our meal time role is important. Even when language skills fall short, there is mutual need, trust and sometimes serendipity.

Laigueglia's budello is quieter and smaller than Alassio's. Often, it seems there are no other visitors, especially in the low season. A handful of merchants wait for business and life to pick up again. Vicos or alleyways thread their way to the National Highway which is more like a luge run than a street. There is the tiniest of sidewalks, an afterthought a few feet wide.

Sometimes we stop and buy a bar of handmade olive soap, a small piece of ceramic tile, a few postcards sharing a couple of moments with a grateful business owner.

On the far side of the highway, tiny passages go under the railroad track, just wide enough for a compact car. A few narrow roads ramp up the hills, one climbing steeply to Colla Micheri. Vacation homes and small apartment houses stake small horizontal plots wedged into the hills. The view from the top is breathtaking. Gallinara Island in the distance looks like a quarter scale Brazilian Sugar Loaf Mountain. The wide expanse of beach between the two towns is a perfect partner with the lovely sea.

You can walk back to Alassio or we usually buy a bus ticket in a handful of bars and newsstands. There is a small train station, but the local regionale stops only once or twice a day. On the street, a small sign and pay phone advertise a local cab we have never seen. On closer inspection, it is the Alassio taxi company.

*****

Alassio is more than a beach. There are sporting events, for spectator and participant, a few concerts and lectures, an occasional art exhibit. Many folks are content to just stroll and relax. Some are so enchanted that they buy a vacation or retirement home or apartment. Few come for "the season" any more. Many return every year for a week or two or whatever interval they can muster. Still others arrive for a day or two and never return. Their paradise might be somewhere else or nowhere.

It is a three-hour drive from Milan or Turin to Alassio. Mental images of palm trees, sea and sand must recur, especially in winter. The British colony has mostly disappeared. From nearly 3,000 in their heyday, now there are only enough to support a church service once a month. There are few French visitors, although their numbers are increasing. The Scandinavians have moved on to other venues. A few Irish and Americans find their way here. Plenty of Germans and Swiss escape cold climes and latch on to this patch of the Mediterranean. A few wealthy Russians buy choice villas in the hills.

Some local hotels are basic and cater to package bus tours. After a short stroll, with a group guide, these folks stay holed up in their hotel lobbies, or on a small stretch of beach front.

151

At night, they choose between two or three adequate but un-inspired courses in their hotel's spartan dining room. Many of these visitors have gray or white hair.

Campers and RVs with foreign plates are found on public highways or berthed at basic camp grounds. But cheap flights and the internet have expanded other options. Italy is no longer that exotic. A younger crowd, mostly Northern Italian, arrive by motor scooter, small car, train or bus on weekends. On temporary reprieve from school, work or lack of work they look for parties and each other. We don't begrudge budget travelers from Eastern Europe or elsewhere their week(s) in the sun. Nor do we mind the young folks looking for a new boy or girl friend.

Each town along the Italian Riviera has its loyalists. Why some go exclusively to Forte di Marmi, Viareggio, Rapallo and others to San Remo, Bordighera, Alassio or several dozen other towns is a mystery. We are just happy with a town we find most agreeable.

Many permanent residents are pensioners, on this sunny coast in their "golden years". We feel affinity for the old and young on the boardwalk holding hands or walking very close together. In their faces, I see glimpses of countless stories we won't learn. Widows and widowers, singly and in clusters, move at their own mostly slower tempo. There is animated talk and shared silence. Dogs are welcome. Cats sun themselves or scamper to their own cadence. Intense joggers and casual cyclists ply the promenade and city streets.

Occasionally, there is an outdoor market in Laigueglia on Sunday. It is smaller and more sedate than the large markets in Alassio, Oneglia, and Bordighera. Once we took special pleasure observing two young couples from Piemonte taking a break from their portable trucks, one offering lovely farm cheeses, the other mountain honeys. Business slowed to a trickle during the lunch hour, so they took a table at Vascello, just a few meters away from their trucks. They were two tables away from us, and their friendship and good spirits were infectious. After lunch, we bought goat cheese and a jar of honey. Both were excellent.

Laigueglia is a quiet and unassuming place we thoroughly enjoy. The Mantellassis, after the busy season, like to bicycle down to the neighboring village for a bowl of pasta or a pizza. It's like going back in time.

Next to the train track in Laigueglia is a magnificent baroque 18th century church, San Matteo. Inside there is beautiful, ornate and moving art, whatever your religious persuasion. The fishermen, whose contributions built this mighty church, had much to be grateful for each time they returned safely home; so too their families. Laigueglia evokes the coast before tourism, filled with fishermen and hardscrabble merchants.

OOO

12

Toward France

Our trips to Alassio consist of alternating bursts of wanderlust and the desire to stay put. The former usually prevails. We feel a strong pull toward the French border 80 kilometers away. But after a long day away via car, or train and bus, any vestige of stress disappears when parked in a local garage or lot, or when we step out of the Alassio train station into the flower bedecked park.

There are only two main roads out of or in to Alassio, the coastal road and a new inland spur through a long tunnel and up to the Autostrada in Albenga. Meandering blacktop wisps climb the hills to hamlets such as Solva, Moglio and the shrine of Madonna Delle Grazie and then dead-end. The main road, if you could call it that, is mostly, but not always wide enough for two very narrow cars. There is almost no place to park. Private houses might have a small sqare indentation, sometimes a flat place over a roof. If you meet the school sized bus or a modest truck on a curve, someone must back up some distance.

Dirt roads constructed for fire safety, hiking and biking, push even further into and along the higher hills. Even with a small and sturdy four-wheel drive vehicle, those paths are dangerous. There are few guard rails. Surfaces are rutted and uneven. Signage is haphazard. Even with a detailed map, it's best to confer with a savvy native. The views of the sea and perched villages are a great reward. Heading inland is difficult. It entails a lengthy trip. East or west to a few numbered and sinuous routes. Over hills and mountains, they wander into Piemonte, the larger province to the North.

Our day trips usually include a search for a good restaurant. We admire the hard work and vulnerability of those inviting you to their public table. It doesn't matter if it is grand or modest, only that it was conceived more from the heart than the cash register. Frankly, the closer you get to France the more likely the restauranteur will be striving for excellence.

Beyond Laigueglia, the Via Aurelia tracks a few short coastal curves, in and out of tunnel galleries. It rises and falls with the hills. One winter we walked as far as Andora, the next town, but that is not for the faint hearted. There is no separate footpath. Inside the tunnels you walk behind the guard rails crouched against the curve of unlit tunnels. Cyclists are even more at risk.

This stretch of road is part of the famous Milano-San Remo cycling race, and the more obscure but endearing Trofie Laigueglia. Hiking the sidewalk free roller coaster road increases your respect for surging cyclists in spandex and the patient engineers who carved a path through the hills.

The road makes a majestic quarter circle turn around Cape Mele and its lighthouse. There is a fleeting 240-degree cliff view of the Mediterranean. Then you descend into the next attractive beach town, Andora. Smaller than Alassio, it is now devoted almost entirely to beach worship. There is some agriculture in the hills behind the town. It is an agreeable, unpretentious venue with a fine beach. It claims Roman origins and a few ruins.

Andora is the last town in Savona Province. Past the town limit, you enter Imperia which extends to the French Border. The TPL bus lines end here. Another company, Riviera Transport will take you as far as San Remo. There you must take another " RT" bus to Ventimiglia and the French border: three busses for some fifty miles! You can't even buy tickets for both companies in the same place. Different cafes or tabac/general stores sell them. Similar challenges lie in the other direction beyond Savona. If you are forced to buy a ticket on board the bus, it roughly doubles the price. It is hard enough for the bus drivers to try to stay on schedule without the additional time of disbursing tickets.

The old National road continues south and west, following the jagged coastline. The towns of Cervo, San Bartolomeo al Mare, and Diano Marina mesh. Rising out of Andora, the road climbs Capo Mimosa then descends into Cervo.

The hill top village of Cervo, founded in the second century B.C., is guarded by medieval walls. The townsfolk had the good grace to not spoil it. The coastal sector is drab. Climbing vertically into the old town, by a series of steep steps or a winding road, you go back in time. A powerful 13th century stone church with 16th century frescoes (Santa Caterina) and a soaring 18th century baroque edifice, the Corallini Church dedicated to Saint John the Baptist, dominate the skyline.

A rabbit warren of residential alleyways is dark and dreary. The shade would be a blessing in summer. A few simple shops provide necessities. A couple of craft stores scrape a living in confined space. Unable to compete in the beach chair business, Cervo opted for preservation. Ancient architecture and atmosphere, and a world class summer music festival in the church courtyard, are strong draws. As pretty as French Eze, and far less snooty, remember Cervo. If you can, book a table at the Michelin starred restaurant San Giorgio.

Alassio and Laigueglia belong, perhaps reluctantly, to Savona Province. Their provincial capital is 50 kilometers to the East. I asked my friend Massimo of Palma why Alassini feel more affinity with the Western towns. His reply: "they are nicer people" (than the Savonese). We have more in common with them. We are Provencale." This mistrust or dislike of many of the neighboring towns is endemic in Italy.

Away from Alassio, we are again transients, susceptible to the same prejudices we find amusing in our Italian friends. There is hardly a town in Italy whose people don't think it is the best or that it has been taken advantage of by outsiders. They don't quite trust the folks in the next town. Still, in an argument, they side with Ligurians over Piemontese. Italians may only come together to support their national football team.

After Diano, you enter Oneglia, a stayed old larger town. With neighboring Puerto Maurizio, merged since Mussolini's days, it forms the provincial capital of Imperia of some 42,000 souls. On the Oneglia side, small factories process olive oil and bottle wine. The large Carli olive oil factory is right across from the old train station. A commercial fishing harbor and warehouse facilities add economic heft. Provincial government, larger bank branches and insurance agencies generate local paychecks.

The main street arcades in the center of Oneglia are reminiscent of northern cities. We come here to window shop old fashioned boutiques almost preserved in aspic; savor beautiful old cafes and sample a slightly higher tempo of activity and purpose than found in the resort towns.

Oneglia's waterfront was once gritty and commercial. Cranes move cargo to modest warehouses and truck bays, a midget version of the large districts of Genoa. Not many tourists came here, although it is gentrifying. Now, substantial yachts tie up with their sterns toward the quay. With home ports in the Cayman Islands, Jersey, Malta and the like, these are not casual day trippers. Many are for charter; others belong to people or companies who prefer to be anonymous.

Homely commercial fishing boats, small freighters and mini-tankers were pushed aside to a perpendicular pier. Good restaurants on the waterfront place linen covered tables outside under the porticos.

A mile down the road, across the elusive Impero River, Porto Maurizio has hill and harbor quarters. The hill sector connects to the waterfront by steep alleys and a few winding streets. It seems cast in amber, dominated by the somber Cathedral of San Maurizio. Now, the harbor is home to large vessels, a modern marina and the remnants of an old fishermen's quarter. We prefer the sea front, but there is a dignified melancholy in the upper town.

In this millennium, the waterfront seemed on the rise with a new kilometer long pier and an ambitious marina. Ocean going yachts, home ported in obscure tax havens, appeared. A tiny but dignified fishermen's church sits on the way to the old budello, a reminder of the neighborhood's origins.

Sadly, the mega marina project is in deep financial trouble and incomplete. Its business architect, the last time I checked, was in jail pending trial for economic fraud. The project is bankrupt and there seems plenty of blame to go around. The city doesn't have the money to complete the project. A small glimmer of hope: the Carli olive merchant family stepped in to help, understanding the impact on the city in precarious times.

From our first visit to Porto Maurizio twenty-five years ago, there is one primary reason we return. Across the street from the local Coast Guard station is a small storefront restaurant: Lanterna Blu Di Tonino. Outside, it looked like other modest nearby taverns. Even graced with fine linens, Ginori China and good crystal in the old days, what made it extraordinary was the owner, Tonino Fiorillo. His wife and son, another Massimo, were also essential to its character.

Now in his eighties, the handsome and spry gray haired Neapolitan has a smile and warmth that is powerful and rare. There is no more gracious host. When he is in a good mood, most of the time, you may even hear a little of his fine tenor in the background. He has recorded some Bel Canto music, and also plays the mandolin. A few of his privately produced CDs are prized possessions. As a young man from Napoli, Tonino opened the restaurant in 1952 starting with borrowed china and tablecloths. We've learned that he used to sing at the legendary Café Roma in Alassio back in the days when Hemingway, Chaplin and other glitterati were regulars. In the restaurant, there is an old black and white picture from the time with a smiling Tonino hoisting a tray. It's reminiscent of a young Frank Sinatra.

On our first visit, he seemed delighted to have some Americans showing up at his restaurant without a reservation. He went back to his office and placed on our table a little place setting with American and Italian flags. It's usually on our table when we return.

The menu was mostly seafood and of the highest quality. We think about his fresh tomato salad with buffalo mozzarella and bottarga all year long. The daily fish, broiled and prepared Ligurian style in the finest olive oil, is the best the region has to offer. With his Sicilian wife making the desserts, and Tonino in the kitchen or in the dining room bantering and pampering us, we were always content. Each meal ended with a Sicilian Cassata or a Neapolitan Rum Cake, a strong espresso; and the house lemoncello.

At least once, Prime Minister Berlusconi hosted a private party there. So to have the heads of substantial Italian corporations. Tonino has the pictures to prove it. I would have loved to hear Berlusconi playing piano and Tonino singing some old songs from Napoli.

The restaurant is a labor of love and can't be replicated. Tonino was often hard on his employees, but no one worked harder. He wanted things to be just so. But one can't entirely escape the impact of growing older and a wobbly economy.

At one time, the restaurant had a Michelin Star. Then and now, it deserves it. When Michelin abruptly dropped the restaurant, we kept writing them saying they had made a mistake. Only years later, from Massimo, we learned of a conversation between Michelin and his Dad. Apparently, the inspectors made suggestions about the need to redecorate the restaurant, and perhaps make some other things. Tonino told them where to go, with perhaps some colorful Neopolitan curses added for good measure.

In 2008, he lured his son back from cooking assignments in the United States and Germany. Since 2010 Massimo has been in charge. Besides having good family teachers, he is his own kitchen virtuoso. He is also a talented pianist with a taste for jazz and a savvy art collector. With Massimo in the kitchen, the food is frankly even better, and there is a more modern vibe.

The marina's collapse and the continuing economic malaise caused Massimo to consider decamping for Valbonne during the winter of 2012. Sadly, Lanterna Blu closed in its 60th year. Tonino was heart broken. An article in the local paper reflected a sadness we had never seen in the man. Several months later, Massimo decided to reopen. There were more wealthy customers in France, but one needs the capital to start a new business. Banks on both sides of the border shun small businesses. Catering to a younger clientele, Massimo is streamlining the restaurant. Tonino still makes appearances, keeping long time customers happy.

We care about this family that has made us truly welcome over two and a half decades. Their fate, like that of Italy, is precarious. We will all be the better, if they prevail.

The latest wrinkle in Imperia's economy is the closing of the two railroad stations in the twin towns and their replacement by a modern station more than a mile inland along the usually dry river bed. Having two straighter tracks is a good thing. There is less time waiting in stations for a train to pass through in the opposing direction. Theoretically, the locations of the old stations and coastal track will foster higher real estate values. But the new station, like several others, is in the middle of nowhere. If you are lucky, one or two taxicabs might be waiting. If not, you will have to call for one.

From Imperia, it is 30 miles to the French border. There are three large towns: San Remo, Bordighera and Ventimiglia. A dozen or so coastal villages in between have their own places in the sun. This is truly the Riviera of Flowers. Hundreds of hothouses and small fields vie for precious space with olive trees and miniature vineyards. We love the crisp white wines, Pigato and Vermentino, coming from tiny estates in hilltop towns like Ranzo and Diano Castello.

San Remo, with over 50,000 residents is bigger than Imperia. In the 1860s, modern tourism arrived, amplified by the completion of the railroad in 1872. Soon, British, Russian and German royalty and well to do visitors made it a favored destination. King Edward VIII, the Tsarina of Russia and Kaiser Frederick III came for extended stays. Alfred Nobel lived there for many years. Luxury hotels and their famous Casino followed.

Today, San Remo is faded, but still charming. Behind tall palm trees, luxuriant gardens and elaborate fences, there are houses, apartments and mansions of some grandeur.

The San Remo Music Festival has had its ups and downs. Italian pop culture and generally mediocre television variety shows provide some reliable economic life blood to the city. For a brief time every year, the Ariston Theater comes to national attention. For the rest of the year, it is a tired movie house.

The heart of San Remo is the ancient and unkempt quarter of Pigna. It climbs the hills and sparkles with gutsy everyday life. It's homey and energetic with the commerce of thousands of human interactions. It is a kaleidoscope fascinating to observe. Wade into its gurgling river of people. Residents shop for groceries in tiny stores, stop for a nearly home cooked meal, buy their household goods in small mom and pop shops and chat with neighbors. Tourists are entirely incidental to what is going on. This is the residents' town, and no one is self-conscious about it. Shops survive on a lifetime or more of reputation and integrity.

The 1905 casino/theater, the Russian Orthodox Church and some of the oldest cafes, none too grand, are a visual bridge to the past. It is too soon to tell whether the town will revive. The casino is in severe financial trouble. But there are a lot of luxury yachts in the harbor and upscale boutiques along the main street. At least some visitors or residents live well.

San Remo now has one of the newer railroad stations replacing a small and much more convenient one. The older one was along the water and close by the casino, the nicest shops and a pretty avenue leading to the Belle Epoque 5-star Royal Hotel. Now, an underground station beneath the hills deposits you in a two-football field sized tunnel. It connects to a parking circle, and ultimately the street, But first you must traverse four horizontal people movers, much as you see in airport terminals. This being Italy, one or two seem always out of order. At the end of this journey, you are a 15-20-minute walk into the heart of the city.

Seven miles closer to France is the smaller, and at one time more exclusive resort, Bordighera. It still has its little railroad station along the beach. It is an easy stroll on to the town's two parallel main shopping streets. Today, the lower part of town looks tired and bewildered. Driving the old National Road, one would have little reason to stop. But up in the flower fragrant hills, there are luxurious villas, exclusive condominiums, a few small hotels and the ruins of grander places from another time. On those steep inclines, you glimpse exquisite private estates only accessible on private roads. Those views inspired Monet. A recent tourism initiative posted reproductions of his work at some of the key vantage points. There is a small ancient hilltop quarter where people still live nearly arms length away from each other, as they have done for 2400 years.

A few pleasant hotels and restaurants cling to the beach on the outskirts of town. Bordighera may never recover its past glory, but it is worth a visit.

Ventimiglia is just east of the French border. It is a large and ancient market town 658 kilometers from Rome and 40 from Nice. Scruffy and unpretentious, some 25,000+ souls call it home.

There is an ugly underside to most of these towns. The Calabrian Mafia has been active in Liguria for a long time. A tourist is unlikely to encounter their shadowy presence, but several mayors have been jailed or removed, and money laundering, intimidation of legitimate business and creation of tainted ones confirm that this is not just a problem in Italy's South.

There is also a growing influx of North African refugees. Work and empathy have been in short supply. These immigrants are resourceful, but many want to move on to France and further north. That has caused considerable tension at the border. Romanians and others from the extreme east of Europe have also drifted in and through. There is mutual distrust.

Most transit passengers see no need to venture into town. They miss something real. Food and household goods merchants stand the test of local customers. A legendary Friday street market stretches for miles through the city. The entire city becomes a down-market bazaar. Parking is almost impossible. The medieval contours weren't designed for cars.

The Hanbury Gardens are on the outskirts of town. Sir Thomas Hanbury, a tea and silk merchant, bought 18 hectares of nearly vertical hillside between Ventimiglia and the French border. He and his family spent over 30 years creating a one of a kind landscape. It showcases thousands of plant species from all over the world. Despite its size, it's an informal place. The comfortable main house has more the feeling of well-worn leather than pomp and circumstance. One imagines the Hanburys settling in, as they did and have. They are discreetly buried on the site. Their son later became a leading figure in the development of the English colony in Alassio.

The Gardens were donated to Genoa University in 1907. It's a working laboratory for the school's botany students, and open to the public. With a modest entrance fee, they merit a visit if you have strong legs and patience with the mountain goat trails. Gardening aficionados may stoop and look at every genus and species. Others marvel at the variety and tenacity of plants coping with little soil, scant shade and daunting slopes. There are benches by tall trees for rest and reflection.

The main axis of activity in Liguria is the sea and coastal roads. Ventimiglia also has major rail and highway arteries heading north into Piemonte Province. The S20 highway wiggles along the Roia River bed (Roya in French). Long ago, this was part of the ancient kingdom of Savoy. In less than 15 miles you're briefly in France on the joint N204/ E74. Another 15 miles, and you are back in Italy. Some 60 miles above Ventimiglia is Cuneo, a handsome old arcaded city, the capital of the Southwestern corner of Piemonte. The mountains loom outside and over the city. The slow railroad line connecting the two cities is one of the most scenic in Europe, chugging through tunnels and clinging to rock ledges over deep valleys.

There are few reasons to stop along the way, unless you like rustic ski, hunting and hiking lodges. We prefer another road, the SP64, staying in Liguria. It arcs into the higher reaches of the Val di Nervia. On road maps, it is highlighted in yellow and green. It's yellow as a secondary road, and green for scenic beauty. Two popular destinations right on the road are Dolceacqua and Pigna. Just off it, are the lovely villages of Apricale and Castelvittorio.

Dolceacqua is an atmospheric medieval hamlet of 2,000 people. It straddles the narrow river 10 kilometers inland. Densely packed houses jumble down the hill to the water. On the left bank, they huddle below a fortified castle once belonging to the Doria family. Most structures, on both sides, are of the same milk white or oatmeal colored stone with red-orange

169

terra cotta tiled roofs. Under deep green leafed trees on the few wide streets, the town seems solid and unchanging. An ancient 33 meter long stone foot bridge gracefully arches across the river connecting the two quarters.

Twenty minutes north, you come to Pigna, an even smaller place surrounded by pine trees, chestnuts and oaks. Steep hills diverge in three directions. A small spa at the far northern edge is nestled over a sulfur spring. The town is a few blocks wide and a half mile long. Wandering those streets, curious locals return your stares. A few postcards are available at the local café, but what little commerce takes place today is mostly amongst the natives.

We were there with an interior motive: dining at a modest local restaurant in the Hotel Terme. Foreign plates on cars in the parking lot and happy diners inside confirmed the popular choice.

We arrived before lunch time and made a reservation. We had forty minutes to drive back into town for an espresso and a stroll. We ambled up the main street for exercise. Then my wife and I stopped simultaneously with a gasp.

A small village hung high on a heavily wooded hill above the town. Peaking out of dark green forest, it was an almost perfect oval of ancient stone buildings, a church tower at one end. Silent and somber, one viscerally understood it was built to repel unwanted visitors. We were ready for a good lunch, but between courses we talked about visiting Castelvittorio. It was where Silvio Viglietti's wife was born.

A very narrow road zigzags up the back side of the hill below Castelvittorio. While Pigna today has 1,000 inhabitants, Castelvittorio is closer to 400. There are traces of the medieval walls and castle. Outside the village is a small parking lot. Most cars and trucks are of the miniature variety. A small shuttle bus intermittently connects the village with Pigna and the world below. Near the center is a tiny square with a town hall, church, a few simple shops. Covered passageways, alleys, flights of steps, and a few modest restaurants lie deeper in the village.

The locals look at you with amusement and mild curiosity. They see a few foreigners taking a brief peak at their town and disappearing. We will never forget this place. It's a study in black, gray and white. It is still rooted in the middle ages, despite television antennas.

On one of our longer day trips, we headed back to Apricale for lunch. The easy road starts in Dolceaqua. A narrow one from Bajardo was closed by landslides and flooding. Faced with reversing course on a long and tedious drive, we naively took off on a "white road", the thinnest squiggle on our map, westward.

There was a small home-made arrow sign: "to Castelvittorio", then no other signs for twenty miles. The rutted dirt road was mostly one lane. It ascended from the valley with spectacular views of other mountain hamlets. But this was barely more than an animal path. Often there was no protection from steep drop offs. There were just a few isolated farm houses and goat or sheep pastures above or below where the hills allowed them.

In forty minutes of white-knuckle driving, we met two other vehicles. Miraculously, it was at places where we could back safely to marginally wider spots. The other drivers were patient, smiled, and perhaps took kindly to the sight of a large French car with a TT plate in their rural patch. It was beautiful and scary. We vowed never to take that road again, nor to venture off numbered highways without irrefutable intelligence.

Dark thoughts of a potential accident, my almost non-existent Italian language skills and our lack of a European cell phone crossed my mind frequently on that harrowing ride. It was unlikely we would reach Apricale, or anywhere else, for lunch. Fear and hunger are not a pretty pair.

Finally, Castelvittorio was in view. We climbed a marginally improving road back to the familiar town parking lot, and then to Pigna and on to the main road to Dolceacqua. It was well past one. A late lunch was still possible.

Apricale, another tiny hillside village, is a short distance east of Dolceaqua. The road climbs another scrubby hill and goes through Isolabona. That village coalesced around an ancient restored castle now used for summer cultural events. For several decades it has hosted an international harp festival. There are a few places to linger, a couple of local restaurants and a nine room two-star hotel. But most travelers press on to Apricale, deemed: "il piu belle villagio d'Italia", one of the prettiest villages in Italy.

The town nestles and ambles on its heavily wooded hill. A thirteenth century church and a small castle are at its core. First you find parking and then navigate on foot via alleys and covered passageways. The houses on the periphery are huddled together like a stone wagon train. The castle and church are neighbors on a delightful sometimes sun-drenched miniature terrace square, the buildings painted in soft Mediterranean pastels. In good weather you can have a coffee or light meal at picnic tables under market umbrellas.

For such a small place, it boasted two Michelin rated restaurants. We enjoy La Capanna-da Baci. This friendly and rustic restaurant overwhelms you with antipasti. Home cooked regional dishes are comfort food. There are rustic wines from Liguria and more elegant ones from Piemonte. But save room for their zabaglione for dessert. Sometime, we will have to try the other restaurants. But there is always the vision of zabaglione, hand stirred with a liberal infusion of Marsala dessert wine!

OOO

13

Savona Province and East to Genoa

From Alassio, we feel an almost magnetic pull northeastward to Genoa and the considerable variety of towns between. Albenga is just 8 kilometers up the coast. We head there frequently for contrast. More than double the size of Alassio, with 24,000 people, its Roman origins are in plain sight. Fragments of the ancient Via Julia Augusta connect the two towns across hilltops. Now, just a wide and fading path, you can imagine chariots, carts and the Legion rumbling to or from Gaul. A few ancient burial grounds along the path confirm its authenticity.

Today, Albenga is a working-class town with a big agricultural backyard. The medieval core makes for an enjoyable stroll. Surrounded by fragments of ancient walls and two millennia old towers, you sense the presence of the ancient garrison post and the Roman street grid. Below today's city, there have been extensive archaeological finds. A small museum displays amphora and wood shards from a Roman cargo ship that sank off the coast more than two thousand years ago.

Some streets are homely with bland modern concrete apartments. But a few avenues are lined with mature trees and mosaic pavers. Behind wrought iron or stone fences there are elegant town houses built in the late 1800s or early 1900s. A few attractive shops sell designer kitchens, modern furniture, second tier designer clothes, and jewelry. There is a measure of prosperity or optimism. But an influx of North Africans and now refugees from the Middle East has generated tension and some petty crime.

On one of our earliest trips to Albenga, we stopped in a main street Alassio bar to buy bus tickets. As the owner handed us the tickets, he said: "be careful there." Newspapers report that foreigners are involved in drugs or domestic violence; as if that didn't happen among Italians!

For many years, we used a coin operated laundry in Albenga. Big Electrolux washers and dryers took Euro coins of all sizes from 5 cents to 2 Euros. One bought detergent and softener by punching in the right vending codes. Clean and austere, with a few plastic chairs and a small folding table, there were detailed operation instructions on large plastic posters on the walls: in Italian, French, German, English and Arabic. A couple of years ago the laundry abruptly closed. Fortunately, for us, two new ones opened in Alassio.

The North Africans have a precarious existence. They work in the agriculture industry and behind the scenes in restaurants and hotels. A few halal butcher shops and ethnic grocery stores offer a sliver of home in a foreign country. We see immigrants with large plastic bags of groceries on the bus, gamely taking them back to some shared home on the outskirts. The women, in abayas or modest dresses and scarves, are accompanied by children and men in more western garb. Each must have a sad tale of why they were compelled to leave their homes.

In Alassio and Albenga, a handful of Africans ply the beach or set up impromptu blanket displays on the street selling cheap jewelry, fake designer bags, toys, umbrellas. Local and federal regulations impose steep fines for those who purchase counterfeit goods, but they are sporadically enforced. At night, a bunch of young, desperate men, filter in and out of the bars and restaurants attempting to sell roses for one or two Euros. Most are Bangladeshis, and supposedly live communally and are forced to turn in all their earnings to their boss.

Now, the old run-down former Army casern in Albenga is being used to house refugees. Here there are no easy solutions for the world's problems.

All along the coast, from Pisa to Nice, peasant soul food includes farinata. It's called socca in Nice. A humble unleavened chickpea crepe or pancake, it may or may not have sea-soning or vegetable topping. A tiny hole in the wall place in old town Albenga, Da Puppo, usually has a line outside. An acquired taste, it is cheap and filling.

There are little niche businesses we love: perhaps the finest cheese shop and salumeria in Liguria run by a cheerful older couple; the showroom of Noberasco, purveyors of fine dried fruits and nuts all over Italy, a one of a kind jewelry store fea-turing estate quality heirlooms and newly designed creations by the owner.

Alassio and Albenga are connected by the "TPL" local bus service. The line runs from Andora to Savona. If you are going that far, the odds are you will have to change buses in Finale Ligure for the last 18 miles. Small half buses provide infrequent service to the hill towns above Alassio, Albenga and other communities on the coast. We have taken the coastal buses many times. When we don't have a car, they are more frequent than trains, and cheaper, but make numerous stops.

The bus drivers are less reckless than their counterparts in the country's South. But grab a stanchion. They take off quickly, making up for time lost along their route. They stop just as quickly when a scooter darts in front of them, or an oncoming vehicle crosses the center line. The recent addition of half heartedly constructed rotaries adds another obstacle to their journeys.

The regular bus clientele are the elderly, foreigners, itinerants, tourists, and school age children. Most of our local friends have never or rarely ridden the bus. Sometimes they are filled with high school students. The service is frequent, reliable, and totally invisible to the local middle and upper class. Each bus ride affords a different assortment of Damon Runyonesque characters. When we have had our fill of the scenery, we can try to piece together the multiple human dramas playing out in the seats around us.

The buses are a bit strange. Seating is peculiar, even haphazard, with mysterious dead spaces, metallic bumps, protrusions and steps. Often there is a front or rear facing seat after a metal partition behind the driver. Some are huge articulated buses. They must be especially awkward to drive on cliff hanging sections of the road and around rotaries. Passengers stamp their tickets in a little punch clock which doesn't always work. Whether there are two or three doors, some are designated for entrance and others for exit, a distinction ignored by most of the passengers.

TPL has a bewildering color-coded system for determining the fare in their little domain. Why they need nine different colored tickets to document slightly different distances and sub-region transit is a mystery to me. The total variance in fare is in fractions of a Euro. We tell a local café owner or shopkeeper we need X bus biglietti to go from Alassio to

Pietra Ligure, and they hand us a different colored ticket than if we were going to Laigueglia or Andora.

Once in a blue moon, two or three inspectors come on board and make sure everyone has a correctly coded and colored ticket. Large fines can be rendered for the scofflaw. Many of the students and elderly have annual or seasonal passes. One evening, we were taking the little school bus size minibus up to the hamlet of Moglio for a meal at a lovely trattoria. As usual, we were the only people on the bus that hadn't been taking it for years. The bus driver greeted every other passenger as one would family or neighbors. A third of the way up the small hill, scarcely five minutes into the ride, two inspectors got on the bus. Of the nine or ten passengers, we were the only ones with tickets to show. No wonder this company is deeply in the red.

The bus ride into Albenga is especially pretty, with sweeping views of the Mediterranean and Gallinara Island. On the Eastern outskirts of the city, flowers, plants, vegetables, grape and olive vines are scattered in regimented rows in small plots or in green houses, often beside little houses. Zoning doesn't seem to be a concept that has caught on. Beyond the wide river valley, glass hot houses perch on terraced hillsides make the most of the strong sun and difficult terrain. A long narrow underutilized beach connects to the next town, Ceriale, a blue-collar makeshift resort with campgrounds and basic apartments.

The railroad track parallels the coast in splashing distance of the sea. Behind the first set of hills is some of the richest agricultural land in the region, the Piana di Albenga. It produces wonderful white wines, lovely olive oil, elegant honey and splendid fruit and vegetables.

Ceriale and Borghetto Santo Spirito, each a community of 5,000 people, seem hard scrabble today. There are more attractive towns further along the coast.

Continuing a condensed overview from thirty years of rambling, Loano is another modest beach resort but with a more interesting and substantial inner core. For five hundred years the Doria family was its protector. This produced imposing churches and civic buildings still in use today. Behind a pleasant beach promenade, the old caruggi stretches parallel for well over a mile. Walking along it and observing everyday life is an enjoyable pastime.

From Loano, all the way to Vado, the coastal road is very sinuous and scenic. Apart from a few mostly ugly modern hotels, isolated homes and businesses respect the craggy shoreline and unencumbered sea views.

East of Loano, Pietra Ligure, is larger than its neighbors. The old center has real character. Byzantines once lived here on a nearby limestone hill. Today, it is more than a beach resort. There is a large regional hospital with a better reputation than the closer one to Alssio in Albenga. Sadly, a large Piaggio plant, with three or four buildings, lies abandoned and forlorn.

Mid-rise hotels, of no particular charm, are lined up along a well-maintained strand. Away from the center, palm trees soften the cityscape and even more modest hotels still have partial ocean views. The budello and mostly perpendicular vicos are homey and inviting. There are mariner tabernas worth finding and modest stores of honest quality. The square next to the imposing Basilica of San Nicolo is ringed with some pleasant cafes with outside tables. A perfect place to observe and be part of the local scene.

Next are two old and intertwined villages: Borgio and Verezzi, each worth exploring.

Further towards Genoa, Finale Ligure has some gravitas. With several neighborhoods and outlying "Frazioni", it has an attractive beach, a large hotel stock and a lively and prosperous center. The hills form a backdrop behind the city with dramatic vistas and some lovely homes. The long waterfront promenade is a memorable stroll, a place to walk, sit on a park bench, and enjoy gelati, a snack and/or a drink. Pensioners, young families, foreign tourists mesh. Many window shop, make small purchases and greet friends and relatives; the town hums.

A few miles inland is the medieval quarter of Final Borgo. It is a well preserved 900-year-old bastion of somber stone palazzos and churches. Enlivened by modern craftsmen and a few restaurants and hostelries, it's a place to savor. It is a minor tourist destination for its beauty and authenticity.

Past Finale, there are two charming old towns straddling Capo Noli: Varigotti and Noli. Varigotti is photogenic and atmospheric. The spirit, if not the reality, of an old Ligurian fishing village lives on. Hemmed in by almost vertical rock walls, it is fixed in size. By sound planning or good luck, there is no road beyond the houses and small hotels along the sand beach. No other town, except Alassio, enjoys this close communion with the water's edge.

Many Italian Riviera postcards are generic and interchangeable. But the old skyline of gelati colored fishermen's houses along the beach in Varigotti is a one of a kind time warp. Artists and photographers are drawn to its beautiful setting.

We once used the microscopic post office here. The postmistress patiently went through all her folders of stamps, finding the best to send to some young children on our mailing list.

Beauty is marketable. There are three- and four-star hotels in this tiny town, together with a dozen more modest hostelries. Despite the onslaught of transients, only 600 souls call it home.

On the other side of the cape, Noli was once a city state. It predates Roman times. With 3,000 inhabitants, it is a handsome and photogenic place. Unlike most Ligurian towns, the main market streets run perpendicular to the water, gradually climbing toward the hills. There are still a few commercial fishing boats and a small sand beach. Solid stone buildings are softened by pastel colors and flower pots.

The church has played an important part in Noli for 15 centuries. By participating in the First Crusade in 1097, it reaped commercial and political rewards. For almost 600 years it was independent. When forced to take sides, it cast its lot with Genoa rather than the closer city of Savona. That turned out to be a good choice.

In 2008, a stunning small hotel opened in the old Bishop's Palace on a seafront cliff. The hotel lured a destination restaurant formerly a few miles inland. Residence Palazzo Vescovale and the restaurant La Fornace di Barbablu are worth a journey from anywhere on the Riviera. The chef and restaurant had been on the site of an old foundry (furnace). I am not sure of why the reference to Bluebeard, a grisly fairytale.

The palazzo is a perfect perch. From a waterfront parking lot, you take an elevator; then a mini-funicular to the palace veranda. In good weather, an outdoor trellised terrace is ideal for drinks or a meal. The dining rooms are painted in soft Mediterranean pastels. They have lovely views over the active sea channel. A few passenger and tanker ships will cross during a meal, and dozens of sea birds. This is one of the best restaurants in Liguria, passionately using the best local ingredients employed by an exceptional and gentle chef, Giuseppe Ricchebuono.

Another 11 miles down the road is the provincial capital and transportation hub, Savona. Busy coastal rail and road intersections head inland as well as along the coast and a new cruise ship terminal leads seaward. I wish I could say nice things about Savona, but it is a remarkably dreary city. I doubt that even the people who live there are very loyal. Most apartment blocks have a Soviet-style bleakness. The railroad station is large, but the homeliest we have seen in Italy.

We spend a few hours here from time to time, often in the old port quarter. It is better to head inland to more interesting towns like Alba, Asti, Acqui Terme and Allesandria. No one has explained to me why there is such an abundance of towns beginning with the letter A! We take the magnificent A6 highway northwest, boring through steep hillsides and hanging suspended over remote valleys. Or we amble down thinner veins of local roads meandering over hills into sparsely populated corners of Liguria and Piemonte.

This Autostrada, and two that are closer to Genoa, connect the coast with Northern Europe. There is a near constant flow of large trucks in both directions. In winter temperatures plunge. Snow and sleet, and more deadly ice, prevail as you press inland.

Savona's waterfront district is jumbled and run down with faint hints of rebirth. A small pleasure boat marina stands cheerily close to an industrial port with warehouses, cranes, and container and cargo ships. A few new piers service passenger ferries and ships. Costa Lines' modern terminal opened in 2003 and is quite snazzy. The tall glass structure, with palm trees, fountains and escalators, looks more like a modern airport terminal or upscale shopping center than a traditional wharf. Airwalks facilitate boardings. Cruise passengers may now walk into the city and new shops have opened in response.

There are museums and venerable churches. But Savona doesn't attract many tourists and has something of a crime problem. The courteous folk in the tourist office have a few pamphlets with not many takers. A grand old theater, Teatro Chiebrera, offers two or three operas a year, and an occasional concert, mostly for local consumption.

From Savona, it is only 48 kilometers to Genoa. While the coast line becomes increasingly industrial, old towns are steeped in their traditions and history.

Just east of Savona are the fraternal towns of Albisola and Albisola Marina, with a ceramic trade that began in the 1500s. Artisans still make elaborately painted pottery and there is a small museum. The beach promenade here is informal and inviting. The town lines are blurred and it feels like an extension of Savona.

Savona Province ends beyond Varazze. The rest is within Genoa's jurisdiction. Some 25 kilometers west, Cogoleto a town of 9,000 and Arenzano, 11,000 strong, sit on either side of Cap San Martino, ever closer to Italy's sixth biggest city of 600,000 residents. They are modest beach resort towns, within commuting distance of the metropolis.

A string of old towns or villages were swallowed up by Genoa but retain their names and memories, and some municipal power. On the west side, Voltri, Pra, Pegli, Sestri Ponente, Cornigliano are heavily industrialized along the water's edge. On little side streets, up in the hills or in an old church or cemetery they retain some charm.

There are glimpses of a blue-collar world not on tour bus itineraries. Residents smell coal dust residue and chemicals daily. They hear the noise of conveyor belts, and endure the exhaust of a constant stream of large trucks and heavy equipment. Tankers, cargo ships and seagoing ferries occupy piers near warehouses and large staging areas. It reminds me of the outskirts of Buffalo or Beaumont. People and towns made sacrifices for jobs that no longer exist. Still, these areas may again be viable. There is some new construction and the ports still have some life. It is too early to write these communities off.

Occasionally, we will stop in one of these industrial outliers, wandering the streets of ship chandleries, import-export stores, hundred-year-old apartments, auto and truck part stores searching for the rare but still present venerable osteria.

OOO

14

Genoa

We often need a big city fix-and Genoa provides it. Three dozen forays into this city over more than forty years are not enough. Look beyond its dour face. Tap into its history and today's attempts at rebirth. There are terrific antiquarian bookstores, museums and one of a kind churches. There is the amazing feeling you are in a place that has been alive and driven for more than 2600 years.

Genoa is not a tourist magnet. There is exasperating highway congestion, somber stone walls and exteriors. Feel free to get lost in the rabbit warren of meandering streets and alleys, at least in daylight. This is a city with a strong sense of place. Perhaps it is fixated on its past, which is worth preserving. The future is more uncertain.

In the narrow harbor quarter are shops and people from nearly every trading nationality in the world. It's an Asian, African and Middle Eastern bazaar. While no longer one of the greatest ports in the world, the maritime character is essential. Plenty of cargo still enters or leaves here. From the sea, high hills wall the city in like a giant arena. The nine-hundred-year-old lighthouse, "Lanterna", is a graceful 117 meters tall. The beam is visible 33 miles at sea. Made obsolescent by satellite navigation, it still is a powerful symbol.

Think of the apprehension and sadness of tens of thousands of people compelled to leave from here on a one-way trip to the Americas or Australia. Many were from Liguria, but all Italian provinces were represented, especially those in the South and Sicily. Refugees from Eastern Europe and North Africa also booked passage from this harbor. All said farewell to family and friends they might never see again.

Those emigrants made new hyphen Italian communities in port cities in Argentina, Uruguay, Chile, Canada, Australia and the United States. The second, third and fourth generations now come back, as tourists, to learn where their ancestors came from.

Transcontinental maritime passenger business declined in the 1950s and early 60s as air travel expanded. Genoa recalibrated. There are new ferry terminals, container facilities, small scale ship, ferry and yacht building and repair, an aquarium and a waterfront convention center. Old Genoa, "La Superba", the Proud, traded with the world and funneled wealth into elegant palaces and churches.

Today, most people enter the city through two large train stations, Principe and Brignole. The core routes are along the coast from Barcelona and Nice on to La Spezia, Rome and to Italy's boot, and North to Turin or Milan, then Venice, Switzerland and Northern and Eastern Europe.

More than a dozen regional train lines spread out to market towns and spas in the hinterlands. These secondary routes daftly have their own schedules, with an infuriating lack of coordination with the Intercity Trains that bring people to or from Genoa. This is not the Swiss or German model of efficiency. Superimposed on this template are a few local commuter lines to the nearby suburbs, and a very short subway line. Sadly, the Italian Railway system and their stations are tired, but slowly they are being spruced up.

Principe dates from 1854, placed close to the thriving port. Genoa hosted a World Exposition in 1905 and built a second station, Brignole, three kilometers east. In French Renaissance architectural style, it is on Piazza Verdi, close to the newer business district. Brignole is still the "second" station, with fewer trains. There are grandiose plans for its rehabilitation which move forward at a snail's pace. But the two stations are connected by the new subway line.

Genoa's Christopher Columbus airport is at the water's edge, straddling the old towns of Sestri Ponente and Cornigliano, about 7 miles west of the city center. You could be downtown with a fifteen-minute cab ride. But there are only nine or ten direct and thin international routes. Commuter flights to Milan and Rome connect to just about anywhere. It's a secondary airport unable or unwilling to compete with Milan and Nice.

Genoa has a dense urban transportation system. The AMT Lines cover 900 kilometers with 140 distinct bus lines, a short subway, a cog railway, two funiculars and ten municipal elevators providing access to places in the nearby hills.

Arriving by car, the best thing to do is quickly park, preferably in a garage or fenced lot. Street parking is ephemeral. Unless you like the grand prix, leave city driving to the taxis, Uber and buses. Walking is the best way to explore this city.

A walk between the two train stations is one of our regular past-times. The stroll includes the once elegant shopping street, Via Venti Settembre. There are still a few lovely small shops. Half way, through homely doors, you enter Genoa's covered food market. The dozens of specialized stalls, selling fish, cheese, mushrooms, poultry, produce, fruit, all put our supermarkets to shame. Small family stands have gone on for generations. If we only had a nearby kitchen!

As a consolation prize, we have a coffee at one of a dozen atmospheric cafes. Better still is attending a concert or opera at Teatro Carlo Felice on Piazzi De Ferrari. Just north of the Opera House is still chic Via Roma. We window shop on the street or wander through the turn of the century Galleria Via Mazzini midst high end clothing, shoes and jewelry.

Late in the day, we choose a route back to Principe. The most direct is past the incomparable palaces along Via Garibaldi or "Balbi"; or, towards the waterfront and into the labyrinthine old sections of the city. Some date from well before the founding of Rome. Phoenicians, Greeks and Etruscans were here first. Some sectors are not safe at dusk and after. Or you can take the Metro.

We zig zag off the carruggi near the harbor. One of a kind shops or stalls run the gamut from pedestrian goods to fine antique furniture. There is no pressure to shop, although you will be welcomed if you do. There are hard to find things, hand crafted bread and pasta molds, fabrics from the Maghreb, CDs of local music in Genoese dialect or from all corners of Africa.

The oldest churches are among the most beautiful that we have seen anywhere. Whether you are religious or not, the artistic skill and piety of the craftsmen comes through. Santa Maria di Castello, a 12th century gem, was built on the ruins of a church that went back another 500 years. San Donato, an exquisite parish church, was built over centuries, starting in the 1100s.

Once we heard a strong and raspy baritone voice wafting from a record store. It was reminiscent of Jacques Brel or Georges Brassens. We were introduced to Fabrizio de Andre, the poet-singer of the Genovese dialect weaving stories of the fishermen, seamen and hard laborers of the region. Born into a wealthy family, he devoted his life to celebrating the outcasts. Two decades after his death, he is still a local and possibly national icon.

A new Carlo Felice Opera House was constructed on top of the ruins of the famous theater destroyed in World War II. The acoustics are marvelous. In Italy, people take their music quite seriously. We attended a matinee performance of Gounod's "Faust". The costumes and sets were loaned from La Scala in Milan. A dapper and elderly gentleman sat down next to us, and opened his briefcase. Inside was a large book he placed on his lap. It was the complete musical score. He sat quietly and followed every note. Today, the theater is struggling financially.

The grand palaces on Garibaldi are now museums, government buildings or the offices of international banks and fashion houses. The museums are worth visiting, and so is peaking through the entrances of the other buildings. Genoa once rivaled Florence, Venice and Rome in wealth and influence. In the 16th and 17th centuries its businesses success generated this exclusive enclave, primarily for six prominent local families. The street still emanates the look and smell of power, confidence and wealth.

In a few corners of the city, funicular trams and elevators climb the steepest hills. Even more ancient and fascinating are the Cruese, narrow cobbled lanes reaching high into the hills and tracing foot and animal paths, some more than 3,000 years old.

An art deco elevator takes you from Piazza del Portello to the top of Monte Albano. At the summit, Castelleto, once a military fortification, there are beautiful views in all directions. It's a fashionable residential area. Nearby Piazza Goffredo Villa intersects the Circonvallazione a Monte, a ring road built in the 1870s. Zigzagging through the hills, the road changes names many times. An electric tram follows the route.

The ultimate stop for some is Staglieno Cemetery. Like Pere La Chaise in Paris or Recoleta in Buenos Aires, this is a very ornate necropolis. Mourning, social status and religious faith converge. It is a baroque bastion, tranquil but unsettling. Outside its tall walls are retail flower stands, bus stops and a large boulevard leading to the outskirts of the city. Through arches and inside the towering and claustrophobic walls, it is a giant city of the dead and a rather class conscious one. There are substantial crypts and monuments with elaborate statues and inscriptions. They record the titles and achievements of these permanent residents. Narrow internal lanes and streets allow for the visits of the living. In the back, hillscapes and trees give something of a country feel. The higher area is for those who could afford burial a little closer to the heavens.

There is a lovely portal out Genoa's backdoor. A 1929 vintage narrow gauge railway line connects Piazza Manin, in the upper reaches of the city, to the village of Casella. The 25-ki-lometer trip takes about an hour. The old engine and cars climb slowly into the mountains. The two toned red and white or blue and white miniature electrical trains make 19 brief stops along the way. The city falls away as the train winds its way up hills and through valleys. Swiveling your head from left to right, there are lovely and steep views on both sides. The short wooden seats are less comfortable than a church pew. Some-times there are sheer drops outside, as if you were in a cable car. Soon you are in peaceful countryside.

Casella is an amiable if not entirely pretty village. A few small stone houses remain of the medieval two-story style from which the hamlet is named. The ground floors were used as a stable for livestock. The living quarters were reached by an outside staircase. Supplies were slowly transported by mule between mountains and shore before the rail link. Long ago, tolls were exacted on the road through town. Today, hiking trails or a rustic meal attract daytrippers.

Another excursion, ten miles north of Genoa, allowed us to indulge two related passions, good food, and adding to our plate collection. East of Casella is the small city of Serra Ric-co, comprising eight villages. A bronze tablet in one of the vil-lages, Pedemonte, dates from 117 B.C. In San Cipriano, there was a more recent treasure, restaurant Ferrando. It served good food for more than sixty years, especially mushroom dishes. It was a warm rural restaurant, the kind of place where the local

Rotary or Kiwanis meet. There is an exquisite outdoor garden for late spring and summer dining. The restaurant eventually closed, replaced by a new establishment in the same building.

Ferrando belonged to the Unione Ristorante del Buon Ricordo. The association of convivial restaurants of "the good memories" seeks to preserve local and regional dishes. If you order the special of the house, you get a commemorative plate as a souvenir. Ferrando's depicts a contented cow chewing grape leaves with a medieval tower and hill in the background. Lovely mushrooms are in the foreground. Their veal was quite tasty. There are currently 123-member restaurants, 109 of them in Italy. From time to time, they change their specialties, and plates. It started with 12 restaurants back in 1964.

East of Genoa, proud neighborhoods are nearly separate towns: Boccadasse, the old fishermen's quarter, Sturla, Quarto dei Mille, Quinto Al Mare and upscale Nervi.

Boccadasse exudes memories of a simpler time. It's a good stop day or night, just off the seafront road. In the midst of real fishermen, restaurants and bars welcome locals and some tourists. The famous Football Club of Buenos Aires, Boca Juniors, refers to this neighborhood and its homesick Ligurians.

There are elegant houses, streets and vistas along the winding road through Sturla, Quarto and Quinto. From a forlorn and rocky point, Garibaldi launched his expedition of "a thousand men" to reinforce the independence movement in Sicily. Nervi is perhaps the most upscale residential quarter, 11 kilometers from Genoa. It was once one of the most fashionable places on the Riviera. A morning or afternoon stroll on its seaside promenade and park is delightful.

That walking route begins at the ancient harbor, Porticciolo. It is now a very narrow outlet to the sea, with a few pleasure boats and surrounded by old houses painted in pastel Ligurian colors. Summer boat tours start here to Portofino, Sant Fruttouso, Camogli and Cinque Terre.

Facing south, a two-kilometer Promenade above the ocean is named after Anita Garibaldi, the General's brave and talented Azorean-Brazilian wife. The sea views are spectacular. For half its length, the Promenade abuts a park and rose gardens filled with palms, pines and exotic trees.

More than museums, the aquarium, the banks, shops and restaurants, I think of the students as Genoa's hope. The University of Genoa was founded in 1481, and has some 40,000 students today. Whether and where those students find jobs will say a lot about the city's future.

When we are in Genoa, we rub shoulders with so many people from all walks of life. It is a living mosaic. The pace is faster. The massive stone buildings and steep steps climbing and descending the sharp hills evokes its tenacity. The city has a presence, a personality, a confidence one doesn't forget.

OOO

15

Sustenance in Alassio

We return to Alassio with increasing frequency and length, now often twice a year for four to six weeks in different seasons. We savor the flowers, sea breezes, quieter tempo and mostly its gentle people. We have been there in every month but those of summer. Simple tasks, buying a paper, a liter of milk, breadsticks bring smiles. The small and peaceful footprint of the town reminds me of the parameters of my childhood neighborhood in Brooklyn. Back then, it was safe for a kid to be out and about on their own, even a dozen blocks from home. Small shopkeepers were neighbors. The foot patrol cop was there if you needed help-and you rarely did.

On each trip, we look for any changes in the everyday cityscape. With so many small stores owned by elderly couples attrition is inevitable. By dusk, on one such day, there was a little sadness too. We had just learned about the "death" of our favorite bar. Even worse, it lives on without its soul.

At home, we don't hang out in bars or cafes, but they are different here. Alassio has plenty. They cater to all permutations of customers. Many are neighborhood spots where tourists are rarely seen; not that they wouldn't be welcome. Hotel bars cater mostly to their guests. Along shopping streets and the promenade people gravitate to a place with decent coffee, snacks, that play a certain kind of music, or where they see similar people. In each, most patrons are of a kind; young, old, preppy, German, blue collar, from Torino, or the neighborhood, etc.

A few watering holes are institutions. "Il Murretto" or the wall of tiles is an Alassio landmark on the back side of the city park. Famous and near famous people have signatures, caricatures and sayings on small plaques on a retaining wall. Mario Berrino, who passed away just before his 91st birthday, was an admired local artist who conceived and promoted the wall. His art studio is around the corner. A friend, Ernest Hemingway, signed the first tile.

The Berrino family's Café Roma, across from the wall, is the most famous in town. Very fashionable in the 1950s, when Hemingway, Charlie Chaplin and other glamorous people visited with some frequency, it once had a rooftop garden which featured society bands and big-name entertainers. It is now much smaller. It still looks cozy and hip. But our experience there has been underwhelming. Perfunctory service and uninspired drinks and hors d'ouveres are the norm. Until recently, it had attitude but no real charm. A change in ownership, or at least management, in 2014, has brought it back from mediocrity to a somewhat higher style.

I've previously mentioned Café Mozart. Fronting the sea and continuing through to a lovely little square, it was the classiest bar in town. With linen covered tables, fancy rattan furniture, ornate curtains and attractive lighting, it exuded quality. Classical music or melodic club music played quietly in the background. On weekends a sophisticated pianist would sing Broadway tunes. The man who first created this elegant space had a heart attack and was forced to retire. When we first visited, a gracious and stylish older couple owned and ran it with panache. After many years, they sold it.

As a consolation prize, for the town and us, they opened the best wine and spirit shop in Alassio in 2002, Carpe Diem. It is a connoisseur's venue. In February 2010 the shop moved from the caruggi to Via Dante and expanded. Now across from the Muretto, a few doors down from Café Roma, they have wine tastings in their spacious cellar and back patio. It is a place where you can buy fine champagnes and wines from Bordeaux and Burgundy as well as fine wines from all over Italy. There are few bargains but plenty of quality.

201

Café Mozart, with its wicker chairs and glass coffee tables both inside and out, stylish green damascene cocktail napkins, profusion of white candles, classical or cool jazz music through the speakers, and live music on weekends, had been our spot. One could make a meal of the lovely hors d'oeuvres served with every long drink, and we often did. Gayle would usually have a premium gin and tonic and I would sample from two dozen aged rums from the Caribbean and the northern mantle of Central America.

For a year or two, the young new owners ran Café Mozart much as it had been done before. Over time, there were fewer customers like us, with a little gray hair and willing to shell out for premium drinks. The younger clientele didn't appreciate jazz and cocktail music played by pianists who knew their Cole Porter and Sondheim.

Another sale took place. The next owners favored a synthetic on-line jazz channel, cheaper drinks and snacks and created another mediocre restaurant. Or perhaps that is what the market demands. They made some money, especially in the summer. We often walked back to our apartment a different way. It was painful to see and hear the newer version. We dreaded the sound of another twenty something singer on weekends with no redeemable voice karaoking their way through American and Italian standards. Mozart must be rolling in his grave.

Eventually, on a quiet afternoon, we returned. They still made a decent club sandwich. The view is the same. The wait staff was courteous and attentive. Perhaps the pendulum would swing back. There were still some long drinks available. Some nights they actually got an adult crowd.

But in 2018 the bar changed hands again. Now it is part of the "Clapsy" empire, a group of cheerful but bland and mediocre restaurants offering pizza, salads and simple fried and grilled seafood entrees of no distinction. These "family restaurants" proliferated as the waterfront has slipped down market.

It took a week or so wandering around feeling forlorn as we looked for a new watering hole. We tried a few places that seemed promising. Despite stylish furniture and glassware, they were merely adequate. Really good waiters are an endangered species in both restaurants and bars. Some are so klutzy they are a major distraction. Industrial or leftover hors d'oeuvres are a further turn off.

On the fourth or fifth try, we had a new hangout. Bombay and Tonic was no problem. Campari and freshly squeezed Blood Orange Juice became a new and viable alternative. But, sadly, no exotic rums. Maybe a Cuba Libre with Havana Club, a grappa or cognac from a shorter list.

Bar Impero has some charm, and decent cookies and chocolates. Two blocks in from the beach, on Via Dante, a busy one way shopping street, the Impero sat across the street from a blue collar competitor. Both have tables spilling on to the sidewalk. Above lively shops are old apartments, most with flower filled terraces. The glassed in enclosure has a ringside view of activity on this heart of the city street. Overhead electric heaters extend the outdoor season.

After walking by many times, we found a table upwind from cigarette smokers and gave it a try. Our young and attentive waiter brought us some homemade focaccia, delicious olives and the usual potato chips and peanuts. The glasses arrived shortly thereafter, and he poured generous rations from the turquoise bottle. Inside, in the early evening, customers bought boxes of chocolate cream filled cookies, macaroons, fruit tarts and butter cookies.

The eight or nine outside tables were full of regulars. A fashionably dressed middle aged California lady was telling her Italian friend, in English, about her next day hair appointment with "the best hairdresser this side of Cannes." Another elegant woman, waiting for someone, read a paperback book, puffed away, and sipped a cocktail. I took another swig of gin and cornered an olive with a toothpick. We wanted to hide our nationality.

Away from the waterfront, the prices are gentler, there are no gypsies or Bangladeshis trying to sell us roses, and the window on local life is instructive.

Over time, we have gotten to know the waiter and waitress that kept this place humming from early morning until around eight in the evening. He is Italian, and she is from Eastern Europe, perhaps Romania or Latvia. They always looked sharp, worked hard, and had a smile and a nod for everyone and a little banter with the regulars. They made the place shine. When it is slow, they might grab a cigarette break. Some high wire stress is defused.

Like many things in life, they are subject to change. The owner of the building raised the rent, and the operator moved on-to the Café Roma no less! After a shaky start, the building owner's son and daughter manage the place. Impero is still a fine stop-and perhaps to trumpet the new regime, they changed their brand of coffee from Lavazza to Illy, to some an improvement.

Just as bars tout the colors and logos of their favorite beers, in Italy, a café's brand of coffee may get you in the door or keep you away. We will stop at a place that serves Hausbrandt, Genovese, Pasqualini, Kimbo or Musetti and skip one serving Vergnano, Esse, or Codem. There is no guarantee that the espresso will be smooth as silk, but at least it could be.

Another virtue of the Impero is that it is next door to the tiny corner Polleria Cunese. It has the best rotisserie chicken in town. Their rabbit, quail, veal, and pork are also first rate, but it is hard to get past the rosemary, olive oil and other herb infused chickens rotating and browning slowly before your eyes. This is a two-generation family operation with father, mother, and son ready to help you. They wear clean white uniforms and radiate friendly appreciation for every customer. At 8 Euros a chicken, it is the best inexpensive meal in town.

There is hardly room for more than two customers at a time in their compact shop. Others queue outside, sit on a small bench, or just look in the windows. Taking a still warm bird back to our apartment, cut in half at the store and served with a salad and wine on Le Terrazze's patio is a regal meal on a backpacker's budget. The white haired pater familias always greeted us with a smile: as "Gli Americani!" My wife gets the best treatment, befitting an attractive blonde.

This is where our lack of Italian is most frustrating. Renato, the owner was always showing a little kindness, throwing in a slice of mountain cheese, a mayonnaise spread. A few times, I have seen him quietly give some food to a couple of forlorn looking street people. I've seen him walk with a painful limp, or bicycle to the store from the other side of the railroad tracks, with never a complaint.

We reciprocated, as best we could, having our friends at Impero deliver an espresso just before his closing time. He would come out of the shop with a smile and toast us with his cup as we sat having a drink. Standing all day in his little shop and kitchen must take a toll. His wife, son and daughter, all who know a little English, radiate hard working integrity and kindness. It makes you feel good to briefly spend time with them.

A few doors down, the other side of Bar Impero, is a narrow Mom and Pop fruit and vegetable stand. They always have some lovely produce sitting outside the shop and a handful of small wicker baskets to bring your selection to the counter. The inside walls are lined with staples; honey, jars of pesto, some dried and frozen pasta. The young man and woman who own and operate "Pantagruel" (The Harlequin), the stock character from Italian Commedia dell'arte, appreciate every small purchase. How they compete with the supermarkets is a combination of tradition, a lack of frills, and a loyal customer base. I might be able to buy a melon or peaches more cheaply elsewhere, but the warm and intelligent look in their eyes when they hand me the change and the exchanged grazies is worth much more.

You may think we have an obsession with food and drink. It is the social interaction we crave. At table, or in a market, we are at the core of someone's livelihood and humanity. They make a living by offering something essential. Even with language and culture barriers, we make contact in a very personal way. We come closer to a stranger, and sometimes make a friend.

Shop owners, restaurant and bar folk are genuinely hospitable in Northern Italy. On the second or third visit the welcome is even warmer. They become interested in who you are.

Conversations go deeper. Many are second or third generation shopkeepers with a wealth of information about the town and environs. When we return, after a four to six-month absence, people smile warmly, and seem genuinely happy to see us again.

Then there is the subject of pizza. As with ice cream, this is a topic of intense debate and passion in Italy. Our hosts believe the best pizza in town is at Italia Restaurant, a humble place a few blocks south along the beach. It doubles in size when tables are placed L shaped around its outdoor periphery. A three-generation family affair, with Neapolitan antecedents, locals and tourists order wood oven fired light and uneven crusted pizza. Having good pizza in a fancy place is almost a contradiction in terms, unless perhaps you are in California.

Half the fun is watching the acrobatic act of young waiters and waitresses taking and delivering orders with a detached efficiency that can only come from serving the masses day in and day out without respite. No one goes away hungry, although the product is only good, not nearly a match for that in Napoli. There are 25 to 30 ingredients you can have on your pie. It is is not wading in melted cheese, like American versions. Smoked salmon, artichokes, mushrooms, ricotta or mozzarella, peppers, full bodied tomatoes, high quality anchovies, the possibilities are wonderful. Besides modest wines, there is good German beer on tap.

There probably wouldn't be a modern Alassio without its beach. While the beach is public, as far as the eye can see there are wooden cabanas and a rainbow of colored umbrellas and beach chairs belonging to dozens of concessions. Some add play structures for small kids and a snack bar. For a small fee, a family can use the little wooden closets to change into bathing suits and for another fee, rent a chair and an umbrella. They can take a cold water shower, get a beverage and a sandwich without leaving their staked out spot, spending the day baking in the sun.

Each "bagni" is a small business, usually a family affair that has been around for several generations. The facilities are almost identical. Through force of habit or the owner's welcome, people go back to the same place. How these concessions were awarded and how much they pay (or don't pay) in taxes is rather murky, shrouded in local politics.

Our bagni of choice is Selin. Dating to 1923, one of the currently owning family is a cheerful grandmotherly Swedish lady who lived for a time in Wisconsin. She is part of the regular table of foreign wives and some widows who meet almost every morning for coffee or tea at Rudy's. Her grandchildren are part Italian, her daughter also married a local. The son-in-law is the lifeguard, "salvataggio", and one of the nicest and hardest working guys on the strand. He is always rearranging the chairs and umbrellas, pulling a heavy plow weight across the sand to make it clean and neat, making sure that the littlest children stay out of harm's way.

It is not warm enough, for local tastes, to sunbathe all year. By city ordinance, the temporary wooden structures can't go up until late spring and must come down in early October. They are assembled and disassembled and put on tiny three-wheel trucks which lumber off to remote garages and storage bays miles away inland.

The beach concessions are a powerful political lobby. Many folks would like to see them gone or reduced, so strollers can see the beautiful littoral. That is not likely. On a glorious day one October, we were walking along the Promenade and most of the cabanas were down. Suddenly, Pizzeria Italia had an unobstructed view of the ocean rather than a back fence of cabanas! The sea breeze was gusty. The sky was nearly cloudless and a glorious blue. While pizza is usually an evening meal, the prospect of sitting a few feet away from the beach for lunch was overpowering. Anchoring paper napkins and tablecloth precariously, we savored the early autumn sun.

There were few customers. Our favorite young waiter was more fluent in English than we suspected. He excitedly told us that he was going to New York City to work in a relative's restaurant in a few months. Would this be another young man leaving the old country, or just a brief experience in America? Today, at least before the uptick in terrorism, Europeans head to the U.S. almost as easily as we do to their countries. With the dollar weaker than the Euro, they may vacation on our side of the Atlantic. Still, limited prospects for work at home may encourage some to buy one-way tickets.

Italians raised ice cream to an art form. Their gelati, sorbetti and Sicilian granita are to ice cream as Broadway is to theater. There are dozens of places to obtain ice cream in our little adopted city. A few make their own. The product must pass muster with demanding locals. When a store announces that theirs is "artigiano", amateur critics arrive. The three biggest rivals in Alassio sit nearly side by side: Balzoa, Cuvea and Alberto Marchetti

Balzoa has a venerable history as Alassio's oldest continuous café and the originator of Baci, a local fondant filled chocolate cookie sold by the truck load to tourists. Purveying espresso to grappa, panini to ice cream sundaes, the café, and its large courtyard, are open a good twelve hours most every day. Across the alleyway, they have a little stand solely devoted to ice cream. Often there is a queue in the street. It is good, and there are several dozen flavors available.

Just down the street, along the same little square, is Cuvea. A self-styled "fruit bar", you can get a mixed drink as well as an ice cream sundae, cone or fresh fruit dessert. The establishment was started by a hard-working Sicilian. In front of the store is an old-fashioned ornate miniature painted wagon advertising Sicilian Ice. In addition to a wonderful variety of gelati and sorbetti, there is a separate frozen case with a dozen

flavors of almost guilt free fruit flavored ice. The light gravel-
ly texture and high water content is a perfect cooler on a hot
summer day. To our disappointment, they close for a month
or so after the first week of January, vacationing back home in
Sicily. Not that we begrudge them their holiday.

It is human nature to choose sides. We and the Mantellassis
favor Cuvea. We continue to work through their 40+ flavors.
The owner passed away in winter of 2010. Fortunately, his
family has kept this wonderful establishment going. A balding,
dignified older man sits at the cash register each evening. You
pay him for whichever size cone, cup or sundae you wish, and
you get a little plastic gettone, different colors for the different
denominations. Then you take it across to the ice cream counter, and one of several handsome young men in their twenties to
thirties fills the order. Early on, I told one of them how much
we enjoyed a vacation in Sicilia, and we crossed the barrier
from tourist to regular. We are often there off-season when
there are few customers. The ice cream men stare into space,
or slowly clean a distant table. I wonder if they are dreaming
of someplace else.

There was a wonderful family owned store, more than
a hundred years old, in the budello. It sold fine silver, china and all sorts of small kitchen wear, including exquisite
chef's knives. After the owner died, the business closed and
lay vacant for a year. Now, some young folks have started a
new gourmet ice cream place, a branch of a famous Torino

establishment, Alberto Marchetti. They sell ice cream and nothing more, mostly in luscious fruit flavors. Inside, there are a few settees and minimalist tables, and a small bar with bar stools. They have earned a following.

Close to the center of Alassio is our favorite pier in Liguria. Almost every town on the Italian Riviera has a Molo. From nothing more than a pile of rocks and a veneer of cement to an engineered structure with deep pilings, a boardwalk, decorative railings and boat access, these walkways out into the sea vary from modest to ornate. None are as big or as crowd drawing as the famous piers of England, New Jersey and California. Our pier is not ornate or terribly fancy, but it reflects the laid back quality and personality of the town. It is a good place to walk off a few calories, or just marvel at the view.

Stretching over 200 yards perpendicular to the promenade, some 150 yards or so out beyond the beach and over the water. It is a fisherman's friend. At any hour there are a few solitary men tending poles, and sometimes a dozen. They congregate at the far end which widens into a T. Below is an infrequently used boat landing, and the clean, shallow waters of the sea. Looking seaward, in the evenings, one sees the small lights of tiny fishing boats, some scarcely bigger than a rowboat. They anchor out or hover in a choice sector. Further, towards the horizon, cruise liners, ferry boats, tankers and container ships pass by on their way to distant ports.

On the T, there is a large compass rose with arrows pointing to and naming destinations in the direction of each major compass point. Seaward, far beyond the horizon, lie Livorno, Elba, Roma, Olbia and Tunis. Landward arrows point to the hillside villages of Solva, Moglio and Testico. Grimacing mythical faces represent the winds blowing from different traditional directions: The Tramontana, Maestrale, Scirocco, Levante, etc.

Benches, some more comfortable than others, are spaced evenly along the north and south sides of the pier, all facing seaward. Senior citizens, young families, lovers of all ages, and the occasional solitary teenager rest, reflect, converse, or use their cell phones as they sit. Sunsets and early evenings are particularly busy. Besides the nearly infinite and changing variety of colors and textures where sea and sky intersect, there is the magnificent coastline to view. At dusk, a string of lantern pole lights, like pearls, extend in both directions to the horizon. Light clusters in the hills embrace hamlets and small villages. In the foreground is a delightful array of pastel colored buildings. None is more than six stories tall; most are shorter. This is the town's stage front.

Near the foot of the pier are posters of the different fish and shellfish found in local waters. A bronze plaque commemorates an early city father and businessman who promoted tourism. Another small memorial recognizes a partisan killed in WWII.

Fanning out in front of and on either side of the pier, like the top bar of an anchor, are a mile-long row of restaurants, hotels, pensiones and bars. Many have outside tables nestled under awnings or umbrellas. Nearly everyone at those tables, when not talking to each other, is looking towards the peaceful ocean. Focus a critical eye on any one building and it may seem dowdy and dated. Together they form a harmonious parade of dignified architectural dowagers. They take in the sun, shade, breezes and rains, nestled among palm trees and gently edging along the strand. Most have roof top gardens where some lucky people look out to the sea.

At night, the promenade is bathed in yellow light from the lamp posts, electric but once gaslights. When the pier needed a major reconstruction, and was closed for nearly a year, the posts on the pier came down. By way of some closed-door meeting between the Sindaco (Mayor) and his town council, the pier posts were replaced with some hideous modern German ones that look like giant sewing needles with fluorescent lights within. They may save electricity, but are ugly and expensive. It will take another Mayor to get rid of them.

From the pier, the buildings do not obscure the steep fist shaped hills beyond the railroad tracks. Bare rock and unruly patches of lush grass and tall trees fill the near horizon. Sometimes scarred by drought and forest fires, the greenery has always come back. Intrepid houses, clusters of vines, olive trees and vegetables, with almost every arable inch put to good use, all vie for a place in the sun.

Many Italians aren't adventurous when it comes to foreign food. Of course, they have many regional cuisines to sample. Restaurants serving other than Italian fare are in short supply. It is quite a contrast with Holland where there is a veritable U.N. of choices. Sure, Italy has some of the best food in the world. But you will be hard pressed to find a culinary change of pace in Alassio, or in most of Liguria.

There is a faux-Mexican restaurant along the beach. A local businessman thought he had found a new way to go after the younger crowd. Quesadillas and Margheritas should be a sure thing? Not so. Often only a few people are inside.

There are two Thai restaurants in town. The older one, which we prefer, is owned by an Italian gentleman and has a fine Thai lady chef. The second earned and lost a Michelin entry. Its owners have a Sushi bar next door. The second is atmospherically decorated. The food is all right, although somewhat ersatz. One of my father's rules was not to eat in an ethnic restaurant if there aren't ethnic servers and customers. Other than one Thai hostess, the restaurant wouldn't meet his test. Many Alassini like to vacation in Thailand. One local owns a small apartment building there in the beach town of Phuket. Perhaps those exotic vacations stoke the interest in Thai food.

216

There used to be two Chinese places on either side of the train station. One soldiers on. It too seems mostly empty; another one of my father's rules as to restaurants to avoid. One day, we decided to give it a try. We won't be going back.

There are a few hole in the wall kebab places in less than prime locations. One supplemented its income by also offering French crepes. I tried a sandwich there one night. I haven't returned.

Along the seacoast, fish and shellfish are an obvious draw. Under Italian law, restaurants must tell you whether what you are eating is fresh or frozen. A "market price" entry suggests the former. Even the modest places do a pretty decent job of simple broiled or fried recipes. Occasionally there is a police raid. Selling frozen fish as fresh brings large fines.

Most restaurants make a respectable simple green salad, or a slightly more elaborate one with tomatoes and a little cheese. You are expected to add the salad dressing, almost always olive oil, vinegar, sometimes balsamic, salt and pepper on the side. The oils and vinegars range from industrial grade to premium. A few side vegetables, "contorni", are noted on the corner of a menu: perhaps grilled peppers, drizzled with a little olive oil and a hint of garlic. For a starch, potatoes are more common than rice. In season, mushrooms, asparagus, artichokes briefly appear.

For us, Alassio's culinary center of gravity is in the Barus-so neighborhood, the southwestern carruggi one block in from the beach. Side by side, the Hotel Panama Ristorante and Sail Inn provide consistently excellent local cuisine.

Panama's glass enclosed L-Shaped dining room is right along and just a few feet above the beach. A no frills décor leaves the focus on the quality of the ingredients and the great ocean view. A platter of calamari and/or a variety of home-made pasta are always superb. The desserts are fine but unre-markable. Fresh fruit is an option, and one can always walk a few blocks for superior ice cream. The restaurant prides itself on using local ingredients. Once in a while, at special dinners, the skills of chef MorenoTavernelli are on greater display. The pensione-hotel has been in the Cosso Family since 1956. They greet every guest of the restaurant with grace and warmth. It is where the locals go.

The Sail Inn takes dining to the next level. Crisp white tablecloths and some flair in preparations raise expectations. Their zuppa di pesce, pasta dishes and well-prepared fresh fish are all of a high standard. The original restaurant is in the budello. A newer annex across the street, on a vico next to Pan-ama, affords diners a side view of the beach through large glass panels. Waiters bring the food out to the annex. In bad weath-er, they usually shut it down. The wine list is more extensive and the tab higher than next door, but worth it. Owner-chef Giampiero Colli and his parents took over the restaurant space in 1988. After his father's passing, he has continued to grow as a chef and a sincere host. He cooks with passion and finesse.

On either side of our pensione, are, or were, U Recantu and Pierrot. The small informal pizzeria/restaurants did a brisk business in light meals and friendly banter late into the night. They catered to transients and locals wth good simple food. Both prepared straight forward fish and pasta. In early 2010 Pierrot abruptly closed after a raid by the Guardia Finanza. The books didn't reflect all the income from a struggling business. Barcala Mare opened in its place, more upscale, and better run. It is an improvement. U Recantu soldiers on in the old traditional mode.

We always hope someone will aim higher. An old hotel on the Albenga side of town, the Lamberti, now has a destination restaurant. The owner's son has a passion for excellent food. It is now the best traditional restaurant in town, with culinary flourishes of style and substance. They attract patrons from well beyond the hotel, discerning locals and well-heeled visitors.

Intense and tempting smells often come from neighboring apartments. Families settle in for a few weeks, and the tiny kitchens are put to full use. Without a stove, options are limited. Our intentions about apartment cooking often evaporate with the wanderlust of moving up and down the coast. A few small gourmet takeout stores cater to those on holiday, or anyone who wants a break from labor intensive cooking.

Along Via Dante several food stores have come and gone as the owners retired or moved on. A tiny band box store run by a young couple from Torino was the most elegant and creative. Each day there were half a dozen entrees and several delectable desserts. Doppio Zero was a true delight, for the wonderful food and the delightful owners. The Scalas previously lived in Monte Carlo, and after a couple of years went back. Then a young Italian chef, returning from New York, took a turn, but after half a year, he closed. In the fourth iteration, an established pasta and ravioli making business moved in and was at least selling quality entrees.

Five tiny meat markets are within a six block walk of our apartment. In each, the butchers have been there for decades. The meats are beautifully displayed, and the customers seem intensely loyal. There are a few small seafood markets as well. None mind and expect that you are shopping for just one meal at a time.

*****

Cafes are an Italian art form and intensely local. There are several dozen places in town to order a cup of coffee, or something stronger. The most traditional is San Lorenzo. The graceful café and tearoom spills out, in good weather, along Via Torino, our favorite little street in town, and on a little courtyard across from the beach. From early morning into the evening one can enjoy coffee or tea in several dozen varieties, perhaps served with a pastry at a table for two or four. A glass of wine, spumanti or grappa are options. Their spremuta, freshly squeezed orange or grapefruit juice, is reason enough to get up in the morning. Frankly, I'm not that fond of their espresso. But the wait staff is kind, the owners are friends of our friends, the Mantellassis. It is a good place to see and be seen.

There are half a dozen park benches along tiny Via Torino. They provide prime viewing space for people and pet watching. Locals converse, catch their breath, watch the world go by, or commune with dogs and infants in strollers. A lovely bridal boutique, clothing stores featuring Missoni, Boggi and other designer fashions, a premier butcher shop, and an internet café with no coffee where I sometimes check e-mails all once graced the street.

While the paved street is wide enough for the occasional car or delivery truck, it is mostly a pedestrian zone. Two blocks inland, stocky metal poles the height of a fire hydrant raise or lower to allow service vehicles, police cars and other stranded motorists to pass. The second, steeper block away from the sea dead ends on the main road. Looking up, there is a lovely view into the hills. Two more local cafes and the largest supermarket in town are just around the corner.

When we first came here, the town's largest supermarket was a Standa. When that chain disappeared, it was taken over by Billa, Austrian/German owned. Lurid red and yellow signs and posters everywhere pointed to low prices. The store was busy right up to closing time around ten o'clock. With odd shaped rooms on different levels, haphazard layouts and makeshift escalators and stairs, finding something was a challenge. We shopped there a bit, but I've never met an employee I wanted to get to know and vice versa. I much prefer the little shops, but for many the price differential is inexorable. Billa eventually pulled out of the Italian market and now the store has been reconfigured as a Carrefour (French). There is a slightly better choice of goods, and the same or similar bored union employees. The newest iteration is open 24/7. With its consistently lower prices and store brand options, they continue to gain market share.

16

Everyday Chores

A t home, everyday tasks may be boring and performed as routine chores or obligations. In a foreign country, we may rediscover their inherent charm or wonder. There is some apprehension in doing them in a different country and language. For example, barber shops, hair salons, even shoe repair shops are places people exchange gossip, discuss their views of the world, and relax. Much of that you lose without mastering the local language. Barbers and bartenders are inherently good listeners, but not so much without a lingua franca. In the Eastern United States, Italian-American barbers have been a fixture, and I have had my hair cut by half a dozen over most of my life. In Italy folks look about the same. But we both struggle to be on the same page.

To have a stranger alter your appearance, particularly overseas, is intimidating. It is especially stressful for my wife.

She has always worn her hair up, beautiful long sandy blonde hair, in what I think of as the Grace Kelly look. Unfortunately, few hairdressers can do this style with great skill. Fortunately, many that do live and work in Italy. But even there, it is not a sure thing. We have had tonsorial duds and a few triumphs. The older the person is with the scissors, the greater is the chance that they will deliver what we are looking for.

When we are traveling somewhere new, we have a routine. We go to two or three of the best hotels, even if we are not staying there, and ask the concierge for a recommendation. If they suggest a shop down the street, we tend to ignore the advice, and try again. There is some likelihood of a kickback or a misperception that we are too lazy to travel any distance for quality. A referral to a chain beauty salon gets the same rejection.

After one underwhelming experience at the fanciest shop in Alassio, we were gun shy. A drive or train ride to San Remo or Nice led to competent salons. With two to three hours on my own, it is a good time for a long walk. When I return, there is either a pleasant transformation, or a temporary setback.

A number of years ago, my wife asked Dr. Mantellassi for a recommendation for a hairdresser. Even though it was around the corner from Villa Firenze, their second hotel, we were hopeful. The salon was clean and busy. Of the dozen or so salons within a half mile walk, there was nothing that would have led us to find it on our own. None of the three hairdressers were fluent in English, and our Italian is still minimal at best. Through sign language and references to a few photos, we hoped for the best. I entrusted her to the fates, and started a long walk on the more obscure streets close by the railroad track.

North of the railroad, running the entire length of Alassio, there isn't much level surface before steep hills. The nearby trains, sometimes three or four an hour, are noisy. Shoulder height rock and cement walls along the right of way keep things fairly safe. The surface train line doesn't help real estate values, but they have been there for 150 years. There are some lovely homes that predated the railway northeast of the station. Westward, large and homely apartment complexes on both sides of the tracks are squeezed into a narrow flat area before the roads spiral upward.

Some of the apartments look sedate and prosperous; others have a tenement feel. This is not the tourist part of town. An outsider sticks out. I walk purposefully, though rambling. Hard working people here live modestly, and some not all that well.

After a long walk, and an espresso at an obscure café, I return to the beauty shop. My wife was pleased, and so was I. We would no longer have to spend an hour or two each way on the train looking for a hairdresser. Recently, we found an even nicer shop where the owner is a virtuoso. Mario Gallo is a master. Perhaps in his fifties, or early sixties, a kindly, greying and distinguished looking man, he has a tall and earnest son in the business. The son helps with the English. Someday we will learn if he has his father's talent-but not now.

I had an equally good turn of fortune in the barbering department, a little shop in the budello. Two older brothers or cousins diligently take care of the locals, waiving to acquaintances passing by through the glass door and windows. Often, someone will step inside for a few minutes banter. The car magazines and weekly news tabloids are similar to my home barbershop, but in Italian. The big swiveling barber chairs, long single blade razors, multiple scissors and tools evoke an ancient art.

After long repartee with the regulars, on politics, sports, cars and who knows what else, we are stuck with short and tentative phrases built on the limited words we both know: "Obama-good or no good?" "How is the new Sindaco (mayor)?" "Tropea-bellissimo". "Volo via Nizza a New York". "Domani piovera." Despite the language barrier, they are perfectionist barbers. They seek permission, and then trim hairs on your ears; nose; eyebrows. I walk out feeling great. Originally from Calabria, their family moved north before they were teenagers. Vacations and relatives bring them back South. In some ways, I suspect they are still immigrants.

Then one fall we returned and saw the shop vacant. They retired and presumably moved south or closer to family. Another little costume jewelry or women's accessory shop squeezed in. Once again, I turned to the Mantellassis for help. Egidio had already switched barbers and recommended a shop with a father and two sons on Via Dante. They are very good, and one of the brothers speaks a little more English.

Banking in Italy can be an ordeal, for natives and tourists. It seems unpleasant for bank employees too. Too many banks chase too few retail customers. That doesn't translate into pampering. While the scene is not as Kafkaesque as we have seen in Portugal or Eastern Europe, a bank visit can be painfully long with unexpected delays. Don't go to the Postal Bank without an hour or two to spare, especially on days when pensions are collected.

At many banks you are buzzed through revolving security doors. Whether in an imposing old building or an austerely modern one, the lobby is uniformly drab, even shabby. Private offices behind partitions aren't any more inviting. Fluorescent lights or a few over worked bulbs in high ceilings cast somber rays.

It looks more like the shipping and receiving department than centers of financial prosperity. Advertising flyers for various bank services show nattily dressed bank representatives and customers. The premises reflect a different reality. Retirees and blue-collar workers stoically wait in long lines, as if in a welfare office.

A small machine dispenses numbers, as at a butcher shop. You queue in a line or sit. There are a large number of teller booths, and only a few tellers. A few Styrofoam or wooden chairs are for the old, infirm or bored. The tellers, dressed in well worn sweaters and jeans, or unfashionable dresses, seem preoccupied and have no incentive to move things along. They may look at a twenty-year-old black and white screen connected to a distant office by a slow dial up connection.

If you want foreign exchange, perhaps one booth is so marked. If not, you will stand in the wrong line for some time. Posted exchange rates may be a day or two old.

Travelers Checks, used for decades, are now shunned and nearly extinct. The banks don't want to cash them, even with a fat fee. ATMs have proliferated, often on a sidewalk wall, with no privacy or security. Some of the machines conduct transactions in four or five languages. I am now less fearful they will swallow my card. Still, I prefer one in an alcove connected to an open bank.

While experiencing bank employee indifference, there can be some human warmth. BNL called our pensione and asked if I would stop back at the bank. They were one of the last to cash traveler's checks. The crisp American Express checks stuck together, and I unwittingly tendered nine checks rather than eight. They wanted me to receive all the Euros due! BNL is now our Italian bank of choice.

With duff loans, thin balance sheets and political drift, retail banking is partially paralyzed. Small businesses and citizens can't get loans and the banks aren't offering very attractive ways to save. A few have received government help. So far, things are not as bad as they are in Greece.

What is there to do on a rainy day in a beach town? Read a book. Linger in the café. Check e-mails. Put your rain gear on and trudge to a store. Don a wet suit and go in the water anyway. The fish don't mind. Go to church; a movie; think; write, watch television.

We love being near the water; but not the kind that is pouring down and hitting us from above and sideways. Puddles, splashes, gusts of wind are everywhere. Nice clothes and shoes get soggy. Damp wool smells like wet dog.

It rarely rains steadily for more than a day in Alassio. Looking at the parched trees and hills, you know rain is a good thing. When it rains for several days, the town slows down. Fewer people are out. They huddle in cafes. In winter, while there is only a dusting of snow, the damp cold is depressing, amplified by a powerful wind. Even with a sturdy raincoat, hat and umbrella, unless you are wearing long boots, water wicks up and gets you. Umbrellas are turned inside out. Large puddles are unavoidable. You wait for the best moment and dart from one door to another. When it stops, you look skyward with deep thanks.

Bad weather must make a terrible dent in the hotel, restaurant and other small business trade. As the high season slips away, little signs appear in their windows: closed for vacation. Some have the courtesy of telling you when they will reopen. Others do not. Perhaps they don't know.

Prolonged rains can bring deadly mudslides on the steep hills. Roads and railway track are suddenly blocked. Dry river and creek beds become torrents. Elegant engineering is not a match for nature run amuck. Wire mesh, concrete stanchions and other shoring repair nature's wounds.

Like most men, I enjoy a ramble through a hardware store. You never know what you might find, then realize you need or want it. If there is a specific object in mind, fine. If not, there will be something interesting. That's not usually possible here.

Most daily shopping is still conducted in little mom and pop stores. There is plenty of inventory on high shelves or in a back-storage room. But browsing in these stores is just not done. Our sorties for odds and ends, a wine cork opener, a small luggage lock, a battery, super glue, have always been successful. You put yourself in the care of an elderly shopkeeper. They know the content of every cardboard box in their tiny store.

Our trips to the pharmacy have been, thankfully, infrequent. Some display apothecary jars and old wooden cabinets. Outdoor signs proudly show starting dates over a century ago. The amount of merchandise on your side of the counter is much less than in the U.S. Non-prescription items, bandages, cough medicine and aspirin require the assistance of a pharmacist. Prices can be double what you are used to paying. The choices are few. Minor poultices and personal hygiene products are now in the supermarket, and at more reasonable prices. Professional privileges are chipped away slowly in this country.

Our need for news in English was somewhat quenched by the *International Herald Tribune*. Printed simultaneously six days a week in Paris, Rome and other European cities, whether it arrived in Alassio on a given day was unpredictable. My wife popped in to a small magazines and stationery store often enough that the owner greeted her with a smile, whether or not the paper was there. A short, swarthy and gruff fellow, he looked more like a jockey or a bookie than a merchant. Jazz music played in his tiny shop. He dispensed local bus tickets, stamps, lottery tickets, tissues, camera batteries and a lot more we weren't aware of. He ordered the paper for us for the duration of our stay. We bought a few magazines and felt a little bit more part of the community. Sadly, a few Januarys ago, the shop was for sale. Our friend said "he was tired". Well into typical retirement age, he had recently lost his Mother. His son lived in Rome. It was time to end the 12-hour work days. Now, we walk to the train station for a paper.

There are a couple of laundromats in Alassio. Laundries/ dry cleaners are quite expensive in Europe. We don't mind an hour or two feeding washers and dryers with underwear and other washables. There is usually a change machine that accepts bills and gives you the right change. The European machines even inject the soap and fabric softener for you and sterilize the equipment between cycles.

Recently we met two twenty something Italian men in our favored laundromat. They were on a several weeks cycling trip through Liguria and Piemonte. Their bikes were parked just outside the door. They consulted their GPS and asked for luncheon suggestions. Another time, I encountered a middle-aged Floridian entrepreneur who had a small house up in the hills with his German girlfriend. The house didn't have a washer and dryer, and like us he was making a fortnightly laundry run.

Some natives come in with big comforters, bags of children's clothes, napkins, towels and consign them to the proprietress for later pick-up. From years on the road, you are more likely to find a laundromat near a marina, in a college town or where there are plenty of immigrants.

Our trips are always enhanced by fresh flowers in our apartment on arrival. Rita Mantellassi is a generous soul. We reciprocated from time to time, using the same cheery flower shop on Via Dante run by a young and talented lady. There were rumors that she might move to another town, and finally she did. Like the flowers, local businesses are perishable. There is another pleasant and professional flower shop a half mile away up on the main road.We don't mind carrying them to our friends.

We have no children nor grandchildren, but that hasn't stopped us from enjoying a dozen or so shops dedicated to spoiling bambinos. It is an Italian tradition. We have bought many gifts for the young offspring of friends. The local shops' clothing is extremely well made, and designed to make you impractical. A lot of children in town, those who live here or are visiting, are fashion plates. Of course, there are many children and families that can't afford these extravagances.

Alassio is known for its upscale clothing and jewelry stores. Some have branches in Monte Carlo and tony ski resorts. Most are small boutiques. Several are more substantial in size and price point. I can't speak for the most frenetic holidays or the summer, but these shops are rarely crowded. Then again, how many Furla bags, Valentino dresses and Gucci shoes are apt to be sold in a nice but not ultra chic beach town? The same limits probably apply to high end watches and jewelry. Still, the merchandise is there, and some very wealthy people in the hills or passing through must keep them in business.

On either side of these high fashion shops, are many more modest stores. Some downright tacky. They have far more customers, even if the margins are thin.

Two big movie theaters in town sit opposite each other on the main street. Both are vacant, one with an ironic sign: "Closed for work." Not that there has been any for years. A few video stores have also disappeared as people gravitate towards the internet and a few suburban megaplexes, just as in the U.S. There is vague talk of turning them into nightclubs or dramatic theaters, but for more than a decade they have stood silent and ignored.

Along the main street/highway through town, there are many empty storefronts. Some have been cheerily covered up by billboard size color photographs of the town's attractions. As in many parts of Italy and elsewhere in Europe, they reflect a struggling economy.

There are medical and dental specialists with generic offices on the busier streets. The hospitals are a long way down the road in distant towns. At one time, Alassio had a small hospital. It was downgraded to a clinic. Now it is open only a few hours on weekdays. Two ambulance services might take you to hospitals in Albenga, Pietra or even Genoa. Those who are seriously ill often travel farther afield: to Milan, Bologna or Nice. Over the years, we have learned that public health services are somewhat adequate. Those who can afford it, however, have private insurance and utilize private hospitals and seek specialists far and wide.

17

The Grand Hotel

E very town and city on the French and Italian
Riviera with a fashionable past or aspirations
to glamour has at least one grand old hotel. The
term has certainly been diluted. Plenty of hotels with
Grand in their name are victims of wishful thinking or
duplicity. They have nothing in common with the Carlton and the Martinez in Cannes, the Negresco in Nice,
the Du Cap in Cap Antibes, the Splendido in Portifino,
all one of a kind, magnificent establishments that truly are 5 Star. Each of these are still a bastion of luxury, and perhaps a bit of snobbery. Come to think of it,
those hotels didn't need to put Grand in their name.

The Italian Riviera versions are often more faded than their
French cousins. The Grand Hotel del Mare in Bordighera, the
Royal in San Remo, even the Imperial Palace in Santa Margherita, offer luxury lodging, without the cachet and celebrity
they may have attained in the Belle Epoque era. A chef friend

aptly skewered the pretensions of some of the fancy places in Forte di Marmi by saying: "they think they are in Cannes; but they are not." Another said they should go to Montecatini or Switzerland and learn what truly is luxury.

Alassio has three or four hotels with Grand in their name. They merit four stars from the Italian government. Though pleasant, none are particularly elegant or memorable.

Since we have been going to Alassio, we were fascinated by the quiet ruins of its first premier hotel, The Grand Hotel Alassio. It never was a Cote d'Azur palace. Still, the graceful Victorian sat in the place of honor near the center of town and on the lovely beige sand beach. The baroque building had been silent and forlorn since the early seventies, and probably in decline for two decades before. There is an iconic poster of the hotel's veranda on a starlit night. A movie star handsome couple, in formal wear, dance alone outside, with a full band and crowd of well-dressed people mingling behind glass doors.

Many plans to bring it back to life simmered and faltered. The family that owned it had fallen on hard times. Two elderly sisters who inherited it could no longer afford to make needed capital improvements. Clientele drifted and/or passed away. After it closed, what remained, beyond a pretty façade, became an eyesore.

At one time, the hotel had a glamorous casino rivaling San Remo if not Monte Carlo. The story is that Mussolini wanted it closed to bolster San Remo's luster.

Over the decades, there were dreams and schemes of restoring the hotel. Lack of vision, money, bureaucratic and political connections caused several syndicates to founder. In the final weeks of 2010, a refurbished hotel finally opened. New investors, from the Piemontese city of Alessandria, gradually cleared regulatory and financial hurdles. For three tedious years, work had started and stopped on the site. Each time we returned to Alassio we looked for clues that the hotel was coming back to life.

First, an underground parking lot, for the benefit of the city as well as the hotel, was completed. Then a new promenade and band stand, with hundreds of folding chairs available, replaced the old and homely parking lot next door to the hotel. A stand-alone state of the art health spa and a completely redone building interior slowly evolved with virtually no outside publicity. In late December, 2010 the hotel opened with the well wishes of most of Alassio.

The detritus of a century had been demolished and carted away. The historical façade was preserved. A new 5 Star luxury hotel emerged. With the hotel open for business, neighboring stores and restaurants hoped to see upscale traffic from the new hotel's guests. In a nice touch, the first official guest was the General Manager of the Splendido, the legendary 5 Star hotel in Portifino. It was his family that once owned the hotel. As a young boy he lived there. Someone saved the original heavy brass keys and massive wooden key shelf and kept them behind the reception desk.

The advent of a new best in show hotel should be good for the local economy. It may even bring back some high-end customers Alassio lost over the years. It could help the handful of upscale restaurants and shops and not interfere with the mainstay lodging establishments.

Of course, the hotel has to earn its stripes. The first signs were wobbly. The lobby, bar and first floor dining room are very modern, even austere. We had two meals there in January 2011, a dinner and a lunch. The food was better than good but less than superb. A Roman chef, with some experience in France, was skillful. But the "Continental/Italian" fare was hotel food without much character. The service was earnest but not polished. The wine list was sketchy and thin.

Reports on their first banquet reflected an ambitious menu less than flawlessly delivered. Staff members we met were pleasant and unpretentious. But much more must be done to be truly a destination hotel.

They began attracting wealthy Russians, Germans and Italians, but perhaps not the kind of visitors we would like to mingle with. Our friend Massimo at Palma had his whole restaurant booked on a weekend night by Russians staying at the Grand. On a few hours' notice, they cancelled leaving him in the lurch. Another friend, in the airline business, suggested they advertise with British Airways to attract British and American travelers. The business office said this was not a market they were interested in. Everyone has an idea of who is persona non grata. At double or more the room rates of most hotels in town, this is an interesting experiment.

The owners are wealthy investors from out of town. Perhaps they will find a dedicated manager who will set the bar high. Without a personal touch, it won't be so grand.

At our third meal there, a lunch, the dining room was sparsely populated. We found ourselves comparing notes with a lovely retired Swiss couple at the next table. They were seasoned travelers, Alassio partisans, and owners of a home in Moglio up in the hills. They too were hoping for the best, but not impressed with the meal and service.

One of the young front desk staff was very pleasant and spoke American English. We chatted with him for awhile and learned that he was from the Dominican Republic.

Whether by governmental choice, local prejudice or economic reality, the main international luxury brands are not present in Liguria. A thirty-year-old Sheraton Convention Hotel next to the Genoa Airport is a competent business hotel, but nothing more. Perhaps it was wishful thinking that a Four Seasons or Ritz Carlton might be attracted to our town. The inexperienced hotel operators will not take business away from the Splendido or the Royal anytime soon. Still, it is pleasing to have the center of Alassio's skyline complete again.

There have been rumors that the owners have been trying to sell the hotel, including to a Middle Eastern sheikh. With many sanctions, the wealthy Russian market is shriveling. The hotel is becoming an isolated island, much like some of the high-end dress shops. Perhaps that is what exclusivity is all about, not making everyone welcome? Judging from some of the fancy sports cars parked in the front, they may have found their market. But they are closed 3-4 months of the year. Most people in town want it to succeed, but perhaps would appreciate a more welcoming and inclusive ambassador for the city.

In the summer, 2016, a wealthy Saudi Princess and her entourage arrived on relatively short notice for a two week stay. More than 40 black tinted window vehicles pulled up and they brought their own security guards for the beach. With a large yacht and other property in Monte Carlo, perhaps they were just passing through. Or maybe it was an assessment.

In September, 2018 for the first time in several years, we stopped by for an outdoor lunch. There is a new Neapolitan chef. The service is still somewhat mechanical, but the food has improved. As it should, at the price.

OOO

18

Getting Out of Town

E ven in a near paradise, people need a vacation! Once there were a dozen travel agencies in Alassio. They were almost as ubiquitous as the real estate agencies catering to people wanting a place here. The few remaining have brochures in the windows picturing exotic lands: Tunisia, Egypt, Sicily, religious pilgrimages to Lourdes, cruises to the Greek Isles, and the temptations of Paris, New York and even Philadelphia! The survivors cobble a living on more complex trips-weddings, business meetings, religious retreats. They are fading through self booked trips on the internet, wholesalers, and discount airlines, as is the case everywhere.

On the main street in Alassio is a little used bus stop. Two austere little signs show a twice a week bus service to and from

Bergamo and Brescia in the North and on demand van service to Romania. The first is for Italian tourists, the second for immigrant workers.

Many Alassini enjoy traveling as much as we do. Phuket, Thailand is very popular, as is Zanzibar. The Thai connection is strong. Some locals own or rent apartments and one businessman owns an apartment house in that Thai beach resort. They disappear for a month or two in the cold and rainy middle of Liguria's winter when the tourism business at home is at its lowest ebb.

Trips to New York, Miami, San Francisco, and Las Vegas are common. But the rest of our country is unknown territory to most.

Years ago, we stayed in an idyllic Swiss chalet hotel in Saas Fee on the back side of the Matterhorn from Zermatt. A mile from town, you must park in a large public garage. From there, you hike, or your hotel picks you up in an electric cart. The objective: no car exhaust in the pristine alpine setting. It was October, their quietest time of year. The still clear air and mountain setting were unforgettable. In a few days, we moved on to see more of Switzerland. As the owner took us back to the garage, I knew they closed for a month before ski and holiday season. I asked him where he goes for vacation. He smiled and said they would be in Hawaii the next week.

Somewhere else is always intriguing. Egidio mentions a trip during his student days at Heidelberg. He and his friends went to the far north of Norway. They were not used to the extreme snow and cold, but wanted to experience life there. He took his guitar but not a winter coat.

Even though he has mostly given up meat, he still raves about the barbeque at Tony Roma's in Florida. Through the wonders of internet marketing, I was able to bring him some of the restaurant's barbeque sauce.

Getting away in the virtual world, high speed internet access has arrived in Italy. From grandmothers to sub-teenagers, everyone seems to have a smart phone. Until a few years ago, I walked two blocks from our pensione to a local internet café and electronics shop. It was a parts and repair store that has three PCs along a wall for internet access. Under Italian law, you must show a photo identification card. For 2 or 3 Euros an hour you could check e-mails, travel arrangements, bank account, etc., under the watchful eye of the resident dachshund. That assumed you got there before the kids. The store, run by a father, mother, twenty something son and the dog, offered pickup and processing of expedited package delivery through TNT, a European courier service. Another way to earn a few Euros as the internet café business faded. Eventually, they saw the electronic handwriting on the wall, closed the café and moved the repair business to a lower rental address.

Le Terrazze now has high speed cable, and wi-fi. Internet cafes in other towns are mostly gathering places for poor foreigners, places for cash transfers; voice over internet phone calls, meeting countrymen and finding news about home. As cell phones become more sophisticated and the price of tablets decline, perhaps these places will go the way of the disappearing video stores.

Nestled on the hillsides above Alassio, like ornaments in a Christmas tree, are a few small hamlets: Moglio, Solva, Vegliasco and Caso. Too small to be called towns, these "frazione" reflect Ligurian tenacity. The sea views and the mountain landscapes are exhilarating. The roads are marginal. Small houses cling to outcroppings of horizontal rock. Before air conditioning, many were summer homes of the local gentry. Now there are many foreign owners.

Olive trees and vines are planted on postage stamp plots. Each village may have a tiny general store, a basic café, a church or chapel, a one or two-person post office and a petrol pump. Can someone scratch a living there? Today these places are pensioners' nests, old family plots, hermit roosts.

We often ride the four or five times a day mini-bus up to the top of Moglio, and walk back down on a marked trail. The little bus is filled with mostly jovial little old ladies who have done some shopping in Alassio. There is a running dialogue with the bus driver, interspersed with taps on the horn as he corkscrews up the narrow road. At almost every turn, a walker along the road waves, with a big smile, at the driver or a passenger on the bus.

Next to the last stop in Moglio is a fine trattoria with a chef who worked in several sophisticated restaurants. A bowl of pasta with local mushrooms, a rabbit stew, a fritto misto is as good as any back in the city.

The upper town has a few dozen small stone buildings huddled together along steep alleyways. Most are adorned with flower pots and colorful hung laundry. On a rainy day, torrents of water course down these passages. Halfway down the hill, on a little rise, is an exquisite and empty seven-hundred-year-old stone church. Gas heaters close to the pews mitigate elderly discomfort.

Narrow roads meander further up the hills, rarely more than two cars wide. Some dead end or turn into dirt fire prevention trails, hardly more than a mule path. One poorly marked road ratchets its way to the summit and through a remote valley to Villanova d'Albenga.

It's an ancient and beautiful town founded in the 13th century. There are vestiges of protective walls. It was originally a fortified outpost protecting the mother city of Albenga. Now, it cultivates violets. Walking through the quiet streets, houses festooned with flower boxes, it is a close but friendly community. Besides the ambiance, there is little to hold the casual visitor.

We have had dinner in a lovely mountain aerie above Moglio. Our Swiss friends have a charming small house overlooking Alassio. At night, they are close to the stars. On a long private road, the homeowners' association chips in for the maintenance costs. They attend the occasional meeting to discuss the cost of gravel or renting heavy equipment. It is a chance to see many local characters in action. Until recently, the only crime involved rampaging wild pigs. Now, an occasional break in has upped the ante.

In contrast to the busy coastal roads and Autostrada, going inland is difficult. A few years ago, a mile-long modern tunnel north from Alassio opened a quicker route to the thousand-year-old village of Garlenda, the small airport near Villanova, and other inland hamlets. It's an alternate way to the Albenga Autostrada interchange. With occasional coastal road landslides and wash outs, the city has another lifeline.

Garlenda is a tourist magnet, with a major golf course, a trotting race track, and other sport facilities such as tennis courts, and a few hotels. That's impressive for a community of scarcely 1200 souls. Six miles from Alassio, it has an entirely different microclimate with more extremes of temperature, humidity and rain.

Young people have moved into the hill towns, able to afford more space than on the coast. Retirees seek Garlenda for the golf and mountain scenery.

Villanova's small airport is named after a World War I hero, Clemente Panero. With a 3300-foot runway, it is suited for small planes. Twice daily, year-round prop service to and from Rome bypasses the major airports. There is a summer route to Olbia, near Sardinia's Costa Smeralda. So far, the airport has had little effect on tourism.

Day and night, there is the rushing sound of trains accelerating or decelerating as they pass through Alassio. The rare freight train may run through the station without stopping. At speed, it is a more urgent sound, accompanied by a warning whistle.

In a narrow city scrunched between ocean and hills, the whistle and the distinctive whoosh of five to twenty metal cars rushing along the track is as reliable as the peeling of the church bells. Even when comfortably ensconced for three to four weeks, it is a reminder that we will be moving on.

At the train station, there is the ritual of announcing the trains. It is not much different from what I heard as a boy with the Long Island Railroad. In Italy, it starts with an electric bell intoning two notes, one high then low, almost like a doorbell. Then a feminine recorded voice states the obvious: "Stazione Alassio" and something about staying behind the yellow line and not crossing the track. This is followed by the less polished but animated voice of a live employee. There is a rushed reference to the incoming train number and its ongoing itinerary. If the train is late, which is quite often, there might be a reference to Train 4071 being "retardo venti minuti." The recitation of stations is fast and slurred or infused with dialect. I make out about 30% of what is being said. Fortunately, we know most of the stops by heart. Also, the train schedule is posted behind plexiglass on yard wide sheets.

In the Alassio station there are only three tracks or "binari". The innermost one is rarely used and then for the slowest of locals. In either direction going out of town, there is only one track. It is a safe bet to stand on the far platform, between tracks two and three, after trudging up two flights of stairs. There is a chair lift for a handicapped person. There are no longer any porters. The indifference to the needs of someone with a disability continues with the rail cars. Most Intercity Trains have three or four steep steps and little luggage storage.

Someday, maybe in our lifetime, dual track improvements will reach Alassio. Most likely, that would mean building a new train station another half mile inland, perhaps underground as the one in San Remo. Then people will be stranded away from the heart of the town to save a few minutes on train schedules. Do I sound like a local?

With the sea to your back, trains heading to the right are bound for Savona or Genoa, and those tending left are moving towards Ventimiglia, with connections, to France, Spain and beyond.

The cash strapped state railway has some "Freccia" or "arrow" high speed trains. But they only run on improved track between some major cities. The shore line, from the French border, was put down some 150 years ago, and in many places, it is still only one track. Service deteriorated with the dicey economy. Gone are the newer Swiss cars on Eurostar running down to the Riviera. A French locomotive used to greet them on the border and take them into France. Tired Italian stock stop for good in Ventimiglia. You now must switch to France's older cars, a TER Regional train, and get a separate ticket, a tedious process for a short trip. Usually, it means another trek down and up staircases to a different platform. One bright spot are the newer Thello trains than run from Milan to Nice and Marseille. At first it was a joint venture between a private French company and Trenitalia, but the former has withdrawn.

Slowly, the Ligurian tracks are being updated and the old equipment carted off to a museum or scrap heap. Many of the Italian cars we ride on are thirty or more years old, and show plenty of signs of wear. Few have air conditioning. Opening a small window for ventilation is either laborious or impossible. In the last year, Bombardier's "Jazz" cars are being introduced, a welcome upgrade.

The comfort difference between second and first class cars is marginal. The oldest intercity cars have compartments taking up three-fourths of the width of the car. This leaves a tiny passageway to walk to the exits, stand or sit on fold down jump seats. Each booth consists of facing bench seats, as comfortable as pews, with a vertical sliding shoulder rest device adjustable to several uncomfortable positions. Towards the ceiling is a metal slightly slanted rack, too tiny for any but the smallest of luggage and coats. On the outside wall is a small metal shelf, barely large enough to handle a few cups, if someone were foolhardy enough to put them there. It probably has the biological characteristics of a Petri dish.

Miniscule reading lights are placed in the ceiling, superfluous in daytime and nearly useless at night. A round and flat perforated speaker device and a nearby metal lever theoretically control the volume on public announcements. A small under foot radiator pumps out considerable heat, especially when you don't want it.

Besides giving us something to complain about, the older trains reflect a fundamental problem with the Italian Railway. Fares are subsidized so the working man and woman can afford them. Little money is put into the system compared to France and Germany. Big infrastructure projects just aren't in the cards for the forseeable future.

The trains trundle along on elderly track. Railroad personnel check tickets, and are mostly courteous and low key. If you accidentally violate an obscure train fare rule, they collect the additional fare or shrug and let it go. A more serious violation is failure to stamp the ticket in the often-malfunctioning punch clocks in each station. This could lead to a punitive fine.

The railroad has entered the internet age. You can check the schedules and buy your ticket on line or at an ATM like device in many stations. You can even display your ticket on a Smart Phone. But most tickets are still sold at a counter. Small bank teller style windows protect the railroad employee from the Mongols. Eventually, you get a ticket resembling an early 1960s era IBM punch card.

Train schedules are printed on large and intricate poster sized yellow or white sheets kept under glass at the station, yellow for departures and white for arrivals. There are elaborate footnotes and abbreviations affecting service, all of course in Italian. Often, there is a crowd straining to find their train and connections. For this reason, and nostalgia, I prefer the written timetable which can be purchased in most tabacs and newsstands.

While the railroad publishes a thick and unwieldy tome, a few obscure Italian companies produce an abbreviated regional schedule you can buy for about 3 Euros. The odd shape periodicals, perhaps five by eight inches, often with a lurid yellow or pink cover and less than newspaper quality paper, contain useful maps.

With the paper timetable, or the internet version, you plan your trip. If you choose to connect from one train to another, don't expect smooth or convenient connections. We sometimes change trains at Genoa Principe and less frequently at Brignole or Savona. The track for a particular train often changes. The schedules ignore the possibility that someone might want to transfer, or they might have luggage too. Mussolini no longer makes the trains run on time, if he ever did.

You have to go down below the track level to find an electronic board listing where the next train might be. A large mechanical board in the main waiting room may be slightly more accurate, if you don't mind walking a hundred yards or so from the tracks to see it.

If you are switching to one of the sleepier lines, like the route to Acqui Terme, the main coastal train typically arrives a few minutes after the local train has departed. There will be another train in an hour or three.

Speaking of waiting, there are waiting rooms in most stations, often frozen in the 1940s or 1950s. They tend to be musty, with the aura of a black and white movie. There is usually a place to buy newspapers and snacks, and sometimes even a small bar or café. Vending machines complete the ensemble of services. Invariably, one or more people are sprawled out sleeping on benches, regardless of the time of day. Some are on a long journey. Others may be temporarily off the street. Eventually, the Train Police separate the latter from the former. It is a far cry from the more enjoyable environs of French and other Northern European stations.

The trains are a vital link for average people who want or need to travel. It affords great people watching. One night we were heading back to Alassio from Ventimiglia. An elderly couple waited for the same train, although we had no idea where they were going. Their flimsy bags and well-worn clothes suggested they were from either Eastern Europe or the deepest part of the Mezzogiorno. Their faces and arms had wrinkles on wrinkles, but an innocent strength. Our train was going at least as far as Rome. From there, there were connections further south; other routes to the Adriatic and even to Sicily. I wondered how far they would travel that night and into the morning, and where they would eventually go. Where had they come from? They were stoic, but I wondered what this trip meant to them. I couldn't speak their language or dialect, nor did I wish to intrude. But it reminded me of our grandparents and great grandparents traveling great distances into the unknown with courage, hope and perhaps some despair.

In fairness to the railroad system, outside vendors have been assigned to clean and disinfect the trains and stations. Newer plastic seats and linoleum floors add a Howard Johnson look, but at least they are clean.

I trust the railroad personnel. From the ticket takers to the train pursers, they could just as well be on AMTRAK or Metro North, even if they belong to a communist leaning union. They are polite, dignified, traveling many miles away from home.

They keep us more or less safe while making the same journey over and over again.

A few years ago, we spotted a luxury Russian train running twice a week from Moscow to Nice. While the tsars are gone, the new elite had money and were willing to spend it on Riviera holidays. While not quite the Orient Express, there was some new glamour on the tracks. In researching the train service, I understand one must buy a visa to travel through Belarus. Visions of ill-tempered police boarding the train, looking for papers and perhaps bribes, punctures some of the potential glamour of the smart looking black and red cars.

A few days before one of our winter trips to Alassio, there was news of a train derailment in Andora. This was eleven miles closer to the French border. After months of heavy rains, a sixty-year-old patio on a villa, and much of a hillside, gave way covering the track in boulders and rubble. An Intercity Train bound for Ventimiglia couldn't stop in time. The smashed engine car came to rest at a 20-degree angle above a sheer drop to the sea, and several cars jumped the tracks. While the engineer was taken away on a stretcher, no passengers were hurt, although they had to walk along the track some distance in the rain. The line was closed for six weeks. Various officials had to investigate the damage and remediation. A huge barge and two giant cranes were brought from Genoa to carefully remove the engine and debris. In the interim, the Railway ran busses around the affected stations. In the long run, this may spur the plans to move the route inland.

Public and private bus lines divvy up the Ligurian routes without competition and still lose vast sums of money. A bus trip from Ventimiglia to Genoa, roughly 102 miles, requires five different buses from three companies. The schedules aren't entirely coordinated.

Clients of the bus lines are mostly a captive audience: the elderly, students, immigrants and occasional tourists. In the larger cities, Genoa, Savona and San Remo, bus lines carry a lot of locals and workers on a daily basis. Frequent strikes reflect the anguish of employees whose salaries are unsupportable. While fares have crept up, they are still relatively cheap. Ultimately, the bus is a lifeline to many who can't drive.

OOO

19

Spring in Alassio

L ike an unsure painter, I am looking at a view of immense beauty and am afraid I can't keep it alive. The large third floor terrace at Le Terrazze is a terra cotta horseshoe surrounded by dozens of planters filled with flowering shrubs. The building's walls are of a slightly deeper earth color. Sturdy green patio furniture and dark green shutters on the large apartment windows enhance the setting. They are framed in a soft cream yellow band and all look out on the sea.

In mid-May, the Mediterranean is at its gentlest. A blue grey glass sheet of tranquil water stretches to the horizon. It softly shades into a lighter steel blue grey sky. Above there is only the slightest hint of thin off-white clouds. Sometimes, the sea and sky are perfectly matched forming a giant infinity pool.

The Alassio pier, just to the left, is on concrete stilts. A few fishermen and strollers peer out to the horizon. There are no boats or ships to be seen. Soft slow swells belie a mighty ocean.

At dusk, lights come on over the molo, tiny candles against the seascape. From two hundred yards away, all of the human forms can be seen, but seem only five to six inches high. The light in the sky gradually fades. By 9 PM, it is not completely dark. There is a small sliver of moon, and countless stars.

On a Sunday night, the town slips back into its sleepy off-season tempo. Saturday, I was afraid we had come too late. Perhaps large crowds had already taken over and would continue through the summer. The streets were filled with so many people. But looking closer, these were a mellower and more local lot.

What a delight to eat outside on the terrace! With vitello tonnato and stuffed zucchini flowers from Doppio Zero, a bottle of local Pigato wine, fresh fruit and a few bread sticks, it's a perfect supper. There are four round tables comfortably spaced on the patio but rarely used. We often have the terrace to ourselves. An occasional seagull watches from the roof. There are kitchen smells and family chatter emanating from the other apartments. The waves sound as soft as the lapping of a canoe paddle, even though they have come all the way from North Africa.

As we finish our meal, the sea has become darker than the sky. The air is soft with a touch of coolness and the slightest breeze. We could stay out until full darkness, but we haven't yet slowed down that much. The air turns cooler. Later in the evening, with no fishing boat lights or passing freighters, the sea and sky is one blue black receding wall.

On the main street, traffic trickles late at night. At any hour, there is the buzz of motor bikes and motorcycles. The evening passegiata through the budello was thick and heavy for an hour or so, and then disappeared. Other streets are deserted. In the window of any two- or three-star hotel's dining room, you see mostly elderly tourists lingering over dessert and coffee. A few late-night bars and cafés nurse serial stragglers. No one drinks to excess. At this time of year, fashionable outdoor cafes are empty.

Shop windows display brief vacation closures, a week or ten days in May. Merchants catch their breath before the relentless summer crowds. The tempo switch from weekday lull to weekend surge is substantial.

Our town and all of Liguria is full of pensioners. They sit in the small parks, alone or with acquaintances, or do light shopping along the avenues. Even when frail, most walk determinedly and alert. We see more elderly couples here than in our country. Perhaps it is the Mediterranean diet or the geographical equivalent of Florida. I will never forget a tall, thin and fragile couple walking gracefully, hand in hand, down a busy street, each with an outboard cane. Not a bad place to pass one's ultimate years.

With my wife in the competent hands of a local hairdresser, I have two hours to walk through the hammock shaped town. A brief trip to the ATM machine, window shopping, a cup of espresso in a different café and half an hour is gone. I hadn't slowed down to local time. There were e-mails to check at the internet café. A pass by the beauty shop; another fifteen-minute walk; then time to give in: I camped on a chair in the beauty shop, half heartedly browsing through Italian fashion magazines.

It's worth the wait, both for the finished product and the look in her eyes. We stop at a mom and pop gastronomia on our way back to the apartment. We buy vitello tonnato for the third time, and some fried egg plant for dinner. What will happen when this elderly couple retires? Will anyone else put in the long hours in the little shop? The next year, the shop was empty.

We head back to our apartment and check the headlines on CNN. A few minutes finishes the *The International Herald Tribune*. It is time for another walk and a quiet lunch overlooking the beach at Ristorante Panama. Grilled peppers, fresh fish or fritto misto and fresh fruit or gelato for dessert are perfetto.

Back in the center of town we return to the windows of Nello, a fine men's sport shop. My wife approves of the sport shirts I have looked at for several days. Inside, the proprietor is happy to dust off his English. It's good enough to dispell any size concerns. With an abundance of nice shirts to try on I wind up buying more than expected. The sign of a good salesman!

We deposit our wares back at the apartment. Instead of going to the beach, we watch the Giro d'Italia on our little television. With or without the cycling, the scenery is breathtaking. Then, gin and tonics at Rudy's Café Romano. There is always the ebb and flow of people strolling by.

Still mourning the loss of the old classy Café Mozart, we give the new version another try. The old furniture is still there. Young and eager waiters and waitresses are on call. A tourist menu, table cloths and silverware replace drink settings on the upper terrace. We settle into a sofa seat in a little glassed in enclave on the beach edge. I had promised Gayle not to say anything about missing the old Café. I ask if they still have any rum drinks. A more senior waiter, in good English, suggests their mojito. I tell him we will save that choice for Miami.

There are only a few of the thirty Caribbean and Central American rums that used to make this a one of a kind bar. We settle for rum and coke with real Havana Club. There is a generous pour and two full cans of Coke. The hors d'ouevres arrive. They are heavy on the potato chips and peanuts. The piped music gradually switches from inane pop to some fairly decent jazz. Our mood brightens; Harry Connick and some other quality musicians fill the air. Our waiter asks if we are ok, and I praise the music and Alassio.

I ask if he is from Alassio. On coaxing, I find out he is from Avellino, near Naples. We know many people whose families are from there in our corner of Massachusetts. Southerners are not always well received and respected in the Italian North. I tell him we know the town, and have American friends from there. He wryly mentions The Sopranos.

So, the Café Mozart is in the hands of folks from Campania. They are working hard and trying to make a go of it. As the rum kicks in, we are grateful it's a short walk back to our apartment. An elderly beggar lady with a terrible widow's hump and matchstick bones comes by with a paper begging cup in her hand. She is dressed for winter. I have seen her camped in front of one of the town chapels. I give her two Euros, and she smiles and moves on with her rounds.

A young foreigner approaches: Perhaps a Kurd or Bangladeshi. He is one of many young men selling roses. They are never too insistent, but I shudder thinking what their life is like. I am prepared to give him some money, but he doesn't catch my eye. Our waiter comes by and takes the three Euros I had left him as a tip; walks a few steps towards the entrance and buys a few roses for another customer.

A few moments later, we get up to go. I seek out our waiter, and hand him a five Euro note and shake his hand. "For you, and thanks for taking care of the flower guy". He turns to my wife and says apologetically: "next time, Madam, the roses are for you."

We sit back down for a few more minutes enjoying the ideal location. With a little alcoholic buzz, we glide back to our apartment. We are a little too full. Dinner on the patio will wait for another night.

There is a more bittersweet experience this trip. We ask Egdio if we can have the pleasure of taking his family out to dinner during our stay. We have had dinner with them several times, and it was always a highlight of the trip. We learn that Rita's Mother had been quite ill through the winter. Over the years, we have known her only as a dignified and courteous woman, usually dressed in black, in a wheel chair. Separated by language and culture, we still exchanged sincere but brief greetings with her from time to time in the lobby.

This year, Rita had greeted us as warmly as ever. Despite the fact that she speaks almost no English and we so very little Italian, we are very fond of her, cherish her sense of humor, generosity and artistic style. It was evident she was carrying a great burden. We know something about taking care of elderly parents and could only silently wish her the best.

She must have been a striking beauty as a young woman with coal black hair and milky white skin. Despite some ongoing health issues that seem to weigh on her, when she smiles and her eyes sparkle, decades disappear and you have a glimpse of the belle of the ball. With some knee and joint problems, she often gets around town by bicycle. Walking is difficult.

A few days later, her beauty shop was closed. There was a small sign on the door with words we did not know. I looked them up: "in mourning". A few blocks away there is a public bulletin board. On it we found a simple white and black family death notice. We had seen this type of notice board in many towns, but had no reason to pay close attention. Even with our primitive Italian, we read the family name of our friends. We missed calling hours the night before. That afternoon at three, there was a funeral at the cathedral.

With no idea of the correct social protocol, we decided to go out of respect for our hosts and an elderly woman we barely knew. It is a large cathedral. We could sit in the back, unobtrusively, and in a small way support our friends.

After lunch, we changed to dark dress clothes and walked the short distance up to the main street. A tall wooden door opened into a cavernous church. It was the first time we had been in this sixteenth century building. From the outside it is a massive, soot stained and stocky stone edifice and not very pretty. From the elevated distance of the railroad station, it had more grace. It was almost two-thirty. There were some large flower displays near the distant altar. Much of the right-hand side of the church interior was encased in scaffolding. A few workers went about some restoration work high on ladders. A small portable radio was on, and it was not playing church music. There were a couple of elderly people in isolated pews. We sat near the back, and were further saddened by the empty church with so few mourners.

Ten or fifteen minutes passed. A priest and someone in a uniform moved a small dolly or platform into one of the aisles, and then disappeared. A few more minutes passed. Angela, who works in the beauty shop, walked past us. She nodded in recognition and went up to the flower display. After a few moments, she turned around and walked back to the far corners of the church. We heard the door open, and she went out, probably for a smoke. A few people came in, mostly older women, and sat scattered amongst various pews.

The priest returned, said something quietly in Latin, and began to sing in a high and fervent tenor. He was in his seventies or more, but had a clear and decent tone. The doors at the back of the church opened and we saw another priest and then a coffin being borne by pallbearers. Some were in uniform, and some appeared to be family members. Behind the coffin several hundred people walked into the church and up the aisle. At the head of the line was Rita, dressed in black. She had been crying but was somewhat composed. Her sister, daughter and other members of the family were beside her. Dr. Mantellassi was further behind. In minutes, most of the pews were full. The coffin was placed on the portable stand close to the altar.

The service went on for quite some time in Latin. We made out bits and pieces. There were a few hymns and prayers by the priest. The congregation stood, sat, responded, were offered the sacrament, and a collection was taken by lay helpers.

The service ended with a final blessing by the priest over and around the coffin. The procession led out of the church. As he left, Dr. Manthellasi saw us, came over, momentarily gripped our arms and quickly said: "Grazie". We said a few stumbling words of condolence. With the rear doors of the church open, we could see the close family enter a limousine, the procession continuing to the cemetery. We stayed behind.

OOO

20

Alassio on Foot; and Stray Thoughts

The next day turned cooler and windier. We walked to the extreme east side of Alassio. A substantial yacht club occupies a large basin close to Gallinara Island. On our first overnight stop we stayed at the nearby Diana Grand Hotel. It was modern, efficient and bland. Smaller family-run hotels such as the Savoia, Lamberti and Aida have warmer atmosphere, personality, and better food.

Past the Diana, the coastal road curves and climbs sturdy rock hills towards Albenga. The grade is steep for a bike or on foot. Far below the highway is a narrow street. At the beach edge, it's a service road and walking path dead ending at the yacht club. Above, small apartment complexes, softened by flowering trees and bushes, attach to the rocks like giant barnacles. Most are ugly cinder block. White paint and glass windows barely soften their facades. Many have small street level garages. They have nice views out to sea and of the Alassio skyline arcing to the West. But these mostly second homes, with German and Swiss cars in the garages, are removed from the community fabric. There are no little stores, generations of neighbors, nor churches and miniature parks that foster local identity. Shuttered and usually empty, they wait.

The warm sunny climate, seacoast attractions, slower pace, and high standard of living, attract more pensioners than anywhere else in Italy. But, fortunately, there are still many baby carriages, toddlers, teenagers, young families, dogs and cats. This is not Sun City, Italy. There is no arbitrary segregation by age, although oldsters may be solitary having outlived family and friends.

A dozen stores sell children's clothing, an ideal resource for doting grandparents. Several boutiques cater to pampered pets. Dogs and cats are nearly as lucky as those who live in France.

Innkeepers and dogs belong together. During all our stays at Le Terrazze, there has been at least one house dog, often two, and now four. First there was Boule, a macho black Italian-American Cocker Spaniel. He was intensely serious about keeping seagulls off his stretch of beach. He barked and chased with a vigor that suggested I am a bigger and tougher dog than you think. He had a raffish reputation for stealing ice cream from distracted toddlers on the street. My wife and I grew up with black cockers, but had never before seen one with such attitude.

Later, Sir Otis was a gentler and more pensive parti-colored English Cocker. He could be petted, unlike Boule, but his mind and focus were elsewhere. When we first met him, he was middle aged, and completely attached to his family.

The third Mantellassi spaniel, an orphan buff colored American Cocker, Lula, has fully charmed us. She had been abandoned and left on the street in Alassio. She had the immense good fortune of finding one of the most loving families for miles around.

At first, she may have been a year or two old, and full of boundless energy, puppy personified. She became more lady like as time went by. The "Contessa", as the Mantellassis call her, is now a lady. No longer an only dog, she has had to cope with a big brother and then a new sister. The spaniels have been the dogs of the female members of the family, Rita and her adult daughter, Anna. Egidio was happiest spending time with his beautiful and gentle Golden Retriever, Arturo. A few years ago, Arturo went on to his reward. After a proper grieving period, a new young Golden Retriever, Benjamin arrived. Benjamin, good natured, was happy to play with Lula, but she barely coped as he grew bigger and bigger. The next year, Polly, another Golden puppy joined the family. Polly has a sense of humor, and plays pranks. Leonardo, another Golden puppy "belongs" to the Mantellassi's real estate agent son Giardano, but more often than not he is with his siblings.

My wife and I adore spaniels, as well as many other dogs. With our work schedules we never thought it fair to have a dog at home. But Gayle's mother had pegged us from the beginning. On our first Christmas together, a large and light package arrived. Inside was a darling stuffed animal, a ginger colored spaniel who we immediately named Chris. His career as a guard dog on the window ledge didn't last long. He is much more comfortable on sofas and pillows. My favorite Aunt added a companion poodle, Phoebe, the following year. These stuffies, and Bret and Bernie, a dimunitive Beagle and a tiny bear, travel with us and have been part of our lives for more than 40 years. They have accompanied close friends in hospital stays, and have been faithful companions. They travel with us in a Pierre Deux Bag, their third by now, and have had plenty of adventures.

The entourage has grown, with four Italian stuffies from our Alassio friends. Various bears have joined the ensemble. We are often accompanied by a menagerie of 16. What people really think about this eccentricity we don't know or care. Fortunately, Anna has more than 50 stuffies in her apartment, so we are told.

Like us, the stuffies are growing old gracefully, with some wear and tear. A few years ago, after an intense search, we found a lady in Rhode Island who we trusted with some major reupholstering. Chris and Phoebe have a new lease on life, and he no longer has to wear one of my ties around his neck to hold it together, or socks to mask his aging feet. With their new coats, the dogs will outlast us.

Other than a kiss from our neighbor's Springer Spaniel, Abigail, Chris never seemed all that interested in other dogs. But it is clear he has lost his heart to Lula, even though he is over 260 years old in dog years.

There are still plenty of things we don't understand about Liguria. They fit no pattern. We accept the fact that butter is never served in restaurants. But why are vegetables relegated to the haphazard and secondary category of contorni on menus? Even in many ambitious restaurants, beautiful food is served without any sides. This is despite a magnificent array in local markets and many back yards.

If you order salad, the bowl comes out dry. Olive oil, vinegar, sometimes balsamic, salt and pepper are on the table. You do with it as you please. Just a few miles to the west, in France, the chef dresses the salad and every sliver of lettuce seems perfectly coated.

At a dinner party or social event, people arrive individually and often late. But when one leaves, all of a sudden, everyone is on their feet and saying good-bye.

Even in mid spring, our city's gardens, next to the town hall, offer some vivid color. With plenty of benches and quiet coves, they feel as comfortable as a pair of well-worn slippers.

The next day was gray and rainy. It was bad for the beach cabanas, the outdoor restaurants and cafes, and visitors seeking the sun. But it was good for the flowers and farmers.

I caught up on e-mails during my wife's weekly visit to the hair dresser. With another hour to kill, I walked up into the low hills in Alassio's San Rocco neighborhood. I saw a few paths and streets for the first time; past the indoor Bocce Ball Club, the town swimming pool and a little neighborhood park. This is a working-class neighborhood, clean, a little austere. It was another corner of the town to appreciate.

The main event of the day was a return to Palma for lunch. A few minutes before one P.M., father Silvio stood outside the restaurant in his highly starched white coat. Was he looking for us, or just getting a little fresh air? After a warm greeting, we are back in the standard ritual. We sit briefly in the waiting room, the beautiful tile floors covered with oriental rugs. We are handed the current menu. The thick wine list sits on the little table to the side. We must choose the traditional menu at 50 Euros or the gourmet one at 85 Euros per person, a five or seven course meal explained, more or less, in four languages.

There will be a pre-menu amuse d'bouche, and another extra tasting. Silvio makes us feel at home. Marina, Massimo's wife, stops by silently and smiles warmly. She doesn't speak English, but I don't think we have ever even heard her voice! Then Massimo takes over. By now, the baton has been passed and he is in charge.

Besides having a fine meal with exceptional wine, we briefly share experiences of food, wine, travel, music and culture with him. There are no other customers today, so we don't feel guilty in monopolizing his time. The conversation runs from Fabrizio de Andre, Genoa's iconic folk singer, to Massimo's diabetic dog, and his dad's aging. We are among friends, people who love Liguria and its traditions.

After a memorable two- and half-hour meal, we step back into the drizzle. We had pledged to return, in fifteen months, to celebrate our 25th year of visiting Alassio. Massimo shares two bottles of reserve white wine that he wants us to try. He shows us a notice from the post office. The package of *Wine Spectators* we mailed two months before is waiting for him.

We walk back to Le Terrazze, and Dr. Mantellassi is behind the counter. We mention our recent visit to Ephrussi, the Rothchild gardens in Cap Ferrat, and he asks whether we know Parranza in Bordighera. We don't, and learn, spiced with his enthusiasm, about the greatest cactus and Mediterranean plant cultivator in Liguria. As usual, he is a man of many talents and interests.

Rather than walk around in the drizzle, we watch the 18th stage of the Giro d'Italia, Italy's premier cycling race. Our primitive language skills are an impediment, but we enjoy the bicycle race and the scenery.

The sands of time speed up. The next day is our last day before heading to Milan and home. We have not done all we had planned to do. We never do. We head to our car, books and maps in hand for a short drive east, a luncheon destination a work in progress.

We look for a restaurant Chuck recommended. Our Boston friend, and former host in Menton, has a knack for finding good but unpretentious places. Toe Drue is an old osteria in Sestri Ponente, an industrial maritime suburb west of Genoa.

The Autostrada dips down within half a mile of the sea. After the toll booths, you maneuver around warehouses, gas stations and somber factory buildings, many abandoned. The avenue changes name every five or six blocks, but follows the coast line towards the heart of Genoa. Older and more interesting parts of town are inland and hidden on one-way streets.

Late morning city traffic builds. There are trucks, buses and drivers in a hurry, knowing where they want to go. Parking spaces are ephemeral. We are now nearly a mile beyond the restaurant. We turn around, and on a hunch and prayer take a narrow street up a hill. There is one space between a gnarled tree and a block long fence beside an old mansion and stately apartments. It's a half mile walk down the hill and then right towards the piers.

Toe Drue is on a corner with a non-descript façade. Opening the door, we are in an ancient house softened with lemon colored paint, red carpet, ceiling fans and comfortable wooden chairs. A young waiter greets us warmly and offers a table towards the back. A few are occupied by regulars, and reserved signs are on other tables.

The restaurant has been in the same family for generations. Each course is heartily prepared and captures the essence of Ligurian flavors: stuffed squid, stockfish, buridda of cuttlefish, pansoti with nuts, and piglet in red wine sauce. At first, it is quiet, and our waiter has time to converse in excellent English. The restaurant name is in Genoese dialect and means "thick table". The strong wooden tables have a down home sense of community, age and informality. By the time we leave, there are no empty tables. Three dozen hungry locals seem quite at home. It's a restaurant to cherish and return to.

Wherever you live, there are attractions and monuments you take for granted. You see them once and only return when entertaining people from out of town. Alassio has its places of interest.

Those with a vague knowledge of the city may know of Il Murreto, a five-foot-high wall of colorful ceramic tiles commemorating visitors great and obscure. It is on the seaward side of the town park along Via Dante. Across the street was the the once famous watering hole, the Café Roma. Hemingway, Chaplin and other notables imbibed the spirit and spirits of the town there. The wall grows at a leisurely pace with new tiles added according to a methodology I haven't deciphered. Some tiles just contain a signature; others a picture, a witticism or salutation. The tiles, many the size of a postcard, require brevity. It's an interesting civilized version of graffiti. Larger mementos, mostly plaques, have been affixed by visiting delegations of clubs, towns, military units and social organizations.

It's not the sidewalk of stars in Hollywood, but it's a nice and festive adornment of an otherwise generic retaining wall. The city tradition included, for many years, an annual beauty pageant to crown a Miss Muretto. The tile tradition started in 1951, and Hemingway's was one of the first three placed on the wall.

The idea and implementation of the wall came from Mario Berrino, who recently passed away in his 91st year. He was a talented painter, with an art gallery on Via Cavour on the same block as Palma. His family also owned the adjacent Café Roma since inception.

The wall also celebrates young love. A sculpture of a young couple holding hands sits on the wall. Larger tiles with love poems add a further element of celebration to the flower filled park. Recently, they started an annual love letter contest. There are small closed locks along the fence, with lover's initials on them, another romantic tradition seen in many European cities.

Now, adjacent to a nearby playground, there is even a new section of wall celebrating favorite pets. The Mantellassi canines have a public tribute among 200 other beloved dogs and a few cats.

Italian cities pride themselves on their ancient churches, particularly if they have important art or religious significance. In the hills above Alassio is the Sanctuary of the Madonna della Guardia. The original oratorio dates from 1226 A.D. and the little church from the 1600s. The views over the sea are beautiful. Behind the sanctuary is a gravel road which becomes a rutted path. It follows the footprint of an old Roman Road. What remains of that ancient thoroughfare is an exhilarating, and not well marked six-kilometer walkway along the cliffs. It passes a few Roman Necropoli and ends in a tiny dirt trail turning inland. One branch then descends into the outskirts of Albenga.

When it comes time to leave Alassio for the last time, perhaps we won't. We have considered making it our final resting place. We have no family here, but for some strange reason it feels like home. It remains to be seen if we can navigate the government and ecclesiastical red tape to find an appropriate niche (literally or figuratively) for non-Catholics. Perhaps we will just have our ashes spread off the town pier when the wind blows seaward or parallel to the shore, or have them taken out by boat to join the remains of Roman and Phoenician vessels on the seabed.

The town cemetery is not exceptional. It is surrounded by a high white painted cement wall. It is behind and above a large parking lot on the wrong side of the railroad tracks. The lot is used on Saturday for the town market. The sound of the trains passing, and perhaps cars gearing up for the upward run into the new mile long tunnel heading into the mountains, would be frequent indignities, if the departed worry about such things.

There are no lovely views, like "the pirate" cemetery in Sete or the hilltop perch in Menton. Hopefully, the need to make such arrangements is a long time off.

My definition of an old codger is someone who spends more time complaining and looking backward than forward. We are not quite there yet. Saddened by the loss of many friends and institutions we cherish, we still continue to look ahead. There is much to learn about our adopted region and layers of culture that aren't readily apparent.

Most of the cemeteries we have seen in Liguria, not that we have made a special effort to look, are austere, if not downright ugly. Horizontal land is at a premium, and fertile plots are much too precious to leave idle for the departed. Clearly, this is a subject on which to procrastinate.

There are quite a few churches, large and small in Alassio, and all are Roman Catholic. We have looked in on a few, mostly to admire the religious art work. The former Anglican Church is now a museum and a hall for occasional cultural events. Protestants must fend for themselves.

There isn't much expat territory left from the 75-80 years in which the English were very much a part of town life. Edward Lear and Richard West came here to paint and Sir Edward Elgar composed *"In the South"* while staying in town. The Scottish General McMurdo built Villa Pergola, a lovely hillside retreat, now an elegant inn. The energetic Hanburys and many other British families are long gone. The Tennis Club and English Book Lending Library with their name remain. There are still some English families in private enclaves in the hills, but English voices are rare along the water's edge.

When we host out of town visitors, we often take them to see West's paintings, and/or those of Carlo Levi. The former are squeezed into makeshift space in what used to be the English Library. Moveable easels and spare wall space are not a fair or fitting tribute to an accomplished artist. The latter are more gracefully displayed in an old mansion. Both depict the town in a simpler and more innocent time. It is rather poignant that West's family donated the paintings to the city. Now, if only the local establishment would find a proper home for them.

The main church of Alassio, Sant Ambrogio (Ambrose) is massive and prettier on the inside than out. It dates from 1507. More to our liking, Alassio is home to the Don Bosco School, begun by the revered priest, and founder of the Salesian Order, in 1870. The Salesians are present in 131 countries, but this was one of their first schools. The school hosts lectures and movies open to the general public.

There is a 50+ year old local hotel school in Alassio, perhaps the equivalent of one of our junior colleges. It prepares earnest young men and women for a career in restaurants and hotels in the region, and according to Dr. Mantellassi, with some success. We have seen these serious young students in action, at dinners in various venues and once at the school itself. Perhaps, there is another Massimo or Sybil Carbone (formerly of Papei di Turta in Alassio) in training who will enchant us in the future.

We are not particularly sport fans. But the city hosts some basketball tournaments, swimming meets, bocce contests and other athletic events in the municipal stadium. Hiking and cycling trails attract many enthusiasts.

OOO

21

Another Departure

In the waning hours of vacation, we pack and move most of our bags to the pensione's garage five blocks away. Dusk turns to night, and we want something to eat. We opt for Italia, the no frills pizza place. A table is set up for some 30 to 40 people. Most seem mellow. We sit down before we see 14 or 15 children, perhaps all under 12, playing games in the alleyways and alongside the restaurant. While the parents and grandparents sit and talk quietly, the well-dressed kids have turned the space into a raucous playground. From the way they are dressed, some have gone or are going to church. They run in and out of the restaurant, playing tag and hide and seek with voices at full throttle. Not a single parent raises a hand or scolds them for unbridled behavior. In France, this would not happen, or if it did, corporal punishment would be swift. We can barely hear ourselves think, much less talk.

The pizza is good, not great. The service is leisurely, and we are nearly deaf by the time we leave. A few blocks away, we return to the more normal decibels of many people out and about and enjoying life. We stop at Cuvea for our last gelati fix until our next trip. At our apartment we open the patio doors. For one more night, we sleep listening to the waves.

Saturday morning, and it is the bittersweet time to leave. For the first time ever, there are no cornettos and paper on the door knob. At a little past eight, I scoot downstairs into the budello to grab a few rolls to go with our coffee. A sea gull flies along and above the caruggi, and then out to sea. On Via Vittorio Veneto, Rudy is wheeling by on a homely bike balancing a large tray of pastries on one hand. He smiles and quickly salutes with his other hand. At Café San Lorenzo, I order two cornettos to go. In the lobby of Le Terrazze, the Saturday leaving ritual has begun. I nod to Dr. Mantellassi, who is settling a bill and supervising a guest family's departure. I head up by elevator the next to last time.

We have a light breakfast, finish the dishes and look around. Though clouds have formed, it will be another beautiful day, and it is hard to leave.

We head downstairs with our luggage. At the counter I settle our bill and give our host some tips for the maids. We tell Egidio that it might not be until the following fall, a year and a half, but we will be back as soon as we can. We step through the corridor to the beauty shop/perfumery and receive hugs from Rita and Anna. We say good-bye to Lula the Cocker Spaniel, who rolls over for some petting. Our stuffie, Chris looks forlorn.

We are to leave the key for the garage at the desk at their sister property, Villa Firenze. Another series of warm good-byes follows at the second hotel. Fifteen minutes later, we are on the road to Albenga. From there we turn east, for Milan and Linate airport. The sky is gray and we choose not to look back.

Past Savona, we take the autoroute north towards Alessandria. Soft rain falls. Lunch was at an old hotel on the outskirts of Tortona. Aurora Girarrosto reminded us we were in Piemonte. Families dug in to hearty meat dishes in a convivial place that has fed generations and countless wedding and anniversary parties. There were no tourists in sight, except for us.

We have to circle around the outskirts of Milan, find our airport hotel, unload and surrender the car. If there is energy to spare, we might go into the city for the evening. Before GPS, even with a detailed city map of Milan, our hotel directions were sketchy-and we paid for it. The rain intensified.

Linate is Milan's second airport, and easy enough to find. But there were no signs to the Holiday Inn, somewhere a few miles southeast. The busy ring road had several rapid-fire exits. After a few extra passes around the airport and on divided avenues leading into town, my wife, the driver, was tired, angry and justifiably so. We were, if not lost, misplaced.

We back tracked a few exits south on the ring road. Then east and north on avenues that appeared on my sketchy map, and then north towards where I thought the hotel should be. Finally, it is the right road. Five minutes drive further on there was a tiny sign for the hotel. A mostly industrial street became a country road. The Holiday Inn looked better than its Internet pictures. It is in what was once some farmer's field. We dropped off our bags, checked out our room, and headed back to the airport to return the car.

It's a short distance north, but the rain hadn't given up. Lease car return at a major airport is usually simple. But there were no signs or they were obscured by the rain and gray skies. Just outside the airport, they were preparing for a major rock concert. Cars were parked every which way on the road. After a few more frustrating passes, we located the correct parking lot. We gave our key and car papers to a caretaker in a booth the size of a caddy shack. With an official looking stamp, he gave us a receipt.

The terminal buildings were a hundred yards ahead. After a cab ride back to the motel, we were stuck there for dinner. Amongst traveling salesmen and stranded tourists, the meal was better than expected. There was fresh pasta, respectable table wine and time to reflect on a fine trip. It was a quiet night, with dull reverberations from the rock concert a few miles away.

The next morning, Italy was 30,000 feet below us. There was a lengthy layover in Amsterdam. Tulips available for purchase shamed most of our flower shops in comparison. The long flight to New York arrived on time, mid evening New York time and more than 21 hours into our day. Heavy rains and wind greeted us and continued through the next morning.

There was the slow march through customs, baggage claim and then up to the monorail to the last stop. A hotel van completed the last mile to the Crowne Plaza. Closed shutters hid a parking lot view. In the bar-restaurant we had our first hamburgers in a month. Then lights out and a very long sleep.

OOO

22

Autumn in Alassio

After a brief prelude in Vence, on a fall Saturday morning, we headed for Italy by car. We timed our arrival to the turnover of apartments. Too early would inconvenience our hosts. A late arrival runs into the evening passegiata and heightened traffic.

The first leg was on the Autoroute. When we descended to provincial roads, our speed would drop dramatically. While my wife drove, I flipped through the pages of the new Michelin Red Guide. The day started cloudy and with a light drizzle. In Italy, patches of blue appeared.

At 75 miles an hour, with moderate traffic, it was a short trip. We were soon at the Andora exit, one of two bracketing Alassio. It was time for a leisurely lunch at Casa Del Priori, up a small private road to a sturdy thirteenth century rock fortress. A long time ago the building had been donated to the Benedictine Monks by a wealthy nobleman. It was a delightfully decadent way to spend Saturday afternoon. There were only a few customers. The portions were substantial, satisfying and it was our main daily meal.

In Alassio, we quickly settle in. While the place itself is very beautiful, if we didn't like the people there it wouldn't matter. The Mantellassis work very hard and yet enjoy life and the little things which make it sparkle. Despite the distances of country, culture and our status as guests, we hoped they were beginning to count us as friends.

We didn't want to interfere with their work, nor assume that anything further was expected. Friendships just happen or don't. Beyond the light pleasantries and courtesies over the years, we saw individuals we wanted to know better. Through them, we understood Alassio as a community and not just a resort.

Several years before, we started a small tradition, asking if we might take the family out to dinner one night on our vacation. The first time, Dr. Mantellassi and Anna his daughter came. He said he hoped we didn't mind the substitution, and of course we were delighted to see Anna. But we were dismayed to learn that Rita had decided not to come. She thought her poor command of English would be a bar. We immediately protested. It was our inability to speak much Italian that was the problem.

Anna is a playfully vivacious russet redhead, then, perhaps in her late 30s, with curly and sometimes unruly hair down over her shoulders. With her father, she is respectful and qui-et--just an occasional oblique or ironic jab when he isn't quite listening. When we speak with her alone, she can be intense, humorous, fatalistic, optimistic, but always engaging.

It was an enjoyable dinner, and perhaps the message got through. The next year Rita did join us for a dinner out. Her sense of humor and spirit sparkled. While Egidio had to do some translating, we loved the conviviality of the evening. For us, it transcended the language barrier. While we were allowed to pick up the tab, flowers were delivered to my wife at table and the wine had been previously paid for.

In 2007, we hoped to continue the tradition. Unfortunately, Rita's mother was very ill. Been there, done that in our own families. It is a sad time when you see a parent slipping away. A few days after the funeral, it was also time for us to leave.

The next year, the mood was distinctly brighter. Again, we soon asked for a dinner date. They accepted and proposed a time a few days later. But at the restaurant, they had previously paid the bill before we could ask for it. We were their guests at a charming neighborhood spot that we had walked by many times. It always seemed busy with a local trade. Osteria Di Angi had a warm glow, partially from its soothing yellow walls and definitely from the friendly and unassuming service. As we thanked our hosts, we asked if we could reciprocate the next week.

Egidio said they had some friends who were going to be in town, and could we join them at their apartment for dinner? Absolutely! This seemed a great honor and an opportunity to see what we expected would be a beautiful home. In France or Italy, it is not common to invite other than your closest friends to your home.

But first there was more sightseeing to do. With a car's convenience, we headed inland several times. Unchained from the erratic and decreasing train service, we didn't have to worry about missing the last train back.

A half an hour inland from the coast, the landscape changes dramatically, and the sea is almost forgotten. Climb over a few rugged hills, and there are scattered towns and more hills and valleys. The land is gentle and intensely cultivated. Further north are the more substantial ancient cities of Asti and Alba. All around them are tens of thousands of vines, platoons of fruit and nut trees. All are cultivated on small farms in undulating valleys. I love this strange topsy-turvy landscape. The hills look like frozen waves, with tiny terraces and narrow roads skimming the top. The earth slopes off in every conceivable direction and angle. Some valleys are narrow, and others gently slope to distant horizons.

There are famous wine towns and namesake vineyards: Barbaresco, Barolo, Gavi and Gattinara, for example. Further south and west are more vineyards and the underground riches of white truffles and porcini mushrooms.

Alba and Asti retain much of their medieval appearance and are a joy to walk through. In the countryside, there are many memorable restaurants. This is the epicenter of the slow food movement.

Even with a car, we often leave it in the garage, especially when visiting the small towns on either side of Genoa. Some are now part of its urban landscape; others retain their ancient independence. Towns east of Genoa have a different feel from those in the west. The hills are steeper and the coastline rockier. If there were five distinct dialects in Alassio, these Ligurian cousins seventy miles away must have their own myriad distinctions. Our Ligurian cookbook, Fred Plotkin's *"Recipes from Paradise"*, has captured eighteen different versions of pesto from various coastal towns.

On the evening of the Mantellassi dinner, Rita and Angela, her assistant and manicurist from the store, met us in the lobby. We had a huge bouquet of white roses for Rita from her favorite florist. We had been the recipient of flowers at her initiative many times. In the elevator, Rita inserted a key, and for the first time we went to the private fourth floor.

The door opened on a delightful and spacious combination living room and dining area. We were greeted by three very friendly dogs: Lula, Polly and Benjamin. A very elegant couple sat talking to Egidio on a spacious sofa. Introductions were made, and we learned that the gentleman was Egidio's grade school friend, a distinguished Milanese physician who lived in a small village near Parma. His wife could have stepped off a fashion page.

The Doctor spoke excellent English, his wife only a few words. Nonetheless, we had a great deal in common: a love of travel, good food, wine and Alassio. The conversation turned to a smattering of politics, literature, music, local history and economics. Egidio and his old friend, "Gigi", kept an intermittent eye on the television. An important football game between Juventus and Inter Milan had begun. Gigi had played soccer in college and had a number of professional atheletes as patients.

Rita gave us a short tour of a stunning garden patio. It had the best vantage point in the building, and perhaps the town, straight out towards the sea. The evening flew by. The meal was extraordinary. Both Rita and Egidio are excellent cooks. Egidio made an outstanding octopus salad. Rita, a Milanese, cooked the best Osso Bucco we had ever had. The wine was from Egidio's brother's estate in Tuscany near Scansano. Close to midnight, we were the first to reluctantly say good night. We felt a step closer to a genuine friendship.

The following week, Rita and Angela made a brief business trip to Sicily, sponsored by one of the perfume houses whose products they sell. Egidio was on a business trip to Genoa on behalf of the city's hotel association of which he was President. That left Anna capably minding the store, the Residences and the dogs.

Anna is the girl next door, with a sharp sense of humor, a keen intellect and a great work ethic. Even when exasperated or stressed, she has a knack for stopping and seeing the humor or incongruity in the situation. I sometimes think she is under appreciated, especially by her bashful, but very decent boy friend. She has lived in Milan, Germany and enjoyed several trips to New York.

Her brother, Giardano, started a real estate business in town, we suspect with considerable help from his parents, and has been quite successful. He does business in Monte Carlo and Milan as well as at home and is focused on the higher end of the market. Charming, perhaps a bit introverted, I wonder if he might someday fly the coop.

Anna does everything in the beauty shop, from massages, manicures, and pedicures, selling jewelry and cosmetics and fills in, as needed at the two pensiones. She is also the principal nurse and caregiver for the dogs. She has the perspective of the next two generations in Alassio, and we value her views and comments. She cares deeply about animals and volunteers in some shelters that take care of abandoned pets.

Egidio's old friends were still in town. On Rita's return, she invited us to join a group for pizza at Ristorante Italia. It was our last night on this brief fall visit. The time was set for 7, and then changed to 8. We arrived at 8, but it had been set back to 7 without our knowing.

While we were embarrassed, everyone was in good spirits. Besides pizza, there were half a dozen dishes of meats, vegetables, antipasti on the table and several opened wine bottles. Other local residents were in attendance, people who we didn't know, but they raised their glasses and welcomed us to the long rectangular table. Rita was at the far end head of the table, with Lula, the Cocker Spaniel resting her head on her feet. We took the last two seats, and I continued my conversation with the doctor who was planning a trip to Guatemala.

On Saturday morning we said good-byes. It was time to head east for our first trip beyond Venice, and on into Slovenia and Croatia. I gave Dr. Mantellassi a deposit for our return in January. We had never been in Liguria in winter. But we were certain it would be more moderate and a good break from New England snow.

Leaving Alassio is always difficult, but we would be back soon. New territory lay ahead. We savored the sea view on the lovely road ascending towards Albenga. By mid morning we were on the autostrada driving towards Genoa and an overnight stop in Piacenza for the first time. The Autostrada carried us north and east, away from the sea. Emila-Romagna, ancient and assured, was different and distinct. Plains, hills and mountains stretched all the way to the Adriatic.

OOO

23

Winter in Liguria

A week before Christmas, 2008 soft steady snow fell on Western Massachusetts. Forecasters predicted 8 to 12 inches by morning. We doubled up on errands, including picking up our Christmas tree. With the tree decorated, my wife prepared a special pre-holiday supper.

We gave up exchanging extensive gifts at Christmas long ago. We would rather make charitable contributions and buy airline tickets. But the tradition of the tree is important to us. We have gone to the same Christmas tree stand for 40 years. Fresh balsam or Douglas fir brings the outdoors into our house. A mélange of Christmas ornaments, some from Gayle's childhood, brings the spirit of the season home and connects us with Christmas' past.

Since I would turn 65 in February '09, we planned one more "pre-Medicare" trip to Europe. The government program doesn't help outside the country. While other coverages were available, it would take awhile to sort it out.

We thought of heading somewhere new: Cyprus, Menorca, the Canaries and other places on our "to do" list. But we wanted to be in Alassio in a season we had not experienced. The quiet month of January was intriguing.

It had been many years since we went out on New Year's Eve. Sometimes there was a mid-evening dinner in a restaurant, and then back home well before midnight. We usually watched the big celebrations on TV, read a book, or even went to sleep before the New Year crossed our path.

This time, we would go out for New Year's Eve, to the airport! While an airplane dinner was nothing to look forward to, the direct Delta flight from JFK to Nice was ideal. What better way to celebrate than over the Atlantic? A couple of days in Nice at our favorite local hotel, Le Grimaldi, and then we would take the coastal train to Alassio.

On a Saturday before Christmas, I spent three hours moving snow dumped on our driveway, roof and shrubs. Even with a trusty snow blower, finish work required an old-fashioned shovel and a roof rake. With 12 inches of snow on the ground, wind and drifts over two feet deep, visions of palm and olive trees were quite appealing. Then we ducked a ferocious ice storm south and east of our home. It brought a state of emergency and days of power outages to the rural counties a short drive away. The Mediterranean beckoned with temperatures in the mid fifties Fahrenheit.

The day before our departure, more snow was coming. We picked up a one-way rental car. The sky was an eerie gray with plenty of moisture in the air. In the morning, we drove to JFK in near blizzard conditions. In southern Connecticut, thankfully the storm turned to rain.

Safely at the airport, there was a beautiful red and orange sunset and only a few planes ahead in the queue. The pilot started a fast run towards the eastern tip of Long Island. Wheels up, and we climbed quickly and banked north.

The next morning, the plane descended into bright sunshine and a warm day in Nice. We gave our bags to a friendly middle-aged taxi driver. Not even taxing our rudimentary French, he cheerfully switched to excellent English. He had taken several American vacations, in San Diego and Miami and regularly spent a month in Florida in their slower season of January-February. The grass must always seem greener elsewhere.

The Grimaldi was as welcoming as ever. Arriving before noon, predictably our room was not ready. The hotel stored our bags and we headed out for a stroll and lunch. The city streets were festooned with holiday decorations. Our stay in Nice was enjoyable and all too short. The only sour note came at the train station Saturday morning. With the New Year's holiday, students thronged from all directions descending on the station in waves. Suprisingly, the number of trains heading east had been cut to "a holiday schedule".

Our train had the least luggage space of any French trains we had been on. My wife got the last seat and I stood in the alcove next to our luggage and close to the doors and stairs. There was a rush hour crowd. It reminded me of my high school days on the New York subways, but then I wasn't anchored to a month's worth of suitcases. I didn't mind standing, but it was uncomfortable and tight. Just a few more people and civility would have completely broken down. The crowds jockeying for position on the platforms and on the train were potentially mutinous.

At Ventimiglia, we let the more energetic run for the next train about to head east. With heavy bags, and trips down and up stairs, we weren't about to compete in the scrum. Another local would depart in twenty minutes or so. The number of passengers decreased dramatically. Dirty windows on the Italian train marred the lovely ocean views.

By mid afternoon we were in Alassio. Our large station wagon taxi squeezed through the narrow pedestrian service road along the beach. It parked next to Le Terrazze, with barely enough room to half open the doors. The encroachment of restaurant and café tables made driving and parking precarious. We walked into the lobby and found two families with little children and numerous packages and bags in tow in front.

Egidio was on the phone patiently providing driving instructions to someone lost somewhere in town. He finished checking in the two families. Then there were warm mutual greetings.

Before heading up to our room, he said we might see a few changes made by Rita. New kitchen countertops, backsplashes, sinks, and cabinets had been installed. "We make a conscious effort to give our customers value. Our regular clients would notice if we don't keep things up." A veteran of the hospitality industry, he understood the competition. With Rita involved, style and quality prevail.

It would be a short but exhilarating stay. Through town, the Christmas decorations were still up. It was a considerably quieter time, although visitors were stretching their Christmas/New Year's holiday. It was cool but not cold.

We unpacked. The bags went on top of the closets, not to be touched until departure. We scooted down the back steps, and over to Piazzetta to buy essentials. At the friendly neighborhood mini-market, the proprietress greeted us with a warm smile and wished us a buon vacanza. Illy coffee, cereal, blood orange juice, fresh milk, a few paper products went into the small hand-held cart, the preliminaries. Then some arugula, goat cheese, and bread sticks.

Perhaps the Sail Inn would squeeze us in early on a busy Saturday night? They did, giving us a small table near the door, the last one. Several groups were gently turned away. Both the old dining room and the newer one angling out to the beach were soon packed with local families.

Pleasant aromas wafted through the narrow confines. The service was courteous and unobtrusive. We opted for beautiful salads with goat cheese. The freshest of fish was prepared Ligurian style, with olives, pine nuts, tomatoes, potatoes, white wine and marjoram. After a dessert of homemade semifreddo with a fresh fruit coulis, we were pleasantly full. Then a stroll back past our residence and on to the town pier. It was bathed in shimmering light blue and green lights, a nice seasonal touch. At our apartment, we opened the windows a bit to hear the waves as we fell asleep.

Should we stay quietly in town, or sortie up and down the coast? We enjoy both. Our many trips to Liguria blend forming a strong mental landscape. There are crystal clear pictures of places we love to visit and a more general sense of others. With temperatures in the fifties during daylight hours, it was often perfect for a long walk in town and elsewhere. But there were damp, rainy and windy days too. The snow and ice of winter was scarcely twenty miles to the north. Liguria rarely sees worse than cold rain. A rare dusting of snow melts within hours.

When there are gray skies, gray and whitecap speckled seas, and a cool moist wind blowing through the streets it makes people linger in cafes and at home. You shop for necessities and long for the return of warmer and brighter days.

After the holidays, there is a brief period of winter store sales. With heavy handed government supervision, merchants have roughly two weeks to offer big discounts, clear inventory and get ready for the quiet months before tourism picks up again. Cash flows dwindle. By mid-January, more and more restaurants go dark. Owners take their own vacations or shut down for maintenance when business is down to a trickle.

Even in an area we know quite well, there were unnoticed corners. We have taken local buses to almost every little town along the near coast in both directions. There may still be un-discovered charm or at least somewhere new to explore.

We sampled Borghetto Santo Spirito, Loano, Pietra Ligure and Borgio Varazze to the east and Cervo, Diano Marina, Arma di Taggia and Ospedaletti to the west. All are just a short distance, an hour or less from home base. We wandered in the everyday commercial districts, mostly window shopped, sometimes peaking into a small church. At lunch time we looked for a local restaurant with competency and character. But like most Italians, we think our town is better.

Stripped of the tourists of fall and spring, we saw a different aspect of places. Most are neither poor nor prosperous. Life goes on, but slower. With fewer customers, each merchant values your presence all the more.

Winter is prime artichoke season. The prize crop, mostly from Albenga, is celebrated in the restaurants that are still open. As in America, out of season produce is brought in from places closer to the equator, Here, that means Sicily, Morocco, Turkey, Tunisia and Israel. In the supermarkets and in the little mom and pop produce stores, there is always a colorful display.

We take Anna out for dinner, and learn a few of the joys and frustrations of her generation. She misses the vitality and variety of Milan, London and even Germany. But family is important, and it is too expensive for a single woman to live in those high-powered cities. She works very hard, our observation, not hers. Her parents have been very good to her, helping her gain a place of her own. She loves to travel and does so from time to time.

On a quiet day, we poke into empty churches, admiring the art work and the ancient piety. As a lapsed Protestant, with millennia of Jewish roots, I don't feel the need for someone to tell me how to worship. Still, I admire these testaments to faith and community. Gayle grew up in the Methodist tradition. While we are no longer regular churchgoers, we believe in God and try to live moral and ethical lives.

The off -season trip was worthwhile. We ducked harsher weather at home. Winter in Liguria is very quiet. With most of the tourists gone, the town and region take on a different aspect.

Our small apartment in Alassio is a tenth the size of our house. We have no lawn or grounds to keep up. It is satisfying living simply for a time. As on a boat, you work with the essentials. Substituting a café or bar for your living room, a restaurant for your dining area, a public garden for your own, they compensate for the slightly cramped quarters.

A charity fundraiser, a Slow Food Dinner, a church concert; they are for local consumption-and all the more pleasant for it. We chip in, as we can. We care that this community thrives despite the buffeting of internal and external forces.

OOO

24

Sharing Alassio

A ll summer, 2009, the dollar sagged against the Euro. Our next Italy trip would be costlier. The season slipped away from us. More daylight hours meant more outdoor chores. Rainy weather and dental/medical appointments took time. Then it was Labor Day.

If you have gotten this far, you can sense that my wife and I are quite content with our own company. When we spend time with friends, it's usually a few at a time. Perhaps being only children, we prefer those who have stuck by us, and we them, for a long time. Respect and affection trump novelty, status and fashion. We avoid tour groups, large crowds and doing things just because others want to do them.

Joe and Sandy have been close friends since Navy days. He was my last reserve commanding officer, and I succeeded him when he retired. Joe is a linebacker of an Irishman. He can extract a laugh or a smile out of most everyone. Before college, he worked in a steel mill, and for awhile studied to be a priest. Sandy, his college sweetheart, then a high school teacher, accepted a marriage proposal over the phone and soon was in Japan where Joe was stationed on a minesweeper. Unlike Joe and me, who view physical fitness as an eccentric obsession, she works out regularly at a local fitness club. They have three fine adult children and a growing crop of grandchildren.

Shortly after I retired from the insurance company in the fall of 2006, they met us in Paris. We had a grand time sharing the big city we most love. This year, as we approached our 40th wedding anniversary and their 45th, they suggested we plan another trip together. Passionate beachcombers, who spend a lot of time in South Carolina and Florida, they were receptive to spending some time in Alassio. It would be their first visit to Italy. They proposed adding some French touring after a one week stay in Alassio. We crafted a rail trip for the second half with two days each in Nice, Marseille, Lyon and then on to Paris for 4 nights and 3 days. As the advance party, we would have a few days in Nice on our own and a week in Alassio before their arrival.

The number of through trains from Nice to Alassio kept going down; then only two a day. We opted for a regional connection in Ventimiglia. The Ligurian local or "regionale" trains were caught in a 1950s-time warp with scruffy cars, in sharp contrast to the newer and cleaner French trains. In Ventimiglia there was time to pick up two generous pannini sandwiches at the station café cum general store. We stood on the platform enjoying the simple pleasures of mozzarella and tomatoes, and sparkling water.

On the regionale, we piled our bags in the end foyer, just in from the doors. There was no specific storage space for heavy luggage. Fortunately, the train was not crowded. I kept an eye on the bags and reasoned the average thief would get a hernia trying to lift them. Rambling through lovely and familiar territory, in less than an hour we were in Alassio.

Our private week flew by. We did things that we suspected our friends wouldn't be interested in: longer trips, fancier restaurants. We enjoy their company, but cherished our solo time.

Joe and Sandy made a tight Friday connection through Paris, and stayed, at our suggestion, at Le Grimaldi in Nice. With the help of a Rick Steves book, they found one of our favorite restaurants, Le Cambuse, along the old market square. They booked the morning through train to Alassio arriving around noon.

It was exhilarating waiting on the platform for our friends. As much as we talk about Alassio, only one other family of American friends had visited us there. A California attorney, her husband and son; they were spending a couple of years in London where her husband had been transferred. They came down for a long weekend. They seemed to like it, and their then young son got an advanced course in Italian gelati.

On a glorious sunny day, the train was only a few minutes late. With nine cars, we weren't sure where our friends would surface. We stood in the center of the platform hedging our bets. Several dozen people got off the train and a similar number queued to get on. We saw Sandy first, and then Joe struggling a bit pulling heavy bags off at the rear end of the train. The steps are steep and narrow and American bags tend to be heavy and large. We jogged down the platform to greet them.

After hugs and a brief torrent of greetings, we all turned around taking in the beautiful landscape. We stood and talked, getting a quick update on their trip. Soon we had the platform to ourselves. We helped with their bags, down the old worn flight of stairs and out to the front of the station. I suggested that Joe, Sandy and Gayle take a cab with the luggage. I would walk to the apartments and meet them there. While check in wasn't until 4, if their room wasn't ready, they could use ours to freshen up and store their bags.

I jogged through the underpass, down Via Dante and through the budello, arriving first. Alessia, a very nice and vivacious young lady and close friend of Anna's, was on the front desk. Our friends' room was ready, and right next to ours on the second floor. They would have a sea view room, and we both had use of the spacious common terrace.

Their check-in was swift. After a half hour, our friends knocked on the door. We showed them the lovely patio, and then headed to the lobby. The first stop, next door at Rudy's for sandwiches and beer.

Then we walked the seaside promenade east towards the marina, weaving in and out of the budello and along the water. The pace was a little slow. Joe was recovering from knee surgery, stoic, but not entirely limber. We carefully climbed slippery stone steps to a little chapel overlooking the sea, just high enough to look down on the marina. A sailing race was in full swing in the harbor. We were a mile and a half from the apartments. On the way back, we had an espresso at a little shaded cafe with prime seaside views. Then back to the Residence. I suggested an early dinner at Sail Inn before the Saturday crowds grew.

Our friends had only a week in Alassio, so we deferred to their priorities. On Sunday, we took a bus to Laigueglia browsing the farmer's market. In the afternoon, another bus brought us to Albenga to wander a bit in the old Roman walled city.

The next day we took a train trip in to Genoa. We walked by the great stone palaces on Via Balbi and returned through the rabbit warren of old streets near the waterfront. Joe clearly enjoyed the ancient churches, both grand and small, in the city's core. He admired both the architecture and the stunning religious art. But he seemed visibly uncomfortable with our brief street encounters with Arabic and African people in foreign dress. Most lived and worked in the old sailor quarters. It was surprising for someone who spent a couple of Navy years immersed in the cultures of Japan, the Phillippines and Vietnam. Of course, western news media don't paint a sympathetic picture of people in djellabas and gandoras, and he had probably never seen folks in this type of clothing, especially moving quickly and inches away from you.

No one approached us in either a menacing or begging sort of way. People were just going about their business. The tight quarters and primitive hole in the wall shops confirmed we were in a different place, as close to a casbah as you would find in Europe. Maybe our friends were not expecting this on their first visit to an Italian city. It didn't stop Sandy from buying costume jewelry in a small Indian shop where the sales women wore pastel colored saris.

It reminded me of my first trip to Harlem-alone, as a teenager, or our wandering briefly in Fez without a guide. Suddenly, we were the minority and not sure of what to expect from the people around us. You instinctively avoid eye contact and try to keep a low profile.

Back in Alassio, Joe suggested a trip to Monte Carlo. On the next day we headed there by train. You learn a lot more about someone's temperament and tastes when you travel with them. I didn't know my friend liked casinos. He wanted to add this famous one to his resume. Monaco's modern train station, built into a rock wall above the city, looks down on a small harbor inlet. A glass elevator descends to the water level. A city bus can take you to the Royal Palace. Our friends suggested a tour of the palace. This was the Rick Steves' Guide Book at work. We would not have gone on our own but it proved worthwhile.

Another bus took us to the other end of the city and the casino. After lunch on a neighboring terrace, we walked into the fabled gambling den. There was no charge to enter the lobby. But to proceed into the upstairs rooms with the gaming tables, there were fees and a "dress code". My wife and I have no interest in gambling, so we were content to wait outside, perhaps doing some window shopping at some of the exclusive stores in the neighborhood.

Joe, as a matter of principle, would not pay the ten- or twenty-Euro fee to gamble his own money in the main casino. He grumbled about putting on a loaner sports jacket too. To gain access to the "public" i.e. private salons, both were required, even though he was prepared to wager more than trivial sums. Somewhat "big and tall" and wearing a polo shirt, he didn't fit my image of a suave Riviera gambler.

There must be plenty of people like my friend. The casino had an alternative. Off in a foyer, opposite the coat room, perhaps once another coat room or storage area, there was a small and cramped room filled with slot machines. You could say you gambled in Monte Carlo without paying the fee or putting on a jacket.

Joe sat down at one of the machines and was content to play for several hours. After Sandy had fed some Euro tokens into another machine for a few minutes, she was done. The three of us left for a stroll, and Joe agreed to meet us outside in a half hour or so.

It was closer to an hour when we all regrouped. A bus took us back to the train station, and after a fifteen-minute wait for the next train, we were on our way to Ventimiglia. Back in Italy, we briefly looked at the departure board and were stunned. The last train heading east was just leaving the station a few minutes before eight PM! I rushed over to the ticket counter and asked about the next train to Alassio. The bored woman behind the counter said 6 A.M. Could it be we were stranded 35 miles from our apartment?

I felt angry and dumb. Dumb because I hadn't checked the return trains and angry that there were no trains during evening hours on what should be a very busy route. I knew that trains came into Alassio from Genoa up until midnight. With my primitive Italian and the ticket agent's English deficiency, the only thing she had to offer was: "Bus!"

The bus system was ridiculously balkanized. Four senior citizens weren't going to hitchhike. Paying perhaps a hundred Euros or more for a taxi wasn't a happy option either. Would we camp at the train station for the night, or break down and look for hotel rooms without luggage?

We stepped into the night. There are two main parallel one-way streets through the long border town. We walked a couple of blocks to the one heading east. The next step was to find a bus stop, and buy bus tickets, usually done only in a café, bar or tobacconist. Both the main streets were dark, and almost every place was closed. I found a bar where someone was mopping the floor before going home. With some urgency I asked where there was a bus stop. She pointed to a spot a block and a half away near the old market. As we regrouped, I saw a bus coming up the street. It said San Remo on the front. I ran down the street following the bus, and shouted back to my travel companions to follow.

The bus driver saw our motley crew, and waited for us to board. The night custom allowed me to pay on board. For about six Euros, the four of us were at least heading in the right direction.

I knew there was a large bus terminal in San Remo. We had never used it. I also knew that we were in Imperia Province, and that this bus company would only go as far as Andora. From there, we would have to switch to another line that would take us the few miles through Laigueglia and back home to Alassio. Assuming we didn't miss the last bus.

There were only a few people on our bus. We caught our breath as we passed through a few villages before Bordighera and then into the outskirts of San Remo. Just to be sure, I walked to the front and asked the driver about a bus to Andora. He nodded and motioned that he would show us where to catch it. In daytime, there was beautiful scenery along our route, but at night there were only glimpses of the coastline and lovely hillside mansions. The bus went right past the big bus station. In a few blocks our driver signaled for us to get off at a tiny bus shelter. He confirmed that the bus to Andora would stop there, but not for an hour. In half an hour, we had advanced a few towns closer to our objective.

Next to the shelter there were timetables posted on a vertical post. In the near dark, with the help of my wife's tiny flashlight, we confirmed that we were at the right stop. But the information was entirely in Italian. We struggled to decipher which the daily, the weekend and the holiday schedule. A bus came by. We debated whether to take it to Oneglia, further along the way. While we hesitated, the bus went on.

We had had a late lunch, and the dinner hour slipped away. Perhaps we were all more anxious than hungry. Sandy said she wouldn't mind a soft drink. I walked a couple of blocks back towards the bus station and found a bar where I bought four small cans of coca cola. We nursed our cokes and joked a bit in the gloom. I told Joe there was another casino here in

San Remo, but at this point we all wanted to just get back to Alassio. A little before ten and behind schedule, an Andora bus pulled up to the shelter.

In late September the bus was heated as if for winter. Strong blasts of hot air came out of several heaters. The bus had a strange configuration inside, unusual metal protuberances, seats wedged in close behind the driver, seats that for no apparent reason were up a few steps, some facing backwards and others forward.

There were a couple of young men on the bus, none Italian. As we walked back to pick out seats, the bus lurched forward. We flew along the road as if we were in a grand prix race. Was the driver in a hurry to get home? Was he practicing to be a sports car driver? We were on a runaway bus. Gayle and I knew the coastal roads, and fortunately our guests didn't. Our driver kept barreling along the highway, often over the double line separating the narrow curving two lanes, and only occasionally tapping his horn as we approached sharp bends or entered small tunnels. We knew there were plenty of sheer drops off the outboard lane we were traveling in, but in the inky dark it was just black space. A few times we stopped abruptly at tiny bus stops in the middle of nowhere, or on empty town streets. One person would get on or off. As the trip moved on, the bulk of our new passengers were clearly foreigners from the Middle East, Eastern Europe or Africa. Some probably worked in kitchens, laundries, or agriculture. I wondered where they would spend the night before another long bus trip in the morning.

We passed by the darkened arcades in the center of Oneglia, the larger twin of Imperia, and I breathed easier. Now we were only 10-12 miles from Alassio. We could almost walk home, although on the coastal highway that would be foolish. A late-night taxicab ride, if necessary, was now more annoying than prohibitive.

We advanced through Diano Marina, San Bartalomeo and Cervo, all mostly asleep. We rode to the very last stop, along the water's edge in Andora. At the very same stop, a Savona bus should pick us up and take us to Alassio. Provided we hadn't missed the last one. Three young men, perhaps Bangladeshi or Pakistani, were waiting at the bus stop. We checked the posted placard. There were two busses left that night.

I crossed the street looking for a bar/café where I could buy tickets. Even they were closed. During the day, TPL line insisted that you have a ticket before you board. I didn't know their night procedure. Everything in town seemed dark. I saw our final bus coming a few blocks away and scrambled back to the bus stop. The night bus driver sold tickets at a premium. We settled in for the last familiar miles.

It was half an hour short of midnight when we arrived in the center of Alassio. There wasn't another soul outside on the several block walk to the waterfront. Anticipating our guests' frame of mind, I said: "we deserve a drink."

On a weekday night, most of the town was shuttered, except for a few waterside watering holes, ones we hadn't frequented. We were the oldest customers by far, but headed for an outside table at Liquid. They were full of twenty somethings, dates, clusters of men and women, a whole range of people trying to look serious and sophisticated. Our orders, Scotch, and Gin and Tonics were quickly and generously filled. A few pretzels and peanuts didn't make up for the missed meal, but helped ease the alcohol's path. Our waiter happily chatted in English for awhile. Later in the week, he waved as we walked by. To this day, my friend Joe thinks I'm too enthusiastic about bus trips. I've reminded him that the new Pope likes to ride the bus too.

The front door at Le Terrazze was closed. I went up the back steps, using my key card, and took the elevator down to open the front door. The next morning started late.

The remainder of the week went quickly. The little bus up to Moglio gave us a chance to peer down at our town through wooded hills. With Joe's bad knees, we weren't about to hike down the slope, so twenty minutes later we rode it back down to town. There were several trips to Cuvea for the best gelati for miles around. Window shopping was a daily occurrence. Sandy bought some small gifts for her coworkers. The Mantellassis confirmed that the Baci di Alassio in our welcome baskets, rich little chocolate filled cookies, were from the

Riviera Café. While there are half a dozen versions in town, these seemed the very best. An order of cookies awaited Sandy when we stopped for panninis on the last Friday.

One evening we were walking through the budello. There was a small and impossibly cluttered little gift shop. Everyone else was closed. Floor to ceiling glass cases were filled with every kind of tchotchke. Behind the tiny counter was a very old, small, crumpled and congenial white-haired man. Sandy eyed some kitchen magnets and small booklets of postcards.

The elderly man chimed in in perfect English. "I took those pictures back in the 1950s when I was working in my Father's shop." He still had a supply. I sensed that this gentleman virtually lived in the store. We all bought a few tiny gifts, and we told him that we would be back in January. He said he would be there, and he was.

On Saturday, we returned to the train station together. Perhaps our friends were not as head over heels in love with Alassio as we were, but they enjoyed it. Sandy had gotten up early and gone for walks along the beach almost every day. Joe settled in to Rudy's, having tried the Italian and German beer, and back to his mainstay, Guinness. How it compared, in their minds, to their regular haunts in the Caribbean, Hilton Head, Florida we don't know. Everyone should have their own place in the sun.

25

Another Winter Journal

S ome day, we may have to give up our New England house. The upkeep and space may be more than what we choose to or can handle. The simple, lean apartment in Alassio might be a template for downsizing; but not yet. We cherish the beauty of our woods, the quiet location, and good neighbors. Western Massachusetts has its charms, along with its shortcomings. As much as we love Alassio, an unstable country and a still foreign culture militate against burning bridges.

Christmas Day, 2009: despite the prior week's northeaster which roared up the eastern seaboard and turned right, we were in a calm, cold and cloudy coda; a safe harbor from the full thrust of winter.

While we were in a cocoon of relatively tranquil winter weather, Northern Europe endured severe bouts of snow, heavy rain and ice. Milan, at Christmas, screeched to a halt under snow storms. Venice had heavy floods, and our favored Liguria was plagued with treacherous mudslides along the coast. There was death and accident dealing ice in the hills North of Savona. Hundreds of trains were canceled or delayed. Shortages of deicing fluid imperiled Italian airports. We prayed for the weather to moderate for everyone's sake, including our own.

There were less people than we expected traveling on New Year's Eve Day, although our plane was full. With 100 miles an hour tail wind for most of the flight, we arrived in Nice half an hour early, around 9AM. The airport was nearly deserted. There were only two scheduled trains into Italy for the day. Of all of the times we have been to Nice, I have never seen it so empty. Folks celebrated the holiday by being away or sleeping in.

The train station was busy, but not the logjam of a year before. The departure board only showed the train schedule for the next three hours. Fortunately, unlike Alassio, the "left luggage" room was open for business. Even train stations now run luggage through a metal detector. With the help of a cheerful attendant, we squeezed four bags into a large locker.

Still groggy, from a long night of no sleep on the plane, we walked around town. On the Boulevard des Anglais, a busy café seemed promising. Warm sun and strong espresso along the beach made us brighter.

On New Year's Day many places were closed. Down at the market place, the Cours Saleya, was our old stand-by, Le Cambuse. An outside blackboard sign listed the daily specials. Near the top, was "a dozen oysters." Voila! We walked through the isinglass curtains, and chose "outside" seats close to a gas floor lamp putting out as much heat as most fireplaces.

Soon, every table was filled. A beautiful green salad, a dozen premium oysters each and a bottle of good Provencal white wine: what else might one need? Oh yes, dessert: a velvety chocolate mouse for me and a slice of swiss chard pie for my lady.

It started to drizzle as we finished lunch. Our umbrellas were a mile away, at the station. The precipitation came and went. Darting under awnings and store fronts, we navigated our way up Avenue Jean Medecin and back to the station just after 3.

The 5:53 PM local train took us, at an ambling pace, to Ventimiglia, just over the border into Italy. Around 7 PM, we boarded the last train east for the day. We had missed that train in September, leading to our three-bus adventure getting back to Alassio. This time we planned to spend the night in San Remo breaking our Nice routine.

By heading into Italy, we avoided the Saturday morning crowds at Nice Station on a holiday weekend. Only a few people got off at San Remo. Outside, there were no taxis at the taxi stand, but a few people queued patiently. In a few minutes, several taxis returned. A cheerful driver stepped out of a Mercedes station wagon. We filled his trunk and were on our way to the Villa Maria at the other end of town.

Four months before, I tried to book a hotel for one night on New Year's Day somewhere West of Alassio. Few would accept a one-night reservation, or claimed to be full. While not in any guide book, the Villa Maria had decent TripAdvisor reviews and was available, at a holiday premium.

Past the old train station, and near the Casino, we made a sharp right turn up a narrow, winding hilly street. Three blocks north, the cab drove past the hotel entrance, stopped briefly, and deftly backed up a slanting driveway. It had the feeling of a large private home in an old but fashionable residential district. The reserved manager greeted us politely by name and requested our passports. He handed us a room key and said there was a lift to the right.

Our room was roughly 15 feet square. Two standard beds formed a faux queen. On the perimeter were old chairs, tables, a large armoire, leaving an 18-inch space to walk around the perimeter of our room. At the far corner, near the windows, there was just enough space to park our bags stacked vertically. The ceiling was 16-18 feet overhead. Beautiful parquet wood floors and old stenciled floral patterns on most of the wood pieces confirmed the building's venerable age. This was no Holiday Inn.

The bathroom was adequate, although sink and toilet were three or four inches lower than expected. A spotless old tub was built for smaller people. All the tub and sink faucets were wrench tight. When closed normally they leaked.

It was oppressively warm in the room. I opened the tall windows to let a little cool air in. We were at the front of the house, overlooking the driveway and parking lot. With the windows closed, we heard every footfall in the hallway and conversations in other rooms. But after 32 hours awake, we quickly fell asleep.

Villa Maria had been a private mansion home. The public rooms were full of antiques, art work, and hints of life in a different era. Breakfast was served in an old-fashioned formal dining room. The hotel offered full board as an option. It had real waiters, with stylish café-au-lait-jackets, and the gravitas from viewing waiting as a profession.

Coffee came in silver pots. Small platters of rolls were brought to the table. We queued for juice, butter, jam, yoghurt, and additional breads and pastries. But the ambiance was better than the breakfast. A very well-dressed older gentleman came down and was greeted like family. A waiter took his luncheon order after bringing him coffee.

Most European vacation rentals are on a Saturday to Saturday basis. With people leaving and arriving, it is fair to the hotel and cleaning crew not to arrive before 4PM. Saturday is also popular with day trippers and weekenders. Our adopted town and others bustle, even in winter. With a car, you worry about parking. Without one, where do you put luggage until check in-time?

The few "left luggage" concessions in Italy close midday taking a long luncheon break. Even when the intercity train arrived in Alassio just before noon, there would be no signs of life at the baggage door. So we took an earlier train.

We left San Remo on the nearly empty 10:07 AM local. Shortly after 11, we reached Alassio. I carried our bags down the steep stairs to street level, one at a time, and then rolled them through the mini-tunnel below the tracks and through the small station. A sharp left outside and in a few additional feet, we were in front of the "Bagagli" door. It was closed with a barred gate across it. I walked around to the ticket counter and inquired. Despite the language barrier, I got the message. There was no baggage attendant. He had gone the way of elevator operators and telephone booths.

We had five hours to kill and a small island of luggage in front of us. Back at the baggage claim door, we vented some uncomplimentary language about the Italian Railway. Another railroad employee, with a smattering of English, was apologetic. Baggage claim was a private concession. A long time ago it closed. You can't blame someone for abandoning a dwindling livelihood.

My wife stayed with the bags at a nearby park bench while I explored our options. At least the sun was out, and it was relatively warm. I headed for Mezze, a delightful restaurant where we had planned to have lunch. Perhaps they would have a table outside and room to park our bags during our meal. I walked down the stairs and through the tunnel beneath the main street. There were throngs on the small streets of town.

Turning towards the water, there was a strange sight. The beach had blown inland, temporarily covering the promenade along the water in wet sand. It was windy, and the water was as close to the buildings as I had ever seen it.

Also, Restaurant Mezze was gone. It was shuttered on our last trip. We hoped that it was merely an extended vacation. Now, in its place was a tacky pizza restaurant. I turned around with disgust, and headed back to the park bench to report.

With wind and sand blowing on the seafront, we needed to get as close as possible to our apartment on inner streets. Wheeling bags through wet sand would make a mess of the baggage wheels, to say nothing of inside floors. Hopes of a civilized lunch were dimming. I remembered the story of an Irish neighborhood in London. It was a few blocks from a train station and as far as people might be able to carry their bags. This was long before wheels were added to luggage.

I suggested walking as far as Via Torino, two and a half blocks from our apartment. We might get a sandwich or light lunch away from the swarms of people in town for the New Year's holiday. We trudged five blocks east, wheeling and carrying our bags past the long-closed movie theaters, beyond the cathedral and found a bench close to our intersection. Gayle, again, sat surrounded by our luggage pile.

I walked toward the beach. It was just as unruly there. The entire slate and concrete walkway was submerged under encroaching sand. The wind was still blowing. Not our picture of a sub tropical oasis. A restaurant at the foot of the street, which we had tried only once, was ¾ full. Theoretically, there was room out in the front of the restaurant to park our bags next to a couple of baby carriages. I walked up to the caruggi, the main pedestrian shopping street and west. Osteria De'Angi, the place the Mantellassis had taken us to dinner, was open for lunch, a rare occasion. There might be room in the front foyer where bags could be placed in plain view, but it would be awkward. Every patron would have to walk by our luggage on the way to their meal. In the other direction on Via Dante, Pasta e Basta, a modest restaurant, was full with large family groups.

We caucused at the second park bench and decided to wheel our bags down Via Torino. The restaurant on the beach was now "full" in the course of an additional ten minutes. You may or may not empathize with all of this emphasis on food.

But the odds are you have been hungry sometime when options have dwindled.

There was a hole in the wall bar next to the beachfront restaurant we hadn't noticed before. A poster pictured some Panini. We rolled our makeshift caravan up to a few outside tables and ordered sandwiches and cokes. It was a modest lunch, but we were grateful for it. While we enjoyed the sun, Gayle glimpsed Anna on her bike swinging right on Via Torino. Anna saw Gayle too. She made a U-Turn and came back to say hello.

We kissed and chatted for a minute. She asked whether we needed help with the bags, and we said no; we were just killing time to check in at a proper hour. After the sandwiches, we inched closer to the Residence. By a back alley, we dodged the wind and came up alongside Rudy's Café, and took a table in front. We squeezed our bags along the wall, right next door to La Terrazze's property. Both of Rudy's sons came over and gave us a warm greeting. We ordered fresh fruit salad, ice cream and good espresso and thus completed our meal. There was no pressure to give up our little table.

After another short session of people watching, including two families checking in to Le Terrazze early, we had waited long enough. It was roughly 3:45 when we walked into the lobby. It was full of beautiful Christmas decorations. Egidio was behind the desk patiently attending to the families whose piles of small bags and strollers filled much of the lobby. Unlike

Americans, arriving with borderline too big bags, many Europeans fill their car with myriad plastic and canvas bags, like they were coming from the supermarket or going to the beach.

When it was our turn, Rita appeared from the corner beauty shop, and greeted us with kisses on the cheeks. After a few pleasantries, I asked about the roads. We had read about closings from mudslides. I had also seen a story about a local priest arrested in town over an allegation of child molestation. Egidio was diplomatic. The allegations were grave, but not proven; the troubled young girl had a sad history, and a man's lifetime reputation was in suspense.

Lula, the ginger colored cocker spaniel, flounced out of the beauty shop and added her welcome, her tail going at a high rpm. We were happy to ride the new more spacious elevator installed since our last trip, and see our enhanced third floor apartment facing the sea.

While Gayle unpacked, I darted to Piazzetta for the usual provisions. A half hour later, we returned to a familiar grazing routine: cocktails at Bar Impero. After generous hors d'oeuvres; we purchased a beautiful rotisserie chicken to take home from Pollero Cuneese. Later we had a nightcap of wonderful gelato from Gelateria Cuvea. It was a delightful and simple meal in three installments. Content, it was time for a long sleep.

The sheer luxury of a no alarm Sunday morning! We had cappucini at Rudy's. While we were there, Anna came over to pick up coffees to go a second time. Earlier in the morning she had brought a cappuccino to Rita in her apartment and went back to the store. Rita was preoccupied. In the meantime, Lula had climbed up on a low table and was slurping the foam laden beverage. The image of the dog with a cream and cinnamon moustache will stay with us for a long while. Any scolding was probably overcome with laughter.

There seems so many options on that first Sunday. We could stay put. But there were so many people wandering through town. We took a short excursion: a bus trip to Loano, three towns beyond Albenga. Loano is a place of some substance, more than just a resort town. It has a distinct patina. Its mile long carrugi and vicos are always entertaining. Older shops, churches, clock towers on former outside walls are geared to the townspeople, not tourists. It also had a restaurant we wanted to try.

We stood in front of Vecchia Trattoria a few minutes before its 12:30 opening time. The lights were on, door locked. We took a short extension to our walk, and returned in ten minutes. Now the doors were open. An older waitress brought us to a cozy table at the far corner of the small stone walled restaurant. Within fifteen minutes, eight of ten tables were full.

The restaurant was a bit formal; taped piano music played in the background. The menu was traditional Ligurian. We chose pasta, a fish course, and a delicious flourless chocolate cake with fresh pear. There was a good Pigato from a local vintner. The food was good, not great. But it was nice dining with local families, no other tourists around. Just 11 miles from our town, the place and people were a little different.

Before catching the bus back to Alassio, we stopped in a local garden shop and bought three packets of Ligurian basil seeds. It might not do so well in New England soil, but we were game to try it the next time we made pesto, and to share the seeds with two friends. We have never had basil as delicious as the local variety. Sadly, they were later confiscated at Kennedy Airport. We answered the question about bringing in agricultural products truthfully. I understand the need to keep us safe from alien blights, but good basil?

On our return bus trip, two thirds of the bus riders were teenaged school kids. Although good natured, they didn't seem terribly bright or courteous. Was this Liguria's future? I gave my seat up to a frail older lady. None of the kids considered doing so. At first, she refused, but I insisted. Then she happily sat down next to my wife. She wanted to chat, despite the language barrier. She was very nice, with probably a lot of wisdom and gossip to share. Unfortunately, little got through.

Monday and Tuesday brought cold, wind and sporadic rain. There was no incentive to go far afield. At Rudy's for coffee, we shared the collective siege mentality of folks whose routines were curtailed. Eventually, we did some window shopping and gravitated towards the Sail Inn for lunch. This was the kind of day that destroyed umbrellas. The restaurant would soon close for their winter vacation. Several folks were already dining at 12:15. We were given a table near the water. Soon the restaurant was full.

Our waiter, who spoke the most English of the staff, responded enthusiastically when I asked if he was ready for "vacanze". He had counted the days for 10 months. He was returning to Thailand, a place warm and inexpensive. Many Alassini, including Rudy, go there frequently.

Sail Inn's red pepper soup with fish and a main course of broiled branzino were splendid. Washed down with bottles of Vermentino and San Pelligrino, all was good with the world despite the foul weather. We returned through the rain to the warmth of our apartment for some television, reading and writing. By evening, it was still gray and damp. Down the back door, through an alleyway, we settled in at Bar Impero for Campari and freshly squeezed blood orange juice and snacks. Then we adopted cooked quails from our favorite Rotisseria.

The wind howled through the night. With more rain and clouds in the morning, we slept past 8. After breakfast, there was a minor mission to find winter gloves. I had left mine in the rental car at JFK. Every small shop in town was having a sale. Both fancy places and discount stores advertised 20, 30 and even 50% off. I found some very nice hand-crafted gloves at a stiff price, even with a 20% reduction. At least they were made in Italy, not Romania, Bulgaria, or China.

The weather marginally improved. We stayed in town and made minor discoveries: a new tea room on the far west corner of town. Even in a gloomy economy some Italians believe they could hew a living from modest food and drink.

Late in the day, we were back at Rudy's. For a change, we tried their hot chocolate. It was like drinking a liquid chocolate bar. Deep and luxurious cocoa coated the cup and stomach, an antidote for winter chill.

A few more days of mediocre weather were predicted. But the low 30s along the coast, with palm and orange trees in sight, was better than the teens with heavy snow on the ground at home and the ice and fog in Piemonte.

That afternoon Lula was wearing a little purple scarf. She was happy to see us. There aren't many better greetings than from a dog full of love. They always have time for some petting.

By mid-morning Wednesday the sun claimed more real estate in the sky. The temperature climbed into the 40 degrees Fahrenheit. With no wind, it was a lovely winter day. It was Epiphany, a bank holiday in Italy. A local town band gave a brief free concert at the foot of the pier. We saw them shuffle rather than march by Rudy's in their worn band uniforms. The music, however, was first rate: a cut above many small town and high school bands. Most of the musicians were old enough to be fathers or grandfathers. There were no women in the band.

After lunch, the sun was still out. The sea was calm. The coldest winter in Europe in fifty years was moderating! People walked a little faster and, like the effect of natural light on flowers, seemed a little taller.

By late afternoon, Rudy's was nearly full. There were a few baby carriages, young and old couples, teenagers; everyone found a brief warm nest out of their cold apartments. It was great to have a friendly bar a few feet from our lodging. We were spending long swaths of the day in a café doing almost nothing but it felt appropriate.

By Thursday, we had the travel itch. With the reduced winter train schedule, we needed to be at the train station early. Still, I am in agreement with an Episcopal Navy Chaplain I once met. If the second coming was before 0900, I would miss it. Our destination was a work in progress. On the way to the station I said: "how about Oneglia?"

The next train was a local. We didn't mind waiting on the platform in the sun, scanning pretty houses in the hills. In a half hour, perhaps the slowest train we had ever been on gradually came to life on track 1. With the Italian's aversion to cold, the cars were sauna warm. It stopped at every minor station and then would expire at Arma di Taggia, still a good distance from the French border. It slowed frequently, as if to catch its breath.

In many places, there is only one track along the Riviera Ponente, and they date from the 1870s. the track is shared by express, local and freight trains. You often wait at a station for an alternating train to whiz by. Many "regionale" were tired and dirty. One wondered about their safety. Makeshift paper signs, with an X scotch taped on a door indicated that it didn't work. Sometimes going through a tunnel all of the lights went out. Two years later, happily the trains were somewhat cleaner and new cars began to appear.

We were in Oneglia in 40 minutes, a place we had visited many times. It's always a trifle warmer in this stretch of land. The old arcaded streets around the center are reminiscent of the north, cities like Torino and Cuneo. Perhaps this is due to its roots in the old kingdom of Savoia. It is a good place to stroll, window shop, or have a coffee at one of a dozen bars, pasticcerias and cafes. In rain or snow, you can walk for blocks without getting wet.

Across the far and hill side of the railroad station is the Carli olive oil plant, perhaps the city's primary industry other than government. Next door, they have a small museum and gift shop. It is worth a visit, with attractive dioramas and exhibits on the harvesting, storing and serving of olive oil over the millennia. From ancient amphora and vials to early commercial packaging, it is an entertaining, amateurish and low-key presentation. Ligurian olive oil is not as well known or marketed as Tuscany's, but locals cherish its delicate taste. As do we.

Once a major commercial fishing port, Oneglia still has the best shrimp on the coast. Every few months, I read about a Coast Guard raid on restaurants selling frozen fish as fresh. The cheaper stock is from Southeast Asia. The better restaurants know and rely on their fishermen and vice versa.

Pride of place in the harbor now goes to half a dozen large yachts for lease. The trawlers have been pushed to the margins. Oneglia is no Cannes or Monte Carlo. A dozen cranes and a few small warehouses are still in operation. Under the waterfront arcades, restaurants occupy former fishermen's tavernas or ship chandlers. In other seasons, the water's edge was a people magnet. In January, it was almost deserted.

We had a good lunch at Pane e Vino. A young oriental gentleman sat at the table next to us. After each course, he took a picture with his cell phone camera. He never looked at us, and scarcely looked around at the restaurant. I wondered how he would describe the food to his friends back home. The three of us were their entire luncheon trade. It must be hard, especially on a restaurant, when business falls to a trickle.

Over the years, we have been to many lavish restaurants. Over time, they seem more theater and less about nourishment. We prefer bistros to haute cuisine. Comfort food, cooked to perfection, generates the most lasting memories. The last time we had been at Pane e Vino, they graciously squeezed us in, even though 80% of the restaurant was filled with a wedding party. We remembered their kindness, and the good food.

We meandered back to the train station. All the stores enroute were closed for their long afternoon break. Under a reduced winter schedule, the next train was more than two hours later. A bewildered Aussie, crew on a yacht, was trying to figure out how to get to Nice to meet a friend. The ticket offices were closed too. The automatic ticket dispensers weren't working, and there were no trains west for a couple of hours too. We told him about the creaky alternative, a couple of buses to the border. As we left, he was still shaking his head in disbelief.

Rather than wait for the train, back in the center of town we boarded the Andora bus. The coastal road is lovely, and we were back in Alassio an hour before the next train would leave Oneglia.

On the walk from the Alassio bus stop, we crossed one of our favorite local streets: Via Diaz. For years, we remembered this short and broad street ramping down to the waterfront for its old sea pines and palm trees. An arch of trees came together almost like a mini Cours Mirabeau in Aix-en-Provence. In summer, it would be a cool and inviting place. This day, the scene was quite different. All of the trees had been sawed off about three feet from the ground. At Le Terrazze, Egidio was at the front desk. We asked about the trees and got a surprisingly sad answer.

The previous year, an 18-year-old boy was riding down the main street on his motor bike on the way to see friends. It was near the end of his two-week vacation. His parents lived in town, but were originally from Modena many hours away. He was living away, at work or school. The family owned a nice little bar on the main street in Alassio. Suddenly, without warning, a hundred-year-old tree cracked and crashed, and the young man was killed almost instantly.

There were no outside signs of tree problems, but the thin roots were severely diseased. The mayor commenced an investigation, and was advised that other trees might be compromised. It would be nearly impossible to determine which were sound. Despite some opposition from local citizens, he ordered all the suspect trees cut down and replaced with young and healthy palms. In responding to critics, he pointed out that he was not responsible for the tragedy. But if there were another injury or fatality, he would be at fault.

Our branch of the Italian Post Office is a monument to inefficiency. On three days, we walked in and were discouraged by long and barely moving lines. On the last time, ten minutes in the queue, we gave up again, as two people had ahead of us.

Part of the problem is mixing banking and postal services; also, the sheer somnolence of the people behind the windows.

They are always courteous. But in a world where postal services are becoming less relevant, there was no sign of heightened customer service. It seemed the same in local banks; pleasant slow-moving people in a bit of a fog. Many of the tellers have been replaced by ATMs. Could the lack of energy be fed by the fact that it is almost impossible to be fired?

Unpleasant weather continued; a stark contrast from the prior January. Was this a more typical winter? I bought a few pieces of fruit and frozen ravioli with pesto from a little store. With a salad it made a simple, economical meal. Lousy weather didn't encourage extravagance.

On Friday morning, in gusts of wind and rain, we steered down the streets like sailboats tacking in the wind. Then we stopped at our favorite newsstand for the *IHT*. We joined the regulars at Rudy's, finding a table close to the glass front. By now, we felt no guilt or impatience whiling away an hour and a half.

A group of older women, Scandinavian, Dutch, German, Swiss, Irish and English, swell and contract in late morning around a communal table. We heard snippets of conversation in Italian, with a few words of English thrown in. These widows or wives started in Alassio as tourists and became permanent residents after marrying Italian lifeguards or men they met on vacation. They smile and nod hellos, and share a few pleasantries. They have known each other for decades, and their "stammtisch" adds a warm spirit to the café. Rudy and his crew know their regular drinks by heart. The few husbands left never appear, although from time to time a grandchild or two is in tow.

One of the ladies is from Sweden, and I have previously mentioned her connection with Bagni Selin. Two of the cheeriest ladies are from Brighton, England and Holland. Over time, they have stopped us for a brief chat on the street or to share a few words about our home or theirs. They spend most of the year in Alassio, but still have families and ties to their homelands. We don't know all the ladies. Over time, we have met more and more of them and they greet us warmly. We hear bits of the conversation without wishing to eavesdrop. After an hour or two, they depart, each going their separate ways.

By now, you know that we often build our days around dining. It would be masochistic to venture far on a windy and rainy day. There was one new (to us) place and chef that we wanted to try. Walking across town to sample the food at the Hotel Lamberti seemed reasonable-until we stepped into the windy street. We pressed on, umbrellas turning inside out a few times. The Tramontana was blowing, but at least there was little rain.

At the fashionable men's store where I had bought the replacement gloves, we had chatted with the dapper salesman. We told him how much we loved the town, and how we had sought out many fine meals in Liguria. He asked whether we had tried the Lamberti, declaring it the best place in Alassio.

Cold and disheveled, we arrived at the Lamberti at noon. The kitchen staff sat at a table having completed their meal, protective of their break time. We stood hesitantly at the door. The entrance to the restaurant was through a terrace. Perhaps the hotel lobby was where we should inquire. I saw a glass door past the staff table. Unhappy about walking past this group, I took a few tentative steps down a closer staircase, not really sure where it led. Someone called a female name twice. Shortly, a very young lady approached us. We asked what time lunch was served. "12:30". We quickly made a reservation.

With a half hour to kill, it was back into the unpleasant weather and a search for a café. Two blocks further, on a corner, was Café San Francisco. The inside was lit with a nice golden glow. It was a quintessential café, small, warm, friendly and family run. On one side was a mini-pasticceria with plenty of temptations in the case. At many tables, a local newspaper was left for the entertainment of patrons. Behind various marble counters, mother, father and son stood separately, quietly, on duty.

A good cup of espresso helped the half hour disappear. I've often wished we could have just one of these real cafes back home. Long hours and minimal profits must make it a tough business. In France and Italy, and elsewhere in Europe, they are neighborhood living rooms. On somewhat neutral territory, there is news, gossip and shared silence.

340

When we returned, the Lamberti staff was ready. The dining room was decorated in understated white, beige and gray. It was smart and elegant, albeit not very original or memorable. The best part, wall to ceiling glass doors opened to a garden patio that should be delightful in a different season. First in German, and then English, our waiter asked in what language would we like our menus. I told him, like music, it sounded better in Italian, and he smiled.

This was a serious upscale restaurant in a modest hotel. The menu and wine list reflected care, ambition, and a higher price point. The proof was in the tasting. The first good omen was the quality of the focaccia and nut bread. We chose appetizers and main courses, reluctantly skipping the pasta course. A four-course meal was too much at this stage in life.

The antipasti were beautiful and delicious, showcasing local crustaceans. The main courses and desserts were equally accomplished. Artistic plates, plating, and especially intense local flavors and ingredients prevailed. The wine list was a mini library of savvy Italian choices. It was a great way to spend a winter afternoon.

Our host, Bruno has spent much of his life in Alassio, but he and his family have also lived in Colombia, and his wife is from Sardinia. Digging deeper, we often find ties broken or unbroken with other places. We are glad they have graced our adopted town with such a classy restaurant.

After lunch, it was still miserable outside. We pressed home through wind and rain. By early evening, the wind was gone and the rain stopped. An evening passegiata began, decimated by the day's bad weather. Our first week was drawing to a close.

On a cold and drizzly Saturday, the weekly turnover at Le Terrazze was in process. With families moving in and out, each week was a slightly different mosaic.

With piles of luggage in the lobby, people reluctantly departed into the rain. At the newsstand, along with the paper, we bought bus tickets for Albenga. Perhaps the weather would improve.

We made another try at the post office. The line was long, but moving. We posted a birthday card to a friend and bought enough stamps to last for the trip. For decades, we have sent postcards to friends, especially a few young children. We hoped it would make them want to travel when they grew up. It seems to be working.

In the wee small hours of Sunday morning, it was suddenly very cold. The heat and electricity had gone off. It was a first in all of our years in Alassio. Outside, the street lamps were on. With my wife's small flashlight, I made a bathroom run. I left the light switch in the restroom on, and hours later the electricity returned. We pulled our winter coats off the coat rack and added them as temporary extra blankets. No one would clean the room on Sunday. Falling back to sleep we woke a little before 9, two hours past our usual schedule.

By mid-morning, we took a short walk. Near the foot of Via Veneto, there is a tiny park with a statue of a fishing boat and a few intrepid fishermen hauling it out of the sea. It's a memorial to a perilous profession, especially those lost at sea. At the back of the park are three benches horseshoed around a table. A plaque indicates an area reserved for the convenience of old fishermen. Rarely have we seen such gatherings. But this Sunday morning, six or seven elderly men sat or stood near the bench engaged in quiet conversation. The sign and the adjacent modest restaurant have the Ligurian phrase: U Recantu. "The corner" in Ligurian dialect, is a place for recalling and recounting.

By Monday, January 11, we were itching to go further afield. We bought train tickets to Bordighera. Closer to the French border it was warmer and the entire sky was blue. Monday mornings are sleepy in commercial districts everywhere in Italy. Stores are often closed, the proprietors and staff partially making up for having worked over the weekend. We walked half the length of that pretty town seeing only a handful of people.

An attractive street leads up to the residential hills. Via Romana, parallel to the sea, and three or four blocks north, is full of old mansions and Victorian hotels, some long closed. They evoke Bordighera's time as a favored resort of the British and other foreigners. Monet painted from vantage points along this street. The local tourist office had put up signs with reproductions of the paintings, right where the artist took inspiration. The views and paintings are still in synch.

From the late 1800s into the 1930s, the town was very fashionable. The present is more precarious. In 2011 or 12, the Mayor was removed for Mafia ties and dodgy public contracts. Wealthy Russians have recently helped the local real estate market. The sources of their money are often obscure.

On this day, the town looked weary. There were a few restoration projects and some new condos, but all the building sites moved at a snail's pace or were quiet. Of course, many little resort towns hibernate out of season. Add warmth to the sunshine and it will come back to life.

We walked further towards the hills. Many lovely houses looked empty or shuttered. Then, we returned to the strand, continuing along the shoreline promenade nearly to the end of the town. It's a pretty place, and even in winter you can have a very fine meal at Ristorante Amarea jutting onto the beach. An eastbound train took us home.

In ten days, we hadn't revisited Laigueglia. The two-mile-long water promenade to the fishing village is ideal for a 40 to 50-minute stroll. The next day we waded through early morning crowds in the budello, stopping for a Cappucino to fortify us for the trip. In a light misty rain, we sat outside under the eaves at Café Barusso sipping and browsing through the newspaper.

Resuming the walk, there were two obstacles. The street was torn up for several blocks. There was a catwalk path around the construction site. Past the work area, dozens of pensioners were out for their walks, at a considerably slower pace. Every twenty or thirty feet, some stopped abruptly to talk, to catch their breath or just inexplicably. Perhaps, in another 10-20 years we would understand. Most were in their seventies, eighties and beyond. The collection of canes, fur coats, wool hats and balaclavas would easily have restocked several of the town's stores.

Beyond the hotels, the strollers thinned out. We increased our pace, enjoying the cool air and clearing sky. Laigueglia, in mid-January was even more deserted than Alassio. We crossed through the whole length of the town's budello without seeing a single person on the street. Most shops and restaurants on this inner street were both modest and of little interest.

One place caught our eye, Le Canard, a ristorante with a French name. An outside blackboard menu listed traditional Ligurian dishes. Like a diner in a Hopper painting, this was a place of some modest warmth. We took another turn along the waterfront. Then past several Venetian style piazzas that add so much to the town's charm. At night, with lantern street lights, it is reminiscent of that distant city.

We circled back to Le Canard. With the door wide open, the small red and white checkerboard tablecloth covered tables were beckoning. As the first customers, our waiter let us choose any table. Tino and Marco are gracious hosts in this family run trattoria. In twenty minutes, there were a dozen diners, both locals and a few Italian tourists. The rustic décor included little wooden plaques of 1950s/60s American automobiles and motorcycles against a cheery tomato red painted and partially exposed stone wall. In many nooks and crannies there were cases or half a dozen bottles of good Italian wine from various regions.

More importantly, the food was splendid. Calameretti, gently grilled and liberally coated with balsamic vinegar, was sublime. My wife's pork filet got equal praise. Both were served with a nice side of grilled vegetables. A bottle of fruity red Nero d'Avola from Sicily added zest. There was only room for a fine cup of espresso. In a town with many competent but uninspired eateries, this one raised the bar.

After lunch, the sky turned unfriendly, with increasing rain. In a bar at the end of the budello, we bought bus tickets back to Alassio. A long walk back would mean getting soaked. We huddled in a minimalist plexiglass bus shelter. Fortunately, the next bus arrived in ten minutes. A five minute ride brought us within four blocks of home.

By evening, the rain subsided. I made a short run for fresh cookies from Bar Impero and some strawberries and pears from the little fruit and vegetable market, Pantagruel. Their little wicker baskets are barely the size of a sheet of paper. With most purchases being a few Euros, I wondered how they make ends meet. In addition to our simple greetings in Italian, the young coal black haired lady store owner gave me change with a "thank you very much!" Repeat customers are appreciated.

Wednesday's weather report and reality were again unpleasant. But our concerns were dwarfed by the unfolding tragedy in Haiti. They sustained its worst earthquake since the 1770s. Television news could only hint at the devastation. I have a deep affection for that country from my Navy days. I was not surprised to see a short, calm and urgent request for help on my laptop. It was from Ophelia Dahl of Partners in Health. Paul Farmer's exemplary relief agency started its world-wide work in that country of epic misfortunes. The scope of the tragedy and the humanitarian response will be with us for decades. With a few clicks, we made a modest contribution.

In light drizzle, we went about routine chores, a trip to the laundromat, the beauty and barber shops, the bank and supermarket, each stop a small contribution to the local economy and a brief contact with town's people. Then back to our spartan but comfortable apartment.

Many years ago, on a Naval Reserve assignment, I led a small group of officers boarding a foreign cargo ship visiting Boston. Of Italian registry, it was a ship that might be protected by NATO's "Naval Control of Shipping" in wartime. Our task was to confirm that the ship had the appropriate communication manuals to respond to coded messages.

The Captain greeted us courteously. After completing our brief business, I told him how much I enjoyed the Italian Riviera ever since my first ship visited La Spezia and Rapallo. He nodded with approval and said his home was in Nervi. I made a mental note as to where this sophisticated seafarer, who had visited most of the world, chose to live.

Thursday morning, we set the alarm early. We told the station ticket agent we were going to Nervi. A local train sitting in the station and leaving momentarily would go there without changing trains. We bought tickets, and rushed up to the platform and climbed aboard. It was 45 minutes late on its schedule, but on time for us.

The elderly train was too warm. The windows were dirty and steamed. Approaching and leaving stations, it jerked, as if the breaks were sticking, or someone inexperienced was changing gears. The first time it did this, it knocked an elderly and plainly dressed lady onto the floor. Several of us passengers rushed to help her up after she signaled she wasn't seriously hurt. Later, we saw her wandering around the train, clueless about the continuing risk. She had other problems.

Approaching Genoa, we were on a track closer to the waterfront than the faster trains we usually take. There were closer views of passenger ships, ferries and cargo vessels in the busy harbor. The train nearly emptied at Principe station. After a few minutes, we trundled on slowly east.

Leaving the train station in Nervi, we walked away from the sea and upward on a pretty tree lined and hilly street. On both sides, behind tall wrought iron fences, large villas sat among dense tropical gardens. Some were beautifully maintained. Unfortunately, others were neglected. Half way up the street, on the left, was a modern garden style hotel.

The first intersection is one of two roughly parallel narrow one-way streets through town. They curve gently with the contours of the land and sea. The sidewalks are an afterthought, perhaps two feet wide at best, scarce protection from nearly constant traffic. On both sides of the street were small smart shops catering to the local community: gastronomias, meat markets, cafes, tobacconists, dress shops, banks and a few local restaurants. The streets and buildings predate motor vehicles.

Further up the hill are larger houses, small apartment buildings, and a church, all well over a century old. Some 80-100 years ago Nervi was a fashionable resort. It is still an upscale suburb.

After lunch at a refurbished old trattoria, we took another stroll down the main shopping street. Then we turned back to the train station. It was too cold and damp for a walk through the pretty park honoring Garibaldi's Brazilian wife and comrade in arms, Anita, or on the sea cliff promenade. No surprise, the train station ticket window was closed and would remain so for several hours. The self serve ticket machine wasn't working. Fortunately, at the little station newsstand, we could buy regionale tickets, but only as far as Savona. Well, that was two-thirds of the way home.

On the local line, Nervi feeds into the "subterranean" part of the main train station in Genova. The regionale made every single stop along the way to Savona. The local trains cost roughly 60% of the Intercities, significant to those on a fixed income or of modest means. At many minor stations, it was the only choice.

A tedious hour and a half later we were in Savona, a dreary and bland modern station. We bought tickets on the next Intercity express and arrived back in Alassio just before 6 PM. It was a long trip for a good meal and a glimpse of another town, but that is often our theme. There was no need for dinner.

Friday morning brought better weather. We kept the alarm clock set for 6:45 AM, allowing time for another long train trip. This time it was to Genova proper, and Brignole Station in the newer part of town. Straight and broad avenues, lined with trees and once elegant four to eight story apartment and office buildings, many with art deco flourishes parade down to the waterfront. They were built in the late nineteenth and early twentieth centuries when Genova was still wealthy. The quarter is still stylish and successful.

The sun was out, and we appreciated it! But strong winds made it another poor day for a leisurely stroll. It was our first visit to La Perlage, a very fashionable restaurant with a celebrated female chef. Small and cozy, instead of art work, the walls were lined with wine cupboards. There were six tables in the first-floor dining room, and another ten on the floor above. Our waiter and the maitre'd co-owner kept things moving at a leisurely but professional pace.

Everything that came out of the kitchen looked and tasted exemplary. In Genoa, almost all restaurants, both fine and modest, are unadorned. People don't flaunt wealth here. The clients, though, were of the expense account or monied variety. They dressed smartly, with the beautiful fabrics and tailoring that put Northern Italy at the pinnacle of the fashion industry.

After lunch, we braved the wind in a longer walk. A stroll along Via XX September to the Fieri, the monumental square below the opera house, has always been a favorite. The covered arcades afford welcome shelter from rain and snow. We browsed through the century old Galleria above the Opera House and then walked back down the fanciest shopping street in town, Via Roma.

The Galleria, a Victorian glass pavilion, has a rare collection of old one of a kind stores. It is like being inside a giant and elaborate glass paperweight. There are specialized antique dealers, exquisite leather goods emporia, high end jewelry shops and a few cafes. In Italy, the custom is not to browse in shops. If you go in, it is because you need something. The proprietor will help you find it. Since we didn't need anything, we were content to window shop. As the sun descended, cold set in. Instead of walking through the shadowy old sailors' quarter to Principe, we took the underground Metro.

At the main train station there was a long line at the biglietera. I bought two second class tickets on the next train, an intercity. It was scheduled to depart in 50 minutes and was already ten minutes late. Waiting for a train in a dreary old station is a chore. You can sit in the musty waiting room among back packers, drifters and the elderly, or stand on the platform, usually in the midst of students, commuters and long-distance travelers. There are a few benches and sometimes a tiny glassed in mini-waiting room. The platform swarms with smokers. Once on the train, it was an hour and a half run to Alassio. It was warmer there, and we were home.

Saturday morning, we woke to a Campari and Orange colored sun popping out of the sea. The sky was extremely clear. For the first time in a week it was warm enough to sit outside on the edge of the beach under an isinglass and metal tent drinking cappuccino.

Lovely days were all the more appreciated, such as the next Monday. Objective: Savona, a town trying to be tourist friendly but not quite having its act together. A very modern deep-water terminal at the foot of downtown, mostly for Costa Lines, was an attractive addition. It resembles a modern airport terminal with plenty of steel and glass and a few potted plants. Slowly, the shops along the ancient arcaded streets in the center have been spruced up in hopes of more commercial activity.

Savona's large and generic train station was a few blocks from any place you would want to be. In all directions, it was surrounded by stark Lego brick gray apartment buildings and extensive parking lots. This was Italy at its ugliest. Beyond a small park was an older and more harmonious cityscape: venerable churches, theaters, fountains, all a little worn. Savona was not, and is never likely to be a destination city. But as the seat of provincial government, it has solidity if not style.

We had a lead on a new restaurant: Suavis. The small, designer elegant and austere bistro was indeed excellent. There were no tourists in sight, just three tables of locals, business types. Our food centric trips bring us close to those who are passionate about their craft. Just as professional musicians need an appreciative audience, culinary artisans crave recognition.

Wednesday morning's sky kept getting darker. After morning coffees, we meant to do a good turn. But it morphed into inadvertent criminal behavior. The previous fall, with our Rhode Island friends, we stopped one evening in a little store overflowing with tourist wares. Anything you could imagine in terms of inexpensive souvenirs was there: plaques, plates, tee-shirts, refrigerator magnets, decals, postcards, inexpensive statuary.

We had passed this shop dozens of times, rarely taking more than a cursory look. Our friends wanted some knick-knacks for grandchildren. The real charm of the shop was not in the merchandise, but in the 80 something proprietor.

He was earnestly working well after 8 on that weekday evening. Clearly, the shop was his life's work and perhaps his financial security was precarious. We all bought a few mementos, and we told him we would return in January.

I had walked by the shop several times in the early days of this winter's trip. The elderly gentleman was always behind the counter in an empty shop. There was little inside of interest to us or most locals for that matter. But I wanted to help this fellow who I imagined might be alone in this world.

That morning, there were a few customers in the shop as we walked by. We looked at the outside display cases. Was there anything we might plausibly buy? A few commemorative plates looked mildly interesting. When the shop cleared out, we walked in and said hello to the gentleman. He looked older and frailer than he had just four months before. Or perhaps it was the daytime light. We had a pleasant conversation, but it was unlikely he remembered us from the fall.

I asked him if he was from Alassio. He said he was from Genoa, and had first come here "for business" with his Father in 1934. He reminded us that the postcard pictures were taken by him in the early 1990s, and he had ordered 1,000 cards. He still had some, and I wasn't sure if they had been reordered or were from his original stash.

After some hesitation, we settled on a plate with raised scenes of some of the principal towns of the Riviera Ponente around the outside, and a terrain map of the region in the center. At 16.5 Euros, it was one of the more expensive items in the shop.

He briefly went back into his storeroom and pulled out a cardboard plate box. He put the plate inside, and without asking wrapped the plate in some colorful gift paper. He slowly folded the paper over and finished the wrapping with scotch tape, in what my father-in-law, who had been a butcher, called a "meat-cutter's wrap"

Other people had entered the shop, and we had no need to tie him up. I handed him a fifty Euro note and one and a half Euros in coins to simplify the change. I didn't see a cash register behind the counter, but there must have been one. The proprietor left the large bill on the counter and searched in his wallet. He drew out three tens and a five and handed them to me and thanked us. He put the wrapped piece in a generic plastic bag and handed it to us.

We brushed by two young men in the shop on the way to the door. They looked rough and not typical customers. As I stepped towards the door, one came up to me and asked: "Parla Italiano?" I hesitated a moment and said "Poco". He pulled his wallet out of a side pocket and showed me a badge: "Guardia Finanza". He asked for my name. I said "we were only trying to help the old man." He said, "Yes, but he didn't give you a receipt."

I handed the young man my business card. He looked at it, and handed it back, perhaps taking my name for his report. The proprietor sensed what was happening, and came to the door with a receipt he should have given us. It would prove that the VAT tax had been accounted for. I knew we were, technically, in trouble, but the tax policemen were not interested in making a case against us. As we left, I heard the old gentleman speaking quickly and in a louder voice, clearly making some kind of excuse. They had caught him red handed. I felt very sorry for him. We bought something that we didn't need, largely to help him, and the net result was trouble. How much trouble he was in, I didn't know. In all of his years in Alassio, he wasn't a stranger to the tax people and vice versa. I don't favor not paying taxes, but I hope the penalty was not severe.

He reminded me of our hard-working shoe man from Napoli with a hole in the wall store near our home town in Massachusetts. He had made Ferragamo shoes in the old country and was a true craftsman. His English was broken, but he always made our shoes look as good as new. The repairs were always for cash and there was no receipt. How and when he explained his earnings to the Commonwealth was a mystery. In the old country, many people felt the state was cheating them, and they felt no guilt in not reporting all of their income. With a population of roughly 20% of that of the United States, Italy's bicameral legislature has 945 highly paid representatives. There are at least 75 more at the European Union. A large middle establishment of 20 regional governments and 120 subsets of provincial governments are roundly disliked. They are often seen as a useless and meddling fifth wheel. Of course, all of these dignitaries have large salaries, well compensated staff, expense accounts and hefty pensions. It had been six years since Italian citizens were able to vote for a government. Huge changes were made in closed door sessions. Is there any wonder why voluntary tax compliance is tetchy and erratic?

Gayle was getting her hair done that afternoon. We had limited time. I suggested walking to the Pallasio Ravizza Stadium. We had bought tickets to a traveling opera performance there for the next week. We had never been to the stadium. From Avenue Diaz, we walked inland under the railroad tracks.

The road to the San Bernardo neighborhood ascends immediately. A small section was marked with cross hatching and a solid line, an inexpensive substitute for a sidewalk. Locals were on foot, often with small plastic bags with logos from various shops and supermarkets on the main streets.

Small trucks, mopeds, and motorcycles sped and revved up as they climbed the steep hill. Distinctive houses perched on flat spots on the hills spread back from the sea. The hills were not steep or dramatic, but green and sprouting fruit, olive and shade trees and pocket gardens.

Just before the Palassio, off to the left was an unusual building with an indoor Baci Ball Court, a bar and restaurant. The chalet style building on a slope seemed a refugee from a different country. Passionate players found a way to play year-round. In one of the big windows eight tall trophies were displayed.

The Palassio was a large and boxy modern structure. It was more accustomed to hosting sports events, such as volleyball and basketball tournaments. The opera season in Genoa was truncated in difficult economic times. No events were scheduled before we left. Seeing a traveling company in our adopted home town was a nice consolation prize. It would be interesting to see how and who supported the event. A flyer said the musicians were from the Milan Opera Symphony Orchestra. While not La Scala, we assumed the performance would be of high quality. This being Italy, even in a town without an opera house we also expected a sophisticated audience.

Next to the Palassio was a huge block sized hole in the ground. It had been a football field and might be again someday. Before putting the soccer stadium back in place, a giant underground garage would provide close in parking for indoor and outdoor events. Grand plans moved slowly in the ailing economy.

On Thursday, we were ready to go exploring again. Our destination: Noli. Their train stop is shared with the next town, Spotorno, and is up in the hills. If we chose that route, it would mean a long walk or a cab ride into the center. Instead, we bought tickets to Finale Ligure, a bigger and closer town along the ocean. With a cluster of buses outside that station, one would take us the short distant two villages further down the coast.

Something strange was going on at the bus stop. A small bus had pulled up and discharged half a dozen passengers. Either from that bus, or a small official car parked in front, there were six or seven uniformed men. Some had insignia for ACTS, the Savona Bus Company, and others with SAR, the company covering the territory from Finale to Andora. A few had badges with Polizia and another word on it. All had clip-boards with multicolored forms and Blackberry cell phones.

Some were clearly checking that passengers had properly stamped tickets. Perhaps others were checking on the check-ers. A lady who had gotten off the bus, perhaps of gypsy stock, was in animated discussions with a few of them. They didn't raise their voices, but occasionally she did. At several points she showed them a driver's license sized plastic card with her picture on it. She rambled on, and I couldn't understand much of what she said, but Genoa came up several times. A few moments later, two municipal police came over, and the conversation continued. Our bus came, and the lady was still surrounded by uniformed men. Two got on our bus, checked tickets and got off. I suspect this was not a good day for her.

Our bus darted quickly along some of the most dramatic Ligurian coastline carved out of limestone cliffs. At some points, steep and jagged hillsides loomed over the road, wire mesh precariously checking loose rock. There were a few mini-tunnels too.

The next town was Varigotti, a pretty and mostly unspoiled fisherman's village. Its pastel stone houses along the water's edge were a painter's and photographer's delight and the subject of the region's most iconic postcards. The highway climbed around or through a few more cliffs and then came down a hill into Noli. The area is prone to rock and mudslides and I always breathe easier when we arrive unscathed.

We have visited Noli many times and never tire of its unique atmosphere. It was an independent republic for six hundred years in the Middle Ages. It is still a very proud and distinct community. While there is some tourist-oriented businesses, most of the small stores are for the locals. I stopped at the local tourist office for a map. The lady there didn't know of the restaurant we were looking for, but identified the street on a photocopied map. We thanked her, and proceeded to thread our way through the winding streets. We should have just walked two blocks to the right and parallel to the sea.

We sought the Palazzo Vescovale, the old bishop's palace. It was on a cliff above the coastal road. In a small parking lot along the water, there was a half glass elevator in a silo. It climbed thirty feet. From there, a small private funicular traveled the rest of the way to the Palazzo. There was a sign for the restaurant and small hotel on the side of the elevator shaft, along with a speaker and a call button.

I have previously mentioned this restaurant, but this was our first trip here. We had dined at the chef's old restaurant in an ancient foundry in the hills above Vado Ligure a few towns away and closer to Savona. The palace was much more elegant digs, the previous home for the Bishops of Noli for three or four hundred years. It had been recently converted into a luxurious bed and breakfast with 8 rooms and suites.

Standing in front of the elevator, there was a cheery greeting via the speaker. While the restaurant did not open until 12:30, we were welcome to come up and take a look around. The hotel owner greeted us and led us out on a spectacular veranda overlooking the sea. Two tiers of tables, one outside and one below, under a portico, were open to the sea. Outdoor dining was possible in spring and summer. We were offered an aperitif, and welcomed the chance to sit outside and take in the extraordinary view.

At opening time, a waiter brought us in to one of the dining rooms. Past four or five grand sitting rooms, we were ushered into a lovely small and square space. There were parquet floors, big windows and stone window seats facing the sea. A magnificent chandelier hung from the tall ceiling, perhaps Murano glass. Below it was a small marquetry table with a vase filled with birds of paradise. There were five tables in the room, and a room of similar size, also set as a dining room, was to our right painted in a different pastel shade.

All the tables had beautiful linens, Ginori China and silver. As we looked at menu and wine options, the chef, Giuseppe Ricchebuono, came out in a beautifully starched white uniform and greeted us. He is a gentle and kindly man, perhaps in his fifties who grew up in the area. He has the presence of a fine doctor or musician. He started by saying that he had just seen us at Suavis in Savona a few days before. It was run by family members. We told him that was a delightful meal, and knew this would be too, having enjoyed his cooking at Fornace a year before.

The meal was indeed memorable. Rooted in Ligurian tradition, it transcended age-old recipes. Their Michelin star was deserved. Home made bread, a wide spectrum of wines, and simple but dramatic food satisfied the most demanding palette.

Three business men entered and dined quietly at one corner of our dining room. In the other room, an older couple savored their meal. In the dead of winter, we enjoyed a masterful meal in sparkling sunlight, probably dining better than the prior occupants, the bishops and their entourage. Below, there were only the faintest ripples in the ocean. A few tankers glided west across the vast track of water and intrepid sea gulls darted in wind currents.

I don't feel guilty investing in wonderful meals. A whole chain of people earn their precarious living from these magnificent efforts: farmers, suppliers, chef and the wait staff. On our next visit, we had the same excellent waiter and learned that he and his family were from Tunisia. It was uncertain when he could safely return to see relatives.

We spent nearly three hours in this luxury cocoon. Back on the waterfront promenade, we saw a bus heading west. Missing the bus meant a long wait for another. But we could sit on a comfortable bench and savor the ocean views. At a newsstand we bought bus tickets back to our town. It was a slow ride through a dozen or so towns, but we were not on a schedule. There was people watching and chances to see more of the environs enroute. In a little over an hour, we walked the last several blocks to our apartment.

OOO

26

The Strada Romana, the Red Arrow Trail & Saturday Market

It was a perfect winter day and Friday to boot. With moderate temperature, a full sun and little wind, an ideal time for something long on our "to do" list, a walk along the Roman Road to Albenga. What was left of this ancient highway started behind the tiny Santa Croce Church in the hills between Alassio and Solva.

Benedictine Monks built the primitive little church in the 11ᵗʰ Century. Only the simple stone shell remains. We ducked under the railroad tracks and hiked up the road towards Solva village. The narrow road climbs steeply. It is an area with some of the most beautiful and sequestered villas in Alassio. Even several wider lanes are marked "Strada Privata." Fancy homes hide behind iron fences and twisting walkways. Parking "boxes" are built into stone walls.

Our map suggested a shortcut we never found. It was a strenuous climb until we came to a small sign at a T intersection. To the right was the Strada Panoramica in the direction of the church. The paved road narrowed, nestled in trees and curved gently along the hill contour.

A couple of motor scooters and a few small cars passed us. Two older couples stood in front of the modest chapel. After taking pictures, they walked past us without saying a word, moving in the direction from which we came. Below the church, on the cliff side, was a large parking area for a dozen cars and perhaps a few buses. A seasonal night club, Paradiso, with an open-air bar sat vacant at the farthest point and overlooking the sea. The lot was empty.

Left of the church, on a narrow concrete pole, was a rusted metal sign with an arrow pointing east: "Strada Romana". Alongside it was a rutted small car width trail. It was a dirt road with a liberal covering of crushed uneven gravel. The trail extended for 5.5 kilometers on the ridge line.

Along the trail, there were extraordinary views of the sea below and steep hills above. At some points, the path climbed a little; then fell steeply. The quality of the surface varied, from a decent road to a muddy and narrow foot path. There were no guard rails, and often the drop off was shear. At those points, fortunately, the road was somewhat wider and flat. You could and should stand a few feet back from the abyss. Our progress was gauged by bearings on Gallinara Island, the fist like rock less than a mile off the beach at Albenga. The bishops, who once ruled this region, had their headquarters on this tiny Gibraltar. Now it is uninhabitated, at least by people.

What is left today of the Via Julius Augustus, named after the Roman Emperor who straddled the time of Jesus Christ, is just a hiking trail. Roman centurions, chariots and wagons had plied this highway to and from Gaul. Now, it is maintained, more or less, by a handful of volunteers.

A few times the road completely disappeared. Vague footpaths went off in several directions. At one point, there were signs for a private road superimposed on the one we had come from. At one fork, a small trail "(Lord) Byron George", headed steeply up a hill. Eventually, we found another makeshift sign for the Strada Romana. The path was now scarcely two feet wide. It tracked behind fences, chicken wire, a number of modest houses and a campground.

A few hundred yards on, it was still just one person wide, a dirt track. A little further, it widened and you come upon the first of four ancient and primitive necropoli dating from the first and second century A.D. There were a few historical markers with approximate dates of construction, and many details, all in Italian. The ruins were small and stark.

Further on, there were glass hothouses on a paved road above and inaccessible from our path. A few hand-painted arrows, hiking markers, indicated where to walk. Then the path squeezed between a rock wall and a long high mesh wire fence. A little further, there was a paved road on the other side of the fence, but no access, except in a few places behind padlocked gates.

Gallinara Island was now in front of us, and the city of Albenga was getting closer. Then, we and the hill veered inland. In just a few hundred meters, the path turned again towards the sea. It descended gradually, still two hundred meters above the coastal highway.

There was a sharp left turn inland. In one of the most remote and implausible places we saw the only other person we encountered on this long walk. A middle-aged woman was coming towards us. She walked as if she knew precisely where she was. Other than a quick blink of eye contact, she continued silently past us.

After another twenty minutes on the deeply worn path, we were above the outskirts of Albenga. The main path veered north towards the broad inland agricultural valleys. But one fork turned sharply down towards a paved road below. We saw the roof of a rural Peugeot dealer we knew.

The last one hundred feet or so was an uneven, semi-paved ramp with small and round thick stones in the Risseu mosaic style of Ligurian fishing towns. It is beautiful to look at and hard to walk on. On a small paved road, we turned towards the sea, and soon were on city streets.

We made a beeline to Restaurant Babette. As we walked in, both the waiter and the chef smiled, remembering us from previous visits. After a three-hour walk, we were ready for a serious lunch. Across the street was the bus stop to take us home.

I wouldn't be surprised if the restaurant's name comes from the wonderful movie, *Babette's Feast*, about a sumptuous banquet prepared by a French refugee in an austere and puritanical Danish village. The restaurant has a French ambiance although the cooking is in refined Ligurian style. The chef, Fabio Bonavia, is an intense and caring young man. He never fails to come out, thank and seek approval from his patrons.

*****

On a Saturday morning sun, blue sky must have warmed the hearts of every restaurant and bar owner along the coast. It was January 23, 2010, and the thermometer topped out at 9 degrees C. Our plan was to take the little bus up to Moglio and walk back into town visiting Alassio's Saturday market.

There were only four or five mini-buses a day, barely the size of a rental car shuttle, to the hamlet two-thirds of the way up to the ridge line. We had taken the bus ride a few times, and stood enjoying the hillside views while the bus driver took a short break. We would then get back on the bus and return to the center of town. The road corkscrews up the hills, and was too dangerous to walk. A marked trail angling down was on our tourist map and recommended by friends.

The agreeable driver confirmed that this was the Moglio bus, but directed us back across the street to the official stop. The two ladies on the bus, presumably locals, had unofficial privileges and were in an animated conversation with him. In a few minutes, the bus made a U-Turn and pulled up to the bus stop. Nearly a dozen more people got on, and it was full. Between making change and chatting with almost every passenger, the bus driver read the sports section of the newspaper.

Underway, after two blocks we took a sharp right turn under the train tracks, then another sharp right turn along a stone wall. Sixty meters on there was a narrow passage to the left with a road sign for Testico, Stellanello and Moglio. The narrow road climbed rapidly and sinuously. The bus was in a very low gear. With a dozen blind turns, the driver only blew the horn twice. There were two close calls, with a small truck and a descending car stomping on the breaks, and then awkwardly backing up the hill until there was enough room for the bus to squeeze by. In a few places, there were cars parked along the narrow road. The bus driver knew, within centimeters, how much clearance he had on both sides.

In less than ten minutes, he stopped at the lower end of Moglio, and half the passengers got off. Many had plastic bags of food and goods from the Saturday Alassio market. There was a tiny post office, a few shops, a small parking lot, and narrow alleys wispily heading off in four directions. The bus climbed higher. Houses were wedged above or under the road. We glimpsed the city below us and the hills ever steeper above. The bus continued up hill for a few kilometers. At the second stop, there was a trattoria/café and a space beyond it just wide enough to back the mini-bus into.

We departed with the rest of the passengers, each thanking the driver. Across the road was a tiny wooden sign on a pole. It said: "Alassio" with a red arrow. On the brick wall was a small red cross, the trail marker on our map. Below the name of our town, in smaller letters was the phrase "40 m" for forty minutes. We crossed the street, between traffic. A narrow cement path descended rapidly wedged between two brick walls. In twenty meters, on a far wall, we saw a trail marker and a red curved arrow. We can do this! After another sharp turn, we descended on a steep path of narrow brick stairs and an asphalt ramp. The narrow street was slightly concave. On either side of the brick were U shaped culverts. In a rainstorm, the street would be a cascade; with snow and ice, treacherous.

The path dropped at a 20 to 25-degree angle. On either side were connected stone row houses and duplexes. Flower pots, fences and windows were cared for and the street was clean, except for occasional dog debris. Laundry hung out on clothes lines. Even narrower streets branched off to the right or left.

No one was in sight. We could see the main road a short distance away. But we descended faster and straighter, as if on a stationary escalator. After awhile, the steps ended. We were at the first bus stop.

Diagonally across the street was the village post office. Behind it, on a building wall, were further markers. Now the descent was on a narrow tarmac lane wide enough for a mini car. We reached a small road on a sharp angle. On the far wall red arrows led to a narrow dirt path. In a short time, we had descended many hundreds of feet.

We walked along the backs of houses on a neglected dirt path. There were several angry barking guard dogs, most behind secure fences. Further along the descent we came to a clearing. Across the town road was a small but graceful chapel. We continued on a still narrower descending dirt path. In ten minutes, the town cemetery was below, and off to the left, the roofs and awnings of dozens and dozens of trucks and trailers at the weekly market. Past a tall wall on one side of the cemetery, we emerged into the market.

On our early trips to Alassio, the weekly market was held in a parking lot west of Via Torino. The space was too small. Alassio was already short on parking. Now the market is north of the railroad tracks by the municipal swimming pool and along the walled cemetery. It's three times larger and sprawls beyond its rectangular center. Trailers and stands snake down a few adjacent side streets like stray strands of fettuccine.

At its core, there were many sellers of vegetables, fruit, flowers, three large cheese trucks and several butchers. Spreading out from this edible interior were dozens of vendors selling modest clothing, shoes, fabric, used books, bric-a-brac, and a myriad array of gadgets, knickknacks and costume jewelry. It was an amalgam of a farmer's and a flea market.

From the trail you could see almost the entire temporary market. Close up, each stall nearly touched the next. The assembly of this giant caravan was a marvel of logistics. Alassio, like many smaller European cities and towns, was not large enough to have such a market more than one day a week. It's a traveling show, heading from town to town on a circuit, a tradition stretching back a thousand years. In its midst, it was much like being in a Middle Eastern souk, the stalls as close as links of sausage.

Small trucks and vans replaced the horses and donkeys of old. From a sanitation point of view, that is a great blessing. Some merchants are local, but many come from distant provinces. Some businesses have been carried down in families for generations and others are new. What substituted for cheap cell phones or generic sneakers in ancient times?

Behind the scenes, there must be licenses, taxes, suppliers, some thriving and others surviving. Perhaps, some of these people live in their trailers, toing and froing along the circuit. For the townspeople, visiting the market is a combination of curiosity, necessity, and seeing friends on either side of the counter.

We entered the market around a quarter to twelve. It had been going on for many hours. After some browsing, we bought cheese for ourselves and tulips for Rita. The cheese truck, one with the largest following had stainless steel fold out trays, glassed in cheese displays, and four or five employees willing and able to parlay free samples into big purchases. They had proudly deployed hand-written signs extolling the origins of several dozen goat and cow cheeses from Piemonte, Liguria and beyond. There was a carnival atmosphere, and a sign above noted that they had been in business since the 1940s.

With others in line, and our limited language skills, we pointed at two of the attractive wheels and used sign language to suggest a portion, adding "por due" to confirm there weren't other hungry members of the family waiting at home. With deft flourishes, wedges of cheese were cut, rapped in butcher paper, again in saran wrap, and handed to us with a smile. The prices were lower than the supermarket, and there was better variety.

We chose one of several flower trucks, again with a big following. We zeroed in on the tulips. They were offered in half a dozen cheery shades. Two dozen made a showy bouquet.

At noon, many merchants started to pack up. While the food and flowers were of interest to us, the rest of the market was not. Egidio had said the market was safe, but be careful of your wallets. The press of people, especially along the bric-a-brac and clothing alleys, reminded me of New York subway cars at rush hour. Everyone tolerated some too close contact. We didn't want to be targets for some inevitable pickpockets. We left quickly down a little path under the railroad track and between large and homely apartment complexes.

The cheese and flower stalls were in direct competition with town merchants. The other stalls were not. The traveling market caters to a bargain basement-railroad salvage sector. There might be some haggling, but the prices were so low there wasn't much to haggle about. No one on either side of the aisle had any allusions about quality or longevity of the merchandise. Some vendors had outfitted themselves, a dubious advertisement for their stock. Frankly, there are more tempting and viable displays in the souks of Morocco and Turkey.

Back at Le Terrazze, Rita wasn't in the shop. We entrusted the flowers to Egidio. He seemed pleased and indicated this was not the best day for her as she was at the dentist.

OOO

27

Edging Toward Spring

In Alassio, we usually set our alarm at 7 AM. But sleeping in on a gray Sunday morning is tempting. After a leisurely breakfast, it was too late to go far on public transportation

It had been several years since we had visited Cervo. Cervo reminded us of Eze in France without the attitude. The town was nearly deserted. A few osterias and cafes were open but empty.

Cervo Cathedral, the focal point of the old hill town, can be seen for some distance. The small modern town sits below on the water and is pretty bland. To get to the historical center, you climb up ladder like stone steps; take a long zig zag back road up through the olive groves on the outside of its walls, or a taxi or rare miniature bus up the latter road.

We took the hard way up, stopping from time to time to look at old historic buildings and catch our breath. Near the Cathedral, we bought a few postcards. Just before noon there was a tremendous clamor. The church bells were rung enthusiastically. We have stood close to the Cathedral many times, but this was the first time when the bells were ringing. While some were out of tune, the overall effect was exhilarating.

We wanted to find San Giorgio Restaurant, an old favorite. My wife wasn't interested in any unnecessary additional climbing. I volunteered. We knew it was near the back entrance to town and I set off on foot to find it. After a few wrong turns, I found our destination. I circled back, and we both returned on a residential street to a small courtyard. When I saw their sign, I immediately turned around. But looking closer now, the restaurant was dark. We used the door knocker, as it was 12:30. There was no response. We stood there, somewhat annoyed. There was no sign saying they were closed. The Michelin Guide indicated they would be open. We vented our displeasure to empty space.

While we were still discussing our frustration, a woman was coming down the path above. She stopped, and in a British accent said, "I believe they are closed." We expressed our displeasure with the typical lack of a notice that they were dark, in contradiction to several guide books. As the conversation continued, we learned she and her husband owned a small hotel in Diano Marina. We exchanged restaurant suggestions in neighboring towns. She mentioned there was a restaurant at the other end of the square which was quite friendly, and "not bad". We thanked her for her help, and gave the Bellavista a try.

The consolation prize was a decent lunch in the type of place a local Rotary or Kiwanis Club might use. Our initial reaction was negative. Two ladies stood outside the front door smoking. When we walked towards them they smiled and returned to business mode.

The big and cheery dining room had fine views and walls covered with art work of varying quality, mostly extolling Cervo. A small bookshelf was full of various food and wine guides, most quite old. The menu was computer prepared, each page covered in plastic. Premium bottles of wine, scotch and grappa, unopened, were on various tables. It was a decent and unmemorable meal.

Despite the misfire, Cervo is a stunning example of an old walled village that has made peace with the present without selling its soul.

We thought about our new British acquaintance. Like so many Brits, she and her husband had staked out a place in the sun. We have met many people like her over the years, in several dozen ports from Fethiye, Turkey to Madeira. They relish their new venue but never quite go native. Neither have we.

It was a nice quiet walk down the back road, with views of beautiful countryside. A large hollow between the road and the vertical walls of the old city was filled with silver green olive trees. In ten minutes, we were on the main road and close by a bus stop waiting for an eastward bus.

Monday morning: there was a slight drizzle, gusts of wind and low temperatures completing a dismal picture. Gray and rainy weather along the sea made doing anything outside an ordeal. In the lobby, Egidio was behind the desk. He asked whether we cared to join his family for an upcoming Slow Food dinner at Panama Restaurant in a few days. "Yes, we would be delighted! "We had been to the Slow Food University complex in Piemonte outside Alba, purchased some of their books and read articles on their philosophy reproaching over processed and fast food. It is telling that it was an Italian who not only was appalled at the march of fast food culture, but chose to do something about it. Now, Carlo Petrini's movement has members in 150 countries.

Egidio grew up in the kitchen of his parent's hotel, the Toscana and is a fine cook in his own right. He has been a world traveler and cherishes food and cultural differences, but he is also a Tuscan and Ligurian patriot. I was not surprised that he was sympathetic to the Slow Food people and knew many farmers, wine makers and restauranteurs that participated.

That night, we were in Le Terrazze's lobby shortly after 7, returning from a few errands. Egidio greeted us warmly, and was in a good mood. He had just completed his annual bookkeeping. He looked forward to a home cooked meal. He mentioned a few of the courses on tap, and you could see them appearing in his head like bubbles in a comic strip. He stopped for a moment and said I must share with you some of our wine. I reminded him that we had enjoyed his family wine before. We knew that his older brother had a vineyard in Tuscany. He scribbled a note, and I knew a bottle or two would appear the next day in our room. It would have been unfair to linger at the end of his workday. We wished him a good evening and headed upstairs.

Italian television is almost uniformly awful: lame quiz shows, old movies, dubious talent shows. At least we had access to a dozen international news channels in English. From the Italian news programs, we barely get the gist of what was happening in the country. We have better luck with English translations of their newspapers through Google Translate.

*****

Tuesday started as a much nicer day. By late afternoon cold and wind returned. We had spent the day in a disappointing outing to Arma di Taggia, more of an agricultural than a tourist destination. Back at our apartment, we turned up the heat as we walked in. On our little table, there was a bottle of red wine from our host family's Scansano Tuscan vineyard. An attached note said:"A good glass of wine on a very cold day in Alassio. Mantellassi."

We intended to follow the good doctor's advice. The temperature slipped to freezing. I scooted down the back stairs and made two stops: to the gastronomia for salami, crackers and fruit; then, across the street for a fresh supply of cookies from Bar Impero. There were a few people out in the caruggi, but not the typical passegiata. No one was out unless they had to be.

I walked briefly along the waterfront, and into our lobby. As usual, in early evening, Egidio was at his desk working on some project or just gathering his thoughts. I told him we were about to follow his advice. He smiled. He briefly discussed his father's way of cooking game. Both of us were working up our appetites.

At the same time, in the late sixties, when I was sailing around the Med, Egidio was back from college, working at the Toscana. At some point, the aircraft carrier *Independence* made a week port call in Alassio, anchored well out in the Bay. Egidio was appointed the Captain's interpreter, a job he was eminently qualified for. I knew he had a lot of respect for our Navy. At one point, I asked him whether he had done military service himself. After a short pause, there was a wistful look. As a young college graduate, he had filled out all the papers and was to be commissioned in the Italian Air Force. It would mean a lengthy school in Rome, but then assignments most anywhere in Europe. He smiled and said the Air Force had better pay than the Army and Navy, and better tailored uniforms!

With his multi-lingual skills and degrees, they wanted him as an interpreter.

He was all set to go, but his father was getting elderly. His mother implored what would we do without you at the hotel? He was managing both the hotel and dining room. The Air Force career didn't materialize. I have seen that look and pause with many people remembering a direction they didn't take.

Weather forecasts can be wrong. By early Wednesday afternoon the temperature was into the mid fifties with a nearly cloudless sky. Keeping out of bursts of wind, spring seemed around the corner. The sea still looked like winter, with whitecaps out to the horizon and the water was the gunmetal color of the Atlantic.

The morning was delegated to chores: chiefly a laundromat trip. With full laundry bags, we waddled on the sunny side of the street, with winter coats buttoned up tight. Our timing was good, three or more washers were available. With forty minutes to wait, we crossed the street to Serena Bar for morning cappuccinos.

Like Rudy's, this little neighborhood place had a following. On a side street in the commercial part of town, the tab was cheap. There was no view, only a dreary building across the street sheathed in scaffolding.

The inside was plain and clean, with a handful of tables. Homely walls were softened by half a dozen old photographs of Alassio in discount store black glass frames. One picture showed the casino, long gone, adjacent to the Grand Hotel. Another captured a narrow path beyond today's yacht club. A third represented our current neighborhood, with no boardwalk or road. Another was of a workman in coveralls with a cart and a donkey.

We read the paper and let time pass. A few local customers came in and carried on a rather loud conversation with the young proprietor. Despite their loud voices, I didn't understand much of what was said. Were they hard of hearing, or just enthusiastic? Had they attended too many rock concerts? Then the young proprietor took a cell phone call, and put the speaker on. His voice was as loud as the customers, and I heard an older woman, perhaps his mother on the other end. It sounded like a lunch order.

It was time to tend to our laundry. I got up and paid, and inadvertently said "thank you" rather than "grazie". The owner responded in crisp English, "you are very welcome", and we both smiled. With our coats on, at the door I got back to my rudimentary Italian, and we exchanged arrividercis.

Our laundry was soon done, and transferred to a huge dryer. In another thirty minutes, we folded and squeezed it into our laundry bags. With the sun shining, the day was brightening too.

Every day, sunny or rainy, Egidio is out walking early, often before 7. This is Benjamin's and Polly's time. The Golden Retrievers cavort and run on the beach, and challenge the shallow breaking waves. With no one else to distract him, they are his and he their's.

For someone who has lived here his whole life, Egidio still proudly shows off pictures he has recently taken of sunrises and sunsets, marveling at a particularly lush color palette. When he is away or tied up in their business, Anna takes over dog walking. She is their second-best friend. Much of the day, they lie down, eyes sometimes open, sometimes closed, as close to Egidio as they can get, patiently waiting for their evening walk.

Lula, the cocker spaniel, on the other hand, eschews any form of exercise, other than a brief stroll around the cosmetics shop before ducking behind the counter for a nap. As a young girl, she was content to ride in the front basket of her mistress's bicycle. She has gotten too big for that. Whether it is arthritis or a true calling to be an indoor dog, trip's outside are a matter of nature's necessity or a reluctant amble to a couple of the closest cafes.

The Joan Shop and "Beauty Farm" is Rita's and Anna's domain. There is a wide array of high end perfumes, cosmetics, men's colognes, soaps and sunscreen, attractive and distinctive costume jewelry, some bags and other gift items. In the back there are small rooms for manicures, pedicures, massage and a sauna. Anna, and the very versatile Angela perform many professional services for their customers. Lula may mingle briefly with the clientele, and then returns to her lounging bed and private space behind the counter.

OOO

28

A Local "Aida"

The show was to begin at 9 PM. A late afternoon's nap helped. When we woke up, it was dark. After a light bite in our apartment, we walked to the far side of town. The streets were nearly deserted during dinner time. Close to the sports arena, there were two large charter busses, and a taxi dropping people off. Several cars jockeyed for limited parking spaces.

Inside, it was like being back at our local state college gym. Plastic chairs were placed along the outside of a waiting area. A little snack bar sold sandwiches and soft drinks. A young man wearing dungarees and a leather jacket had a photo badge on his belt. His role was to hold people back from the seating areas until the appointed time. An ambulance crew, in chartreuse reflective gear, stood around. They were bored but on call. A young lady timidly walked around with an armful of programs. After awhile she made a gentle sales pitch in a soft and tentative voice. This was a far cry from the impassioned audiences at La Scala, or even the fashionable San Felice in Genova.

The first time we attended a matinee in Genova, we were fortunate to have third row center seats. We sat and took in the sleek modern theater built to replace the ornate and eminent 1828 musical temple destroyed by bombs and fire in World War II. The theater was filled with people of all ages, from long haired and bearded college students to frail and stoic octogenarians. They radiated an interest and knowledge you rarely experience elsewhere.

Most of the people waiting around in the Alassio arena were dressed for a sports event. Only a few were fashionably attired. I had never before seen a fur coat worn over dungarees, sometimes with stiletto heeled shoes or what I call Italian cowboy boots. It was good to see a few children and young couples, but the bulk of patrons were in their golden or silver years.

At twenty minutes to 9 we were all let in. No need to rummage around for spare change to offer an attendant, everyone had to find their own seats. We came down through bleacher seats, and on the gym floor were two large clusters of folding chairs. Rows of some 15 or so metal folding seats each were about a dozen rows deep. We quickly understood the improvised seating arrangement. One section was A, the other B. Our seats, B36 and B37 were half a dozen rows back and slightly to the left. The seat numbers were scotch taped to the folding chairs. We had an excellent angle view of the temporary stage. The closer in "orchestra seats" were also folding chairs. They were two deep, squeezed in within a few feet of the stage. Someone had thoughtfully placed thin cushions on all the folding chairs. emblazoned with an ad for a local children's furniture store. People continued to leisurely come in and arrange themselves, many of all ages, fidgeting with their cell phones or chatting with their neighbors. Nine o'clock went by, and the front sections were only half filled. At nine fifteen, the lights were raised and then dimmed. The orchestra, many of whom had been tuning up out of sight, straggled in, as did more patrons. With the lights down to movie theater minimum, the first violinist came in and made a final tuning. A few moments later, the very young conductor strode in to center stage.

The traveling orchestra was quite good. A regional chorus did a credible job in backing up a solid company of mostly young professionals. I imagined this was the single or double A League, on their way up or down in the opera world, but ready and willing to bring Verdi to the masses.

There were simple but striking sets, brilliant lighting and costumes that sometimes worked and sometimes looked ridiculous. The show featured multi-media, slides and film, projected on to semi-transparent curtains. Familiar pictures of ancient Egyptian artifacts and tourism style outdoor scenes were sometimes effective, often distracting.

This was our first four act opera in Italian without subtitles. We concentrated on the music, voices and the emotions. We knew the gist of the opera. But watching it in real time, it seemed static. Of course, all of the blood and guts action takes place off stage. Unlike its debut in Cairo in 1871, or its triumphal openings in Milan, Buenos Aires and New York City, the staging and the players were not top tier. It was only a one-night stand in the provinces. Still, Verdi would have approved of bringing his music to the hinterland. The audience was polite and perhaps disoriented, like a group of people in church for the first time in many years and trying to remember the sequence of the service and how they were to behave.

There was polite clapping at the end, even a few bravos and bravas. But this wasn't a passionate opera audience. They left their seats like people leaving a town hall or school board meeting. They had done their duty and could now go home.

As the opera drew to a close, past midnight, we had no concern about our safety walking home. Four or five hundred people headed quietly into the night, many to their cars and buses. The rest of us walked through empty streets. We passed a few bars with a handful of taciturn patrons. On the main street, cars and motorcycles streamed by as if they were on a major highway, which they were. The last four or five blocks were empty, except for two patrons sitting outside a pizza shop puffing on cigarettes, no longer welcome inside.

This was the latest we had ever come back to our apartment. The front door was fully locked. We opened the metal gate in the back and placed our plastic key card in the receptor. After walking up three flights, in record time, we were soon asleep.

29

Savoring the Remainder of a Vacation

Friday was another fine day, once fortified with breakfast and cappuccini. The main event would be the Slow Food dinner as guests of the Mantellassis. After the late opera evening, we took an easy day in Alassio.

On vacation, there are few obligations, but things that should be accomplished. Sending postcards to friends and buying small and unexpected gifts for people who may never see this part of the world were on the agenda. A neighbor's young daughter has nurtured our bonsai plant whenever we are away. Now that she is almost twelve, we looked for a special gift at the Joan Shop, the beauty shop attached to our Residence and owned by the Mantellassi family.

We have to be careful stopping in the store when Rita is around. Often and spontaneously, we will be given gifts rather than allowed to purchase them. They have a wonderful selection of fine cosmetics, soaps, perfumes, costume jewelry and handbags. Anna, their cheerful and savvy daughter gave us a fine suggestion, a pink jewelry box for our young neighbor.

For a little exercise. we walked to the the eastern end of town. There were views of elegant homes in the hills and alleys to the sea. The gelati colored houses of Liguria stay in mind long after we return home. The colors are universal throughout the region. Egidio referred to the subtle soft red as Rosso di Genovese. It is the color of cream of tomato soup. The mustardy gold is called the yellow of Chiavari. Other towns must have the lock on the traditional shades of green and blue.

The length and width of our little town reminds me of the parameters of my neighborhood growing up in Brooklyn. Or what I later felt was my part of Manhattan and New Orleans. Beyond certain distances anywhere you live is another place, with different people, where things are less familiar, less comfortable.

We had a simple lunch at Matteti Osteria. It is a jovial and bustling local venue There were no tourists in sight. With the strapped economic times, its modest prices, generous portions, decent carafe wine and complimentary dessert make it popular. The greying owner walks around with a buttoned-down dark sweater and a warm smile. There is always a little banter with your order.

A plate of well-turned pasta, fresh salad greens, agreeable wine and fried dough with several fillings for dessert, at 30 Euros for two, this was the Ligurian equivalent of the blue plate special. This was a hangout for the working men and women, cash only, plenty of food and easy on the budget.

The special dinner was to commence at 8:30. When we arrived in the lobby, Egidio was already there. In seconds Rita appeared. She handed us both beautiful shopping bags. Inside were birthday presents. I mentioned the prior fall that we would be back for our birthdays, and Egidio dutifully remembered the dates, perhaps from our passports. In the bags were two lovely wool scarves. They would be pressed into service the next day.

Anna soon joined us, and we all set off on the ten-minute stroll along the beach to Panama Restaurant. As usual, Rita led the way by bicycle, easier on her hips and knees than walking. The restaurant had been closed for vacation for several weeks. What a way to end their vacation, with a challenging dinner filling the restaurant with the local gentry!

At the front door, we were greeted warmly by the owner couple and another gentleman. In perfect English he said "Egidio has been telling me about your dining in all of the great restaurants in the region." I responded, "We were always happiest in Alassio, and Panama.was a favorite." This fellow, Mr. Scarpa, was the president of the local Slow Food Society and especially involved in the protection of the Albenga Violet Asparagus, a rare and delightful local varietal.

Standing around, in a brief cocktail party environment, we looked to see if there was anyone we knew. There was Giampiero, the hard working and gentle owner chef of the Sail Inn, the next door competitor which was closed for several months in winter. We saw Massimo, our good friend from Palma, and he introduced us to one of his buddies, the owner of a Laigueglia restaurant.

It was a complete ecosystem, the restauranteurs, wine merchants, food producers, the intense and mildly interested well healed burghers and professionals of the town. We all shared a passion for exemplary food. For some it was also their livelihood; for others, an important part of their identity.

All the tables were assigned. Ours, furthest from the door, and overlooking the water, was a place of honor. Gayle and I sat with our back to the beach, and Mr. Scarpa asked would we not prefer the sea view? We told him we had been privileged to have it many times. Along with the Mantellassis, a woman and her adult daughter at our table were the owners of a small vineyard. Another woman, who was Dutch, had been coming to Alassio on vacation since 1968. She married an Italian from town. She is still here a few years after her husband passed on.

She is part of the circle of lady friends that have their coffee or tea most mornings at Rudy's.

Scarpa was a very suave and handsome retired business-man. I subsequently learned from Egidio, that he had held a high position in a multinational company and had traveled the world extensively and in style. He clearly enjoyed speaking, almost lecturing, savoring and sharing insights into little hidden corners of the food world. There was nothing pretentious about him, just jovial and brimming with enthusiasm; perhaps just a little bit lonely.

We were familiar with the Slow Food Movement, but not the Presidi. These are small groups of producers dedicated to preserving and making viable the production of rare local delicacies. The Italian Guide to the Presidia has 108 pages of these local treasures. While that seems a lot, the Guide notes that 95% of the world is fed through 30 basic foods, but over 300,000 local varieties have already become extinct.

The dinner showcased a rare white bean from the hinterlands, a mountain cheese (Toma di Pecora Bregasca) and a unique garlic from the village of Vessalica. These ingredients were components of dishes, but made them unique. Two traditional seafood dishes and a risotto were presented in a more elegant style. A semifreddo dessert, melding camomille, zabaglione and moscat wine, would have been a crowd pleaser at any upscale restaurant. Panama has always insisted on quality ingredients, but usually a more casual culinary style. This night, they were at the top of their game.

The conversation switched to wine and dogs, two topics all enjoyed. Egidio mentioned how sad their three dogs were when they knew everyone was heading out for the evening without them. Benjamin, the older Golden Retriever, refused to eat, even when tempted with his favorite snack, a piece of Parmesan-Reggiano cheese. All would be forgiven when they got home.

We were surrounded by people who really cared about distinctive and transcendant good food. There was the same spirit and camaraderie you would find amongst a gathering of bird watchers or antique collectors. This was a banquet where what was presented at table really was creative and memorable. All around the dining room, conversations and good wine flowed.

I can't say with certainty that it came from this dinner, but the next year two important collaborations started amongst rival restaurants. There was a special series of theme dinners, celebrating particular ingredients or foods from a different corner of a region. The remarkable thing was that the chef of one fine restaurant was invited to prepare his feast in the kitchen of another. The whole series was advertised with flyers and posters. As Massimo confided, we began to see each other not as enemies, but as friends all needing to encourage our clients to support fine dining.

After the success of that series, the chefs put together several "Street Food Fairs". The expensive restaurant facades might intimidate some people, but who could resist tempting finger food or samples served outside and with a hearty welcome?

The dinner ended just as quickly as it began. Or so it seemed. Everyone got up almost together, exchanged a few pleasant words and headed off into the night. Anna took off in the direction of her new apartment in the hills. Rita said goodnight and got on her bike. With our limited language skills, I asked her if she was ready for the Trofeo di Laigueglia, a famous bicycle race starting in two weeks. She smiled and said: "naturalmente".

Egidio walked back with us. I asked him about the abandoned old hotel next door to their other property, Villa Firenze. At one time, the Ideale Hotel must have been a very nice establishment. There was still a beach section, Bagni Ideale. He said the lady owner lived there for nearly fifty years. She was like a second mother to him. She lost her husband, and then her only son was the center of her world. The son was a good friend of his, although slightly younger.

At one time Egidio had a motorcycle, a Ducati. His friend decided he wanted a motorcycle too, and purchased a B.S.A., British bike. Sadly, after a few months, he was killed in a motor vehicle accident.

Many years later, when the hotel became too much for the widow, she offered to sell it to Egidio. To obtain financing to do the extensive renovation work required, and turn it into a modern residence would have been very costly and not within his means. He thought it would take some twenty years to be profitable. He regrettably and apologetically declined.

There were signs of activity at the derelict hotel. Wealthy out of town doctors had purchased it. They would turn it into apartments to sell and make a lot of money. A small and gracious business would be replaced by an absentee investment. It was one more hidden story in a town rich with memories.

Monday, February 1st, was a beautiful day, and just happened to be my birthday. My wife brought a charming birthday card from home. The picture of a young boy and girl holding hands and walking down a path, with the message: "I'm not letting go…ever". We have been married more than 45 years, and I hope we are granted many more.

It might seem a strange thing to do on your birthday, but our destination was the most important cemetery in Genoa, Staglieno. The statuary and sanctuaries, and the many famous permanent residents, make it the Italian equivalent of Pere La Chaise in Paris. Admired in their day by Mark Twain and Nietzsche, on a sunny morning it was a good place for a walk; especially not burdened with visiting family or friends there. When we left the Genoa Principe Station, the bus to Stagliano was sitting on the corner.

Shortly before noon, we saw a ten-foot-high wall, extending longer than a football field. On the outside were many large stalls selling flowers. Through several arched gates you walk into a lovely wooden and hilly park filled with graves. Thirty or forty minutes gave us some exercise and perspective on this important part of Genovese culture. Many tombs and monuments were grandiose, some graceful or theatric. They ranged from a simple headstone to a three-story tower. Since 1851, this has been a necropolis for the rich, powerful and once famous.

Outside, a different bus brought us to the other train station, Brignoles. Six blocks away, on the corner of a little piazza, was our dining destination, Galletto al Mattoni, a Tuscan pub. Their signature chicken dish and an interesting lamb presentation on the menu were not available. The explanation, it was Monday, and they didn't have all of their provisions for the week. Despite that uncertain start, we came to trust our friendly waiter.

Pasta with bottarga, and pork cutlets with onions were good comfort food. Almost every inch of the restaurant walls was covered with paintings, old menus and memorabilia. It was a cosy neighborhood place, and the eccentric older couple a few tables down, I imagined a retired professor and his long-suffering wife, just added to the milieu.

I told our waiter that I had first visited Genoa in the Navy more than forty years before. He had spent a year in the Italian

Navy stationed in La Maddellena. We exchanged superlatives about Sardegna's beauty.

After the long train trip home, three barking dogs greeted us as we entered Le Terrazze, all friendly barks. Lula was wearing a kerchief with an American flag. She got up on a little black chair, making it easier to be petted and for pride of place over the two golden retrievers on the floor. She knows we are spaniel people. It was a perfect birthday greeting.

The next night we made a foray trying to find a better pizza. The go to place seemed tired, and was closed that evening anyway. Early in the week the town was still. The budello was empty after the shops closed. Even on the waterfront, nearly all the restaurants were dark. After a fruitless walk towards the east of town, looking for something new, we took a few steps up Via Torino towards the main street. My wife was a bit hungry and running out of patience. I mentioned a place near the municipal parking lot. Skeptical, she continued to walk with me.

We ran into Rudy, the café owner, walking with nearly a dozen filled plastic bags. He stopped to regain his balance. We said hello and asked if we could help. He said no, he was fine and would see us in the morning. It would be as beautiful as today-did we see the lovely sunrise? We said yes. He asks if we were heading home. "Le passegiata, then pizza." He nodded approvingly and said good night.

On Via Dante, a modest pizza place I had spied and we had not tried was closed. It was past eight thirty. Empty places might close for the night. We turned left along the municipal parking lot. Standards are lowered as prospects dwindle and hunger sets in.

A small and plain pizzeria was open. One customer sat at a table talking with the restaurant staff. We walked by once, gathered courage and stepped in. A very young man was behind a modestly stocked bar and another stood on our side, talking to the bartender, a waiter. There were eight or nine simple tables in the narrow room, and a small overhead television tuned to a local Italian station.

The waiter pointed to all of the tables, implying we could sit wherever we liked. When we hesitated, he pointed to the table lined up with the television and just behind the other patron.

It was a basic menu. There were roughly a dozen pizza choices between 6 and 9 euros. In Italy, these would be individual sized pies. As we debated our options, the fellow at the other table turned in our direction and asked in Italian if we were German. Emphatically, I said no, American. He seemed elated. He announced we were Americans to the staff. Then, in a laborious mix of Italian and English, mostly Italian, he said he was going to Miami in two days.

I looked at the man and tried to get some sense of him. In his early fifties, he was gaunt and looked like he had lived a hard life. Modestly dressed, perhaps he was a traveling salesman. With some effort, I followed what he said. He was from out of town and stumbled on this place. Did we know it? Was it recommended? While he talked, his pizza arrived, and with a polite excuse, he turned for a moment to sample his dinner. He told the waiter that it was very hot and good.

There was something about this man. He was trying to be the hale fellow well met. He didn't seem a drinker, but he tried to bring us and the restaurant staff into his conversation. It was attention that we didn't particularly want. He commented on the poor quality of the television program. After a few minutes he asked the bartender if the television could be turned off, and turned to us for support.

He seemed curious to know more about us, without trying to pry. We reluctantly said we were from Boston, better understood than our little town. With big gestures, he indicated that he would fly from Milan to Boston, then on to Miami. I asked whether he was on vacation, but it was unclear why he was going there. I asked whether he had family in the Estati Uniti, and for a moment he hesitated and looked sad.

While the language was fragmented, we soon understood. He had lost his wife and children in an automobile accident. I wanted to say something comforting, something appropriate, but we were both hobbled by a language barrier. What could one say? I hope he could see the genuine concern and feeling in our faces and hearts.

Our pizza arrived, and it was good, with a firm light crust, generous anchovies, tomato, oregano, and olives on top of a thick coating of melted cheese. We ordered coca cola, somewhat self consciously because of the American connection, but that night we didn't want wine or beer. No one minded.

The other diner finished his pizza. Then a plate of meat arrived for him. He commented, for our benefit, about the wonderful Piemontese crudo. Then he praised the olive oil. He was obviously lonely. I suspect there had been many lonely nights, and this one would end that way.

We finished our pizza and were ready to go back to our apartment. I asked for our bill, and it came quickly. It was all of 20 Euros for pizza and soda. I left a generous tip, and wished our almost dining partner a buon viaggio.

As we left, he sat silently at his table. Part of me wanted to to say something more and part of me wanted to leave.

As Rudy promised, the next morning was beautiful. We selected an outdoor table in the sun and out of the breeze. Rudy stepped out of the bar carrying a tray of beverages for another table. After setting it down he comes over to us and said: "two pizzas!" and smiled. We savored his gold standard cappuccini.

Later in the day, I tried to complete another item on our checklist, a gift for the Mantellassis. Our friends who own the wine shop, Carpe Diem, had just moved from the budello to a store front on Via Dante across from the famous Muretto, the wall of tiles.

The move was a monumental undertaking with thousands of bottles of wine and hard liquor to be gently transported. Everything in their well stocked store in the old town was fragile and valuable. A few days before, the old store appeared almost empty. Now, the center of gravity had definitely moved to the new one.

The door was open, but the floor was covered with boxes of stock not yet put in their proper place. A workman brought in shelves. I thought a sale might be appreciated. They had been out of business for two weeks. If my Italian was better, I would have asked in a more tactful way. I spoke about a regalo (gift), perhaps old rum and Chateauneuf du Pape.

We located a bottle of 15-year-old Barbancourt Rum from Haiti on a tall shelf, and my dapper silver haired friend waded through the boxes to pull it down. He then went into the cellar, and brought up an unopened wooden case of French wine. He pried it open with a screwdriver. It was a 2007 vintage, which he said was a very good year.

I realized I had caused more trouble than I had wished. I took out my wallet and credit card, and he frowned. Instantly, I realized their phone lines hadn't been hooked up. So, I paid in cash. The proprietor offered to deliver the gift to Le Terrazze, and I filled out a gift card. With my recent experience with the Guardia Finanza, I asked for a receipt. I would have to return the next day. The price for the two bottles was steeper that what I would pay at home. But I knew the business was appreciated, and so would be the gifts.

With just a few nights left of our trip, that evening we returned to the Lamberti for a superb dinner. Three men in suits came in. They were on the expense account trail. They sat down next to us, and their conversation was mostly in English. Whether we wanted to or not, we couldn't help hearing all of it. They were in the charter airplane business and traveled far and wide. One was a native Ligurian, a second from perhaps Milan, and the third an American, a pilot. They enjoyed their food, and were oblivious to the fact that everything they said was understood at the next table. It was an interesting discourse, even if one we would have preferred not to hear. When everyone nearby is speaking a different language, you never know who is listening. We rambled home, content on a chilly and windy night.

Thursday morning was fundamentally grey, with a sliver of blue sky on the horizon. During the night, I turned the corner on a cold that had been around for a couple of days, but at a price. Sleep didn't come until the early hours.

In the morning, Egidio was at the front desk. He asked whether we would join Rita and him for a dinner and a musical concert at the Aida Hotel on Friday night. Certainly! It was our last night in town, but we wouldn't pass on the opportunity to experience more of the local community. He briefly went to the door of the Joan Shop and said something to Rita. She quickly came around the corner with two packages, and handed them to my wife. More birthday presents! This time, for Gayle whose birthday is less than a week after mine. One was three lovely small artificial plants, reminiscent of herbs, in white porcelain dishes. The other bigger bag was a present from Lula, their cocker spaniel. Inside was a large and playful stuffed animal dog to add to our menagerie.

Umberto is the biggest in our family now, white with café-au-lait spots, remarkably pliable and excessively cute. He is a full 21 inches tall when upright, which isn't often. A loose paunch looks good on a stuffed animal. The rest of our animals would have a tighter trip home in their Pierre Deux bag. With Anna's help we christened him with his Italian name that of our favorite hometown shoe repairman from Napoli. The name seemed to fit.

A little before one, we walked down the back stairs and over to Restaurant Palma, our first stop in Alassio some 28 years before. We couldn't come to Alassio without dining at this very special restaurant. Father Silvio greeted us at the front door. Still in a starched white uniform, and with a great smile, his role had become mostly ceremonial. After greeting us and another party, he retreated to his home around the corner.

The reins were firmly with son Massimo. For many years, we had a small ritual of bringing a handful of "Wine Spectator" magazines to Massimo who is passionate and knowledgeable about wines. The magazine is not readily available in Italy, at least in small towns.

The brief anteroom ceremony hadn't changed. We were seated and shown the menu. We opted for the gourmet menu, seven small tasting courses. Rather than show us the wine list, Massimo asked what kind of wine we would like. Since all but one of the courses involved fish, I asked that he propose an interesting white. He suggested a small producer's pinot noir blanc. It was spectacular, a damascene colored wine reminiscent of a superior rose' or a fine german riesling.

Between delectable courses, we exchanged information about the town, his family, the region. His father had a serious medical condition with a blood clot in the fall, but thankfully was now fine. Massimo had difficulties with his knee, so much so that he even suggested that in a year or so he might question whether he could still do the demanding work of "chasing the stars."

He said, perhaps he and his wife would just run a nice wine bar with tapas. That would be a sad day for us and many others who admire his creative and cutting-edge food. But the reality and toll of his demanding and perhaps lonely work is understandable. I hoped it would not soon be the end of a four-generation family business.

While he and we love Alassio, perhaps the town is too provincial to appreciate a destination restaurant. I asked about the Grand Hotel for perhaps the umpteenth time, certainly a source of well-heeled customers. Massimo thought they should have studied hotels in Monte Carlo, not Rimini. "Do they really know what makes a truly grand hotel successful?" He said the "mentality" was still that of pension-rented rooms, not fashionable hotels". For good or bad, he was right.

After another sublime meal, we told Massimo we would be back in September. We told him whether it was a restaurant or a wine bar, we would return. He said the people he has in the kitchen now were good. But they don't understand his vision. After Massimo, there is no one to carry this on.

Like us, Massimo has no children. At present, there is no young and creative apprentice to collaborate with and eventually bring into the chain of succession. Several other young chefs apprenticed there and went on to earn Michelin stars of their own. For us, Palma is part of the very soul of Alassio. On a pinnacle, it transcends the many very good but more typical kitchens.

The Vigliettis have made sacrifices. Their aim has not been to maximize receipts. They create interesting and sometimes ethereal food. Are there enough customers who care? The current difficult economy was not helping.

Back at Le Terrazze's front desk, Dr. Mantellassi started with a profuse thank you for our wine and rum selections. I had visited the Barbancourt estate when I was in Haiti. With the challenges that Haiti has today, I wanted in some small way to support them too.

Friday morning was damp and cold. I brought the suitcases down from on top of the closets. Late morning, we went for a stroll, half hearted window shopping and just a little exercise. We walked by the post office and along a number of streets we would not see again until the fall. We stopped at a plain looking fruit and vegetable market recommended by the Mantellassis. The quiet young man lit up like a Christmas tree when my wife mentioned that it was a recommendation from our hosts. The young man had a good command of English, and we sought his help on salad greens, tomatoes and fruit for the day. There was time for one last roast chicken from our corner rotisseria, a fine lunch for less than the cost of one main course in a modest restaurant.

By late afternoon, the packing was finished, and we awaited an interesting evening. We had walked by the Aida many times. In front of the hotel was a poster indicating the concert was for the Valentine season. Romantic songs would be sung by a tenor and a soprano. The poster recounted the menu and noted that the festivities would start at 7:45.

When we asked what time we should meet in the lobby, Egidio suggested a little before 8. We wondered whether like many things in Italy, the event would start late. To be on the safe side, we were in the lobby at 7:30. Eight o'clock came and went. Some fifteen or twenty minutes later, Egidio came down, apologizing profusely for being late. He had been in Savona on business, and was caught in traffic.

We asked about Rita, and he said she had a sinus infection. It was particularly annoying for her, since the lady owner of the Aida was perhaps her best friend. We told him, he shouldn't feel obligated to go, and we would gladly accept a rain check. But he was insistent.

It was windy, and Egidio suggested walking along the little path in front of the beach. This would protect us from the Tramontana wind coming down from the hills. The Aida is on one side of a narrow street and the Hotel Toscana, which his cousin now owns is on the other. From a distance, the Aida always seemed well cared for, with lovely flower boxes on each little balcony

The lobby was packed with well dressed people, mostly sitting or standing in a stylish lounge area. It was a much smarter crowd than at the traveling opera a few weeks before. Here were the local doctors, lawyers, business owners and some politicians in what looked like their equivalent of a country club. It was a night to see and be seen, cutting a "bella figura". The lobby was decorated with many discrete and attractive opera mementos, programs, posters, all in keeping with the hotel owners' affinity for music.

Never had we sen so many nattily dressed people in Alassio. Superlative hors d'ouevres were being served by smartly dressed waiters. At the buffet, there were lightly fried vegetables, small fried fish, a huge wheel of parmesan cheese with dozens of slivers and chunks pre-cut for ease. At a large slicing machine, Giovanni, one of the owner's sons was cheerfully and theatrically cutting slices of beautiful crudo and bantering with guests.

Giovanni is one of those people who lights up a party with good humor and high spirits. He is somewhat of a man about town with an eye to grand gestures. One is his 1930s vintage chocolate brown Bentley, parked in front of the hotel on special occasions.

A substantial array of enthusiastic guests mingled in anticipation. Waiters maneuvered, serving prosecco. A number of animated conversations were going on. We had stepped into a fashionable club and cocktail party, at least for that evening.

An attractive and stiletto thin woman in a black designer dress came up to Egidio and exchanged a warm greeting. Later, he told us she was a passionate tango dancer and because of it no longer went to the gym for exercise. Alessandra has become our friend too. A single mother, her gentle pre-teen son and daughter were there, quiet, respectful and thoughtful among all the adults.

Mr. Scarpa, of the local slow food club greeted us warmly. I had thought that he had something to do with Panama Restaurant, but learned he was a retired Phillips Electronics executive from Milan. He and his Dutch wife lived in Garlenda, and were friends of the Mantellassis.

He introduced us to another tall and elegant gentleman, a retired Merchant Marine Captain and currently the mayor of Garlenda. I was happy to talk with another mariner. He had commanded huge LNG tankers. Now, he steered people around the best regional golf course.

Half an hour later, we were ushered into the dining room. The lady who arranged the concert introduced the singers, a pianist and a lady violinist. Part of the concert would be at the outset, and the remainder towards the end of dinner.

The young singers were enthusiastic, with perhaps the soprano more talented than the tenor. The songs ranged from popular American show tunes sung in Italian, famous opera arias, and a few older Italian songs in which the audience was invited to sing along. The pianist and the violinist were earnest, and as the evening wore on got better, despite poor acoustics. It had a strange resemblance to someone else's wedding or anniversary party.

The dinner was adequate but uninspired. The wine flowed easily, everyone was in good spirits, and we lost track of time. Dessert consisted of special cookies for the Italian equivalent of Mardi Gras. The owner of the vineyard from which the Piemontese wine had come was asked to say a few words, and answer some questions. He did so, at greater length than most cared to hear.

It was past midnight as we walked back to the Residence. We thanked Egidio for a lovely evening, and he sent us up in the elevator.

No matter how many weeks we spend in Alassio, the last day comes too soon. Early on Saturday morning I went down the back stairs with our final trash for the recycling bins. The caruggi was empty. I ran down the street, and heard something coming up behind me. A seagull, moving like a luge driver, sailed over my left shoulder, barreling down the street as if late for a meeting.

On the way back, I savored the beauty of Via Torino, our favorite short street which ends at the beach. Tiny orange trees, planted by the British for their marmalade, glowed in the early morning light. The street lamps, too, had a yellow- orange aura. The sun was coming up strong and the sky was a radiant Mediterranen blue. A beautiful day would help business in the restaurants, cafes and shops.

The weekend IHT had not arrived at our newsstand. My wide told the owner we would be back in September, and he wished us a buon viaggio. He was a short gruff man but seemed to have a soft spot for my wife. Italian men appreciate beauty. There was no time for cappuccinos at Rudy's, but we both stopped in to say goodbye, and both got hugs. Until September!

We brought our luggage down in two shifts and waited as a few other departing guests finished their accounts. I told Egidio we still wanted to take all the family members to the Lamberti for a nice meal in September, and he immediately responded we must have you to our house so Rita can cook the meat and I the fish.

A big station wagon cab took us up to the train station. We punched our tickets and climbed the old stone stairs. On the platform, we waited in the sun, taking in the beauty of the surrounding hills and old homes nestled in the olive and pine trees. From the platform one can't see the sea, but its presence is palpable. Soon we were on our way back to France and then home.

30

Fall 2010

For weeks we had been getting our house in order. As homeowners, we want to leave things in respectable condition. With windows washed, the house clean and bags packed, we returned to JFK and the only non-stop flight to Nice.

The long in the tooth 767 was a bus in the sky, even if not an Airbus. First light was over western France. Then a glide down through sunny skies and wind dappled sea. Summer was still in full swing in September. We ducked a transportation strike by a couple of days.

The direct bus to the train station was jam packed. Due to construction, we had to change trains in Monaco on the way to Ventigmiglia. Both were full like a New York rush hour subway with day trippers to the Friday market in Ventimiglia and further destinations in Italy. I stood in a pile of luggage, squeezed like a canned sardine. A lady got on who hadn't taken a shower in a long time. Her aroma made me almost wish for the smell of tobacco.

In Ventimiglia, an equally dense throng tried to get on our train heading back to France as we were trying to get off. They needed persuasion to let us leave. After being jammed in a standing position for an hour, I was anxious to get us and our luggage safely off the train without being caught in a stampede. It would take a couple of transits up and down the narrow stairs. When the new mob got on, it would be a one way current. I made some warning noises, and when no one moved, I jumped down towards them holding two bags, about a hundred pounds of luggage and dangerously close to their chests. It was a Charles Bronson moment, and I wish I regretted it. But I didn't. In a confusion of languages, I could tell some middle-aged women disapproved. They did, however, move.

We spent the night in San Remo and were in Alassio just before noon. On the side of the municipal park was a little café and luncheon spot that had been there as long as we remember, but one we had never tried. The café was under the wing of a couple perhaps well into their seventies. Inside was an array of town folk regulars who were there for the long haul.

We took an outside table. With luggage piled next to us, we were temporary homeless people. Panninis and iced coffee, enjoyed in the shade of orange and palm trees, made it more of a picnic. With plenty of time to kill, we followed up with fresh macedonia of fruit. The fruit salads were cut especially for us, and the brandy snifter sized portions were delicious. After a leisurely hour, we walked slowly along the main street, stopping to rest every hundred feet or so with our heavy bags. Making the turn on Via Torino, the gentle slope and view towards the water were exhilarating. At another way station, an outdoor table in the shade at Café San Lorenzo, we killed another hour. Nursing freshly squeezed orange juice, we were yards away from our apartment around the corner. This slow-motion procession would make no sense in the U.S., but here it seemed quite normal. At precisely 4 PM, we ambled the remaining yards to Le Terrazze and received the warmest of welcomes.

In Alassio, we have few obligations. We plan some outings and time to spend in town. Life fills in the rest. At first, the days go slowly. Then they seem to speed up. The remaining time slips like sand in an hour glass. A coffee at Rudy's or a cocktail at Bar Impero can turn into an hour or more of people watching, a little conversation and a lot of reflection. Without fail, soon it is almost time to leave. Four weeks have flown by.

Little by little we learn more about the town and its citizens. It is small enough that almost everyone knows each other. Or they know someone who knows or is related to the person they haven't met. It is big enough to feel the political and economic strains on the region and country.

We invited Anna out to dinner, and had a lovely evening at the Lamberti. Her boy friend, a commercial artist, was invited too, but we were told he was too shy to accept. In subsequent years, he would come and we got to know and appreciate Alberto.

Anna and her girlfriend Alesia, had made a trip to Manhattan, and ostensibly we were getting a debriefing on their adventures in New York. Our interest in what is going on in town is always high, and Anna has the next generation's perspective. People's ambitions, strengths and failings underlie most human endeavors. Whether you call it intelligence or gossip, it is always interesting to know the back stories.

Anna related a rumor that someone wanted to build an 8 or 10 story condo on an underutilized lot a block or so back from the Grand Hotel. Like Paris, Alassio's low skyline is central to its charm. We were all appalled, as was most of the town. Thankfully, it hasn't happened...yet.

Strangely, the then mayor, "Il Professore", decided to reverse the direction of Via Dante, which is parallel to the main street and add bicycle lanes. It was not a popular move, being against the main flow of traffic and what people knew for as far as memories go. Several hundred thousand Euros later, the street was returned to its original pattern, about the time the mayor was deposed.

The Mayor, who started in a collegial and open-minded way, had become authoritarian in his second term. The owner of a very modest one-star hotel, whose letters and phone calls on a zoning dispute went unanswered, saw him on the street and punched him in the face.

Anna would love to spend some time in San Francisco, and we have encouraged her. Her boy friend doesn't have the same passion for travel, and her girl friend has had difficulties getting paid by a company she has worked for in Loano. The company is shaky financially, but if she leaves, she would forfeit priorities under Italian law. It is a difficult situation and one that is depriving Anna of a travel companion.

We really like Anna, a younger, articulate and perhaps under appreciated version of her Mother. Her English is perfect, and we sense she both likes us and the opportunity to speak and sometimes vent frankly and discretely. There must be a nearly universal blind spot. Parents can love their adult children completely without giving them full credit for being adults with their own judgment and sense of direction.

She loves and respects her parents completely, but perhaps feels hurt about the extra support given to her younger brother, set up in a real estate business with considerable help. Now, Giardano is having some success and independence, swanning around a bit, while she is pretty much tied to her Mother's shop. Those words have never been said, but are merely my conjecture. She is part of a generation in limbo. Fast forward, and I am sure she could run the businesses quite well, given the chance.

For the first time, in all these years, we went to the beach, renting chairs and umbrellas. The folks at Bagni Selin were especially kind, and have plenty of repeat customers. This is the "bagni" owned by the "Swedish-American" lady we met at Rudy's. As a widow, she and her daughter and Italian son in law continue providing good cheer and service on the sand. We grilled slightly in the sun; I took a swim in the shallow ocean water, a long walk in the wet sand along the beach followed by a vain attempt to read in the sun's glare.

Our pensione looked all the more solid and secure from the wind-swept beach. I briefly paraded my knobby knees and aging body amidst the oblivious overweight German fraus and equally preoccupied Italian teenagers.

By mid-fall, shops and beach cabanas for sun worshippers hibernate. The little wood changing huts, temporary walls, chairs and umbrellas are taken down and hauled off in miniature trucks to sheds and garages in the hills. People still walk the beaches and swim, but they don't settle in for the day. It was a little like the end of summer camp.

Exceptional places attract artists, whether their medium is paint, music or words. Extraordinary visitors to Alassio have left their imprint. Two memorable painters lived here and have small local museums dedicated to their work.

Carlo Levi was a physician, journalist, politician and writer. He was also a fine painter. Dr. Levi is perhaps best known for his account of exile during World War II. He describes his experiences in the remote reaches of Basilicata, especially the village of Aliano, in the novel "*Christ Stopped at Eboli*". While primarily associated with Turin, Levi spent some of his childhood in Alassio, and returned later in life. There are 22 of his paintings in the Palazzo Morteo, a lovely old building in the eastern quarter of town. Some depict people and places in Alassio.

The Irish artist, Richard Whateley West, lived in Alassio during the 1890s and passed away in 1905. There are 76 of his beautiful landscapes in the cramped and makeshift venue of the old English Lending Library. The building is on the main street, Via Hanbury. The paintings are an exceptional gift to the town from his friends and his daughter. They depict a much simpler time. It's a pity that they are so precariously displayed, many on makeshift easels.

The popular local artist Mario Berrino passed way in 2011 at 91. He conceived and implemented the Muretto. The wall of tiles, across the road from his family owned Café Roma. It has become a symbol of the town. The art gallery continues around the corner and close by Restaurant Palma. Many of his paintings are large and filled with primary colors and a deep affection for the local seafront.

Image Gallery in Alassio has one of the finest collections of Art Deco posters anywhere in the world. Beautiful prints, many with travel and fashion themes, have been lovingly collected. A picture of the Alassio Grand Hotel in its heyday, a moonlit night, a man in a tuxedo and a beautiful woman in an elegant dress, with a band and the beach as background captures the town at the height of its glory.

While not an artist in the traditional sense, Sir Thomas Hanbury, along with his brother Daniel, recognized the beauty of the natural world. Sir Thomas' land purchases around Alassio helped bring the railroad to town in the 1870s. Alassio's most exclusive little hotel, Villa della Pergola, was once Hanbury property. The house and 22,000 square meters of vibrant gardens are a joyous tribute to its setting. Even if you are not a guest of the hotel, from time to time their gardens are open for limited tours.

The better known Hanbury Gardens, just east of Ventimiglia are a unique, sometimes vertical, botanical preserve now under the care of the University of Genoa. It is also the final resting place of Sir Thomas and Lady Dorothy Hanbury.

In a recent book about the English and foreign visitors and residents in Alassio, I stumbled on the discovery that Andrew Dickson White spent a few winters in Alassio writing his memoirs. The educator and diplomat was the first President of my Alma Mater, Cornell University. I tracked down a copy of those memoirs. His references to Alassio are brief, complimentary, and a bit dull. They don't reveal much about his time there. Perhaps he was preoccupied by more monumental events in his life. About that time, there was a cholera outbreak on the very young school's campus. It dictated an urgent trip back to New York State.

The important English composer, Sir Edward Elgar, spent a winter with his family in Alassio in 1903-04. During that period, he wrote the lovely tone poem and concert overture: "In the South (Alassio)".

In all the years we have been coming here, we haven't taken the plunge and made it a permanent home. Perhaps we will always be outsiders, but certainly sympathetic ones. We haven't gone native. We should take an intense language course, so we can carry on or listen to a full conversation in Italian. But we don't. Still, we feel that we are more than tourists. Inexorably, it seems more and more like home, and harder to leave. But we do. Then think about our return.

The last Friday of this trip came quickly. We packed and wrote the final postcards. We said goodbyes to a number of our favorite merchants. Knowing we would be back in three months was some comfort.

We had one last dinner with the Mantellassis' and a few of their friends on our last Friday night, a mushroom themed dinner at a local restaurant. What we lost in language translation was made up in good will, spirit and humor. Alessandra would love to go on a shopping trip to New York. Anna has gotten Alberto, her boyfriend, to agree on a weekend trip to Verona. It's a start. I encourage Egidio to take Rita on a little holiday before their winter projects for upkeep of their hotels. We both think and talk wistfully about Marrakech and Mallorca.

Each time, at table, we learn a few more homely facts. Benjamin, the senior golden retriever, has a weakness for small chunks of Parmigiano Reggiano, as long as it isn't too old and strong. Anna has 48 stuffed animals, at last count (to our 20). Pierrot, a longstanding modest ristorante and pizzeria next door, closed after the tax authorities figured out they were grossly underreporting.

Egidio and Anna are taking Russian lessons. With their traditional markets flat or diminishing, they feel the hotels, stores and restaurants in town muct be more welcoming to guests from a place that might fill some of the gap.

On Saturday morning, we said our good-byes. Back in Nice for two nights before heading home, we celebrated with a Saturday night dinner at L'Ane Rouge, perhaps Nice's most venerable restaurant. We sat outside, despite the October cool air, right along the old inner harbor. The restaurant had made one of those informal patioes that impinge on the sidewalk.

I thought of how I walked this area as a poor Ensign some 41 years ago. I didn't know then I would return frequently with the love of my life. It has all turned out quite well. This little corner of the world still excites.

OOO

31

Closer to Home

We are usually at arms length away from home, nearly oblivious to the strange machinations of Italian politics. They seem even more ineffective than our own. Italy is so much a family-oriented country and we have no family there. We have little family at home either. So, our friendships are especially cherished. In a foreign culture they can't be rushed.

In our most recent fall trips, our bonds to Alassio deepened. Resort towns are inherently transient and, on some levels, interchangeable. Those returning serially to the same one are drawn by something satisfying and timeless, even as the world changes around us. Of course, these places are not impervious to change themselves. It is like those summer vacations you ached for in school. Of course, there is something artificial, somewhat ideal, about a resort. Can or should it be taken seriously?

In September 2011 the weather on the Italian coast was nearly perfect. Long walks and time spent in outdoor cafes were a daily routine. There were posters about an upcoming fashion show on the beach. Looking closer we saw that the Joan Shop and Rita were involved. We knew she was active in the Women's Business Association and charitable organization, Alassio Donna. We had seen her creative touches in the shop and the two residences. We knew this event was carefully planned and would be executed with style. Most of the upscale shops in town were listed as participants. We were pleased when Egidio said we were invited to attend. It was on a Friday afternoon in several weeks.

Our pattern continued of several day trips out of town and a day or so closer to our apartment. When we were in town, we would often visit the Joan Shop. Anna and Angela do lovely manicures, something my wife enjoys on vacation. There were soaps, cosmetics and costume jewelry to buy, often as gifts. It was a chance to play with Lula, the Cocker Spaniel and/ or have a simple visit with Rita, still restricted by mutual language barriers.

Almost every day Anna or Rita kept reminding us of the show, wanting to be sure we planned on attending. From our apartment, we saw the outdoor preparations. By October 1st, the beach concessions mostly complied with the town law, taking down their changing cabanas. Most of the umbrellas and chairs were stowed, then hauled away in tiny three-wheel trucks. Bagni Salin had volunteered to host the show, they were allowed to keep some of the cabanas open a little longer in compensation for the disruption..

An L shaped wooden runway was placed on the beach. Lights and speakers were hoisted on poles, and several hundred folding chairs were put on the sand around the runway. Our only experience with fashion shows was from newspapers and an occasional television film clip. We assumed people coming to such a show would think and dress stylishly, so we tried to blend in, Gayle wore a pretty lemon lime full dress, and I put on an Italian sports shirt bought in Alassio and dress slacks. About a half an hour before the festivities began, we gingerly walked out on the sand. Egidio, camera in hand was standing in the second row. He smiled, and motioned us to some seats just behind him.

Soon most of the beach seats were filled with a wide variety of folks: elderly women with fur coats; young mothers with several children on a short leash; young men straining to see the lovely and strutting big city models. Photographers, amateur and professional, jockeyed for the best vantage point. The theme:" Alassio, non solo estate" (not only in summer) was emblazoned on tee shirts and banners.

At the end of the runway, many chairs were reserved with paper signs attached for the various shops. Rita and a few ladies we knew from town were at tables near an impromptu stage. They were being arranged for later refreshments. There was a phalanx of speakers, electronic boxes and a DJ wearing a headset. A dapper and athletic suntanned gentleman in a themed tee and khakis, the host and emcee, was conferring with a few ladies we didn't know. We later learned he was the town's Minister for Tourism and the long time President of the Yacht Club. From the enthusiasm and delivery, perhaps in a prior life he had been a carnival barker or auctioneer. A long trailer was set up next to the promenade for the models to dress and change.

The town and/or the trade association had contracted with a modeling agency from Milan, and the dozen or more models were very young and beautiful. The professional cadre was supplemented by a smaller group of young local children, perhaps those of the shop owners.

Not too long after the appointed time, the emcee turned on his microphone and heartily greeted those sitting in the beach chairs, and curious onlookers along the boardwalk. He rambled on, and even though it was all in Italian, we could tell he was thanking several dozen people for various contributions to the festivities.

Eventually, after a nod from a lady standing at the entrance to the trailer, he asked us all to welcome "le ragazze e ragazzi di Vaniglia!" Vanilla was a wonderful little shop offering beautiful home furnishings and gifts. Half a dozen children, all pre-teens came out of the trailer draped in bathrobes, beach towels and pajamas. Some were clutching stuffed animals.

They got a rousing round of applause, and smiled back at us with fear turning to fun and triumph. They had been taught a little about how to walk on the runway, and some did it more stylishly than others, but they all added refreshing informality to the event. Kids and stuffed animals sell!

Then. bed sheets, bath towels and fancy linens were also draped on the first of the professional models. They walked on the runway with panache. For more than an hour, the town's fanciest dress, shoe, and jewelry shops, beach ware and hand bag dealers had their wares presented by stunning young ladies with beautiful hair styles, makeup and poise. Most of the models were so pretty that they made even the more outlandish clothing temporarily plausible.

A young popular singer who grew up in the town, but had moved to the big-time cities, was welcomed on stage and sang two or three songs which he had recorded to a sympathetic crowd.

There was no written program, and we followed along as best we could in the high speed and animated delivery of the emcee, and with the distraction of squirming children and sometimes equally rambunctious adults in our section.

It was time for just a few more announcements before a half time break. Suddenly, I heard him call our names! "Alan and Gayle Fridkin: Please come to the stage!" We didn't know what this was about, but surely Rita had something to do with it. We hobbled, as best we could through the sand and shook hands with Mr. Dagostino.

First in Italian, and then in English for our benefit, he told the crowd that the town relied on its many repeat visitors, and that he had it on good authority that we were world travelers, but had been visiting the town for more than twenty years. On behalf of the mayor, he presented us with a metal plaque. It recognized us for our fedelta', (loyalty) to the town. He asked if I would say a few words, and being a lawyer, I did. I said that we had been privileged to see most of the coastline of Europe from Sweden to Portugal and Spain to Greece and Turkey. For us, Alassio is the best, not just for the beach, but for the people. A photographer took a few photos. Rita smiled and applauded, and we smiled back.

The fashion show went on into the early evening. After it ended, there was wine and trays of hors d'ouvres served by young men from the local hotel and restaurant school. We thanked Rita and Egidio and left them amongst a crowd of local people we didn't know. Just a few blocks away we blended into the weekend throngs.

For many years, Egidio was President of the local hotelier's association. As a professional mediator, I saw he had the diplomatic skills and unthreatening nature to be accepted by polar opposites. He got along well with the alternating mayors from parties of left and right. He had both the access, intellect, history and discipline to make suggestions on what was in the best interests of the town. Even the most publicly minded grow tired of the fray. He stepped down during a particularly heated debate about noise from weekend bands in bars along the beach.

We had a dog in that fight so to speak. Staying at Le Terrazze, we were, regrettably center stage, on some nights when the local bars sought a young and enthusiastic crowd. On some "white nights" the bands and/or taped music played on until one or two in the morning. There was usually a residue of inebriated young people who continued to loiter and talk loudly even later. In other towns, night clubs for this demographic were some distance from residential areas. In Alassio, they were cheek by jowl with the residences and small hotels. Attempts to restrict the decibel level of the bands were contentious. Neither side was happy with compromise. It was too personal when your own bedroom is on the front line. For a time, Egidio left these headaches to others.

The town's future, like many in Italy, was buffeted by the country's economic and political problems. Italian tourists have thinner wallets today and have cut their vacations short. Germans, Swiss, British and others have so many options. While loyal fans return year after year, the hospitality industry and merchants need new sources of revenue. Egidio had the vision and discipline to court the Russian market. While some we have spoken with over the years have disliked their encounters with big spending Russians, others want their trade.

Two years earlier Egidio started taking Russian lessons. The following year, he and his son attended two different trade fairs/conferences in Moscow and Saint Petersburg. Now, Egidio was helping assemble a delegation of more than two dozen hoteliers, restauranteurs, and wine and food suppliers. They would go to a major tourism exposition in Moscow with attractive brochures, in Russian, and specialty foods and wines from Liguria. Working with the Russian consulate in Genoa, they invited Russian chefs to spend some time in Alassio. More Russian guests began to show up in town.

A big challenge was fostering cooperation between traditional competitors. Egidio invited us to participate in their "Team Building" exercise last fall. The details were a little vague, but we would go to a beautiful vineyard in the hills near Ranzo, a tiny village 10 or so miles north of Imperia. We would pick a few grapes; meet some interesting people, followed by refreshments and good times. What's not to like? An added bonus, Egidio's long time friend, John, Another American, was coming too.

Our only concerns were what was expected of us and what to wear. Like someone invited to go sailing for the first time, there was anxiety about keeping a low profile and acting like we knew what we were doing, even if we didn't. We have sampled a lot of wine over the years, but have never been in a muddy field harvesting grapes. Visions of Peter Mayle's encounters with hailstones, an old truck with defective brakes, sweating in the hot sun and backpack sized wicker baskets brimming with just cut grapes came to mind. We certainly didn't want to do anything to muck up the harvest or embarrass our host.

It was a beautiful sunny day. Egidio was running late and asked us to walk over to Villa Firenze to meet John. He would pick us up there. John was standing in the courtyard of the sister property, and we were soon friends. He is a Californian of our vintage who has lived in Manhattan for many years. We quickly learned that his wife, Maria, who we would meet that evening, is a Cuban-American. Her Mother lived in Spain when the Spanish Civil War broke out. Her family sent her Mother to a church run school in Alassio to be out of harm's way.

Six decades later, well into her 80s, she told her daughter she would like to revisit Alassio. They stayed at the Aida hotel, and sought information about the Spanish children of the thirties. Giovanni mentioned a local professor-historian who might have some information. They tried to reach the gentleman, but he was out of town. The person who answered was his wife, and she was one of Maria's Mother's classmates! Maria fell in love with the town, and views Giovanni as a brother. When she decided to marry John, after getting Giovanni's opinion, he became a great fan as well. They had worked for British Airways for 36 and 40 years respectively, and have traveled extensively-our kind of people.

By the time Egidio picked us up, we were in synch. After driving the back road via Garlenda, Egidio took secondary roads climbing into the hills. In half an hour we pulled up to a small parking lot next to Ranzo's town hall. It was surprising to us that a town of less than 600 people had a town hall, and a beautiful old chapel-church.

Thirty or forty people were milling around, and others were trickling in. Egidio introduced us briefly to the lady mayor; and the manager of the fanciest hotel in San Remo. There were owners of restaurants we knew, proprietors of vineyards, and some politicians. Natasha, Egidio's Russian instructor was there. She was the wife of a Russian engineer who worked with the Piaggio Aviation Company in Finale. From people's stylish casual dress, this was beginning to look like a cocktail party without cocktails. But the presence of a camera man from a regional television station suggested something of consequence was going on.

Half an hour later we were invited to head up to one of the vineyards. We climbed into a small station wagon driven by someone we didn't know. He drove further up the hill, and then a sharp left down a rutted dirt road with a vineyard on one side and a steep hill on the other. After a half mile he turned again, along another trail, and parked across from a miniature barn. There was a vineyard gradually sloping up towards a hill on one side and a steep drop with nettled bushes on the other side descending into a valley below.

Small wicker and large plastic baskets sat along the side of the road. We were offered dark green aprons with a reference to the Team Building "In Vigna", and incorporating the names of half a dozen of the local growers. A few of the real vineyard workers cautiously handed out a dozen small gardening shears or snippers. The vineyard owner gave us a short lesson on where and how to cut grape clusters. Then they let us loose on some beautiful grapes destined to become lovely Pigato white wine, if we didn't screw up.

We took turns, filling a dozen baseball glove size baskets and dumping them into the larger containers, a little bigger than a wine case. The ground was dry, with a few muddy spots avoidable with care. We sampled a few sweet and firm grapes right off the vines. We were no match for the folks who did this for a living, but it was good to be that close to the source of a revered wine. The country side was beautiful and peaceful radiating in the glow of sun and light blue sky. A number of pictures were taken with people smiling and mugging.

After an hour, it was time to move on. Some decided to walk back, and the rest of us were convoyed down to the wine cooperative, a large warehouse, half set up as a country tavern. The other half, the business end, with a concrete floor, had a long metal conveyor belt, a big vertical aluminum silo, a crushing machine and numerous steel and wooden casks for storing and maturing wine. Forklift trucks, boxes and palettes for wine bottles were piled along the outer walls.

We had a brief tour of the building, and saw a truckload, including our grapes, arrive and head to the conveyor belt. Outside the tavern area, large picnic tables were set up for food and wine tasting. There was some logistical delay, but eventually, very young students from the local hotel school, dressed in smart uniforms, dispensed food, and adult members of the cooperative poured the wines. Surprisingly, there were few, if any, announcements, and people were free to mingle or not and enjoy the early fall evening.

Not knowing many people, and not fluent in Italian, Gayle, John and I eyed the exits. Besides, John wanted to reconnect with Maria, who had spent the day at a spa and shopping. They were only in town for a week, and had committed to a dinner at the Aida. At John's invitation, we agreed to head over to their hotel for a drink before their supper.

Back at the Aida, we met Maria for the first time, had a good chat, exchanging stories about our experiences in the town. While we both had plans that evening, we were going to a choral concert, we agreed to meet the next day for a brief shopping trip to Albenga. Our circle of friends had just expanded.

Every visit, I regret my lack of Italian language skills, but not enough to do much about it. In recent years, we would see Senor Giuseppe and his elderly wife, delicately making their way down one street or another, leaning on each other, or sitting placidly on a local bus. Senor Giuseppe was the very first person we met at Le Terrazze. Serving as the night manager, he had shown us an apartment when Silvio Viglietti had walked us over to the property. Now, presumably well into his eighties, he was completely retired.

The occasional grimaces of old age pains would change to smiles when we saw each other. He would often spend a few hours on a stone bench just outside his son's costume jewelry shop in the heart of the budello. We would stretch our vocabulary to the limit inquiring about each other's health and the weather. Despite his cherubic face, I knew there were eight or nine decades of experience I so wanted to hear about. I never did learn about his earlier years. He seemed an ideal grandfather. In the fall of 2013, we walked by the shop many times and he wasn't there. Anna confirmed our worries. He was gone, although his wife soldiers on. Even the Mantellassis only found out about his passing well after the fact.

Speaking of Anna, we finally had our dinner with her and her boyfriend, Alberto. We could tell how much they cared for each other. They seem to both love and be limited by the town. There are deep layers of family ties and business relationships that can be both supportive and stultifying. When Alberto's customers for his custom sign painting and design business don't pay or take a long time to pay for services rendered, one doesn't just sue or drop them.

Alberto's family owns San Lorenzo, perhaps the classiest café in town. His parents and sister work very hard and have earned their fine reputation. Both are from hard working families and see some of their contemporaries coasting or taking advantage of their parents. Both might do very well in Milan, Turin or New York, but they won't leave their aging parents in the lurch.

They have dreams of starting a small retail business together in town, but the rents and difficulty of obtaining bank financing make that hard to realize. At some distant point, their parents may turn over the residences and the fine café to their children, but that is beyond our ken and perhaps theirs. Meanwhile, Alassio provides a safe but limiting harbor for their life and dreams.

Alberto is a man of few, but well selected words. His English is better than he believes it to be. Conscientious and thoughtful, he has some health issues that contribute to his reluctance to travel far. He is a good man.

Despite the barriers of language and culture, we know and enjoy more people in Alassio than we do in our American home town of more than 40 years. In both venues, people are preoccupied with their families, their work, perhaps their worries about the future. We will never be Ligurian or Italian. But in some subtle way, perhaps we have become a part of its mosaic.

OOO

32

Crimes and Hopes

W e have been blessed. All of our travel experiences over 44 years have been good ones. But now, there was a small exception, one that didn't seem that minor at the time. On the way home, we had just boarded a French train in the Ventimiglia station in February, 2012 and swiftly became the victims of pickpockets. In a few seconds my wallet was gone. Passport, credit cards, identity papers and cash were in the hands of fleeing thieves. They also managed to get a change purse out of my wife's pocket book that had quite a bit of cash in it and some cherished earrings.

My first reaction, boy they were damn good, getting a wallet out of my front pants pocket. Then a more sickening feeling took over. It was stupid to have everything I needed in one place, and it was now gone. I had separate photos of my

Passport and credit cards, but was my identity about to be stolen too?

The Italian Railway Police were helpful. They would have been even more so if they were on the platform, or going through the trains as the French do. Four of them were in their office sixty or seventy yards away drinking coffee. The two thirty something perpetrators were most likely foreigners, perhaps Romanians. A policeman showed me a foriegn passport picture that could have been one of the men. That morning, a handle on one of our heavy bags had broken, making its movement awkward. It was excessively warm on the train and I had unbuttoned my topcoat as we tried to wedge our bags in some narrow storage areas. The two strangers began to help despite our refusal. Then, we saw them running down the car and out the next exit.

I filed a written Complaint and immediately contacted all my principal credit card companies. The Police conveniently had the 800 numbers on their wall! Within half an hour, my cards were shut down, after the somewhat uneasy experience of giving my credit card and social security numbers to people in call centers in India and the Philippines!

We were on our way to Nice on a Saturday before heading home on Monday. With the relaxed Schengen borders and our tickets still in hand, we could get to France. But we learned that afternoon that the American Consulate in Nice had been closed due to budget cuts. A several hour trip to the one in

Marseille, one hundred miles away, on a Tuesday (Monday was an American holiday) was needed to get a Temporary Passport. I couldn't get on a plane without one. Rescheduling our flight, at additional expense, and a few extra days in France were minor inconveniences. A temporary credit card was overnighted to me by Visa from Germany.

It is unsettling to have to prove who you are in a foreign country without a passport, driver's license, and credit cards. Photos of those documents, your Affidavit and that of your spouse help to make your case, but suddenly you are a suppliant subject to the vagaries of a bureaucratic machine. Hello, Mr. Kafka.

The Consulate in Marseille is located in an old building in a seedy part of the city. Surrounded by Jersey Barriers, barbed wire and a control booth, one is not quite sure if you are safer inside or out. As we waded through the red tape, I studied historical documents displayed on the Consulate walls. More than 2,000 lives were saved in 1940 and 1941 through the extraordinary efforts of Varian Fry, a private citizen and journalist, and Hiram Bingham, Vice Consul. Fry's exploits have been compared to Oskar Schindler. They arranged transit and exit visas and hid many who would otherwise have been killed by the Nazis. Their efforts were in contradiction to callow or callous official U.S. Policy at the time. As we spent several hours at the Consulate on my predicament, the wartime situation put my problem in perspective.

When we came home, it took several months to sort everything out. It appears the bad guys just wanted the cash. To our knowledge, there have been no other repercussions. As I replaced various documents, each time I heard stories of similar encounters. Each victim I met had the same wistful look recalling their painful memories. Of course, pickpocketing is a perennial and ancient crime. It could as easily happened in New York or our hometown.

The incident hasn't dimmed our love of travel, although we have tried to be more careful. My valuables are now dispersed, and I use a hidden wallet. We have also started using a car service to a less dangerous station when tied down with heavy luggage.

While the pickpocketing incident could have occurred anywhere, Ventimiglia has become a more troubled venue as waves of desperate East Europeans, Middle Easterners and North Africans transit Greece and Italy. Most want to go further, to France, England and beyond. In some respects, that has been the case for close to two hundred years. While most of these refugees/migrants are law abiding, some are not. With plenty of their own problems, Italy is not fully equipped to cope with the uptick in crime. There are more and more boat people now from Syria, Somalia, Yemen and Afghanistan.

There is another culture of crime in Italy which has seeped into Liguria, the Mafia. While Americans think of Sicily as the heart of this underworld, there are distinct crime organizations around Napoli, Calabria and Bari as well. The Calabrian crime families have had tentacles along the Ligurian coast for decades. The Ventimiglia and Bordighera mayors were removed from office over their roles in entering government contracts with crime family businesses. Extortion and infiltration of large projects by criminal elements surface with some frequency. Protection money is paid by some small businesses. The mafia is in our town too. The extent of its influence is not a topic of idle conversation. But it is far less pervasive than in the South. The police, courts and some citizens fight back and they seem to be making some headway.

The mega marina project in Porto Maurizio, central to that town's future, was shut down after embezzlement and shoddy engineering work. A wealthy principal is in jail pending further hearings. Dozens of super yachts for lease sit idle. New taxes give them an incentive to leave. That is probably not the result of organized crime, but gross business misconduct. Several high-end hotels, under the same logo, including one in Alassio, are shuttered. We have heard only vague comments about improprieties.

The unelected Monti government substantially increased tax enforcement. Now, almost every restaurant, bar and merchant provides you with a receipt. Before, many of those transactions didn't make it into the public purse. The former Prime Minister, Berlusconi, was convicted of tax fraud and sex crimes; although it's unlikely he will ever see the inside of a jail.

Still, the good life goes on in Liguria. People are strapped and worried, but there isn't the level of gloom and despair we found in Greece. Unemployment is too high, politicians are feckless and people cautious about expenditures. But they still live with some style and grace. Living next to the sea can be precarious. Mankind has made it more so. Calm or angry, it reminds you that you are alive and fortunate to be so close to the edge.

Perhaps I didn't quite step into paradise 46 years ago, or in all the years since then. But when the warm sun, gentle sea and pastel scenario are at their prime, it is close enough. Add beautiful music, today's catch on the grill and a bottle of Pigato, and you are almost there. Of all the hundreds of ports of call I have been privileged to see, Alassio is the hardest to leave. We can see the imperfections. But that doesn't matter when you have friends and feel at home.

At this stage in life, we go to more funerals than weddings. Some long-time friends are coping with difficult medical problems. Many, but not all, younger folks don't have the time or interest to engage with seniors. We still get up most days with a keen sense of anticipation, enjoying life, physically and mentally. We will continue to do so, until the lights go out.

OOO

33

A Tale of Two Massimos

Perhaps inertia or laziness has gotten in the way. After all these decades, our Italian language skills are limited to menus, music and a few choice conversational phrases. Still, I believe we have deciphered some of the "mentality" of the people, to focus on an English word one of my Massimo friends often uses.

Back at our Italian apartment, I called Massimo Viglietti, and asked if we could book a table on Thursday or Friday. After a warm greeting, in a strange tone, he said we are closed. I asked about the next week. Somberly, he said: "we are closed forever; at least now. I am working in Roma." As the enormity of what he said hit me, I asked further questions. On February 4th, he was taking up a position with a well regarded Enoteca in the heart of Rome. There would be some cooking, and a chance to display his great passion for the best wines of Italy and beyond.

As this sank in, I asked if he had a place to stay and how his wife felt about the move. With some enthusiasm, he said that his new partners had found them a nice little apartment over-looking the Piazza Navona. There were only two windows, but a little balcony and the apartment was only a five-minute walk to the Enoteca. That tony address suggested that he would be doing ok. As expected, he ducked his wife's reaction.

The conversation trailed off. I told him we had many wonder-ful memories of Palma, that we wished him the very best and that we would come to Rome some time and drink wine with him. I told him, as usual, we had brought some *Wine Spectators* for him from the U.S. He said his Father and Mother would still be at home on Via Cavour. I sensed I was talking to a man now between two places. Not only was his restaurant closing, it was also his home-upstairs.

A very good meal and warm hospitality had drawn us to Alassio. Learning this winter that Palma, a 75-year-old fam-ily run restaurant, had closed, hit us with the force of losing a close friend. As we walked the familiar streets of Alassio, we stopped in front of the restaurant façade. In recent winters, they had reduced their hours to three or four days a week in recognition of the fewer people in town out of season. In truth, the restaurant was rarely full. Now, there was a long essay, in

Italian, taped inside the glass door about the new restaurant in Roma and the closure of Palma. Even with my limited language skills, the message was bittersweet.

The next day, while Gayle was getting her hair done, I found myself standing in front of the restaurant and feeling very sad. How had Silvio, Massimo's Father taken the news? We had hoped to celebrate my 70th birthday at this quirky but inspiring restaurant. Suddenly, the door opened, and Massimo stood there, smiling. He stepped out on to the street, in casual clothes, and gave me a warm handshake.

I told him I was sad to see so many little stores in town closed since our last visit just a few months ago. He confirmed that the region and country were going through difficult times. I picked up on the theme and said, "at least in Rome, you will have a large core of sophisticated Romans who will support your talents." He shook his head negatively. "I don't care for the Roman people. But there will be people from all over the world who come to Rome." Massimo had always seemed happy when invited to cook in Genoa, Mougins, Milan, Merano for a few days, but even happier to return to Alassio. His culinary role models were in Spain and France. Now he was packing his bags, leaving the small town perhaps for good.

As we talked, his Father came by, back from a walk with his elderly dog. Silvio seemed frail but composed. He gave me a warm greeting and handshake and stood silent, listening to his son. After a few minutes, he excused himself and went into his house.

I asked Massimo how his Father felt. He said: "he understands, and supports me." Three generations of Vigliettis had presided over countless celebrations in their restaurant. No one went to Palma for an everyday meal. But, in truth, Massimo took the restaurant in a direction more appreciated by "stranieri" or outsiders, the French, Germans, Swiss, Russians and wealthy people from Milan and Turin. Many Alassini did not like Palma's theatrical and modernistic riffs. They prefer traditional cooking. Over time, there were fewer of those wealthy visitors coming to Alassio with fat wallets. Palma had earned two Michelin stars. After a few years, Michelin took one away. Massimo once told me that they had suggested he should spend more to upgrade the dining room. They apparently didn't have Italian bankers.

Massimo said on his blog website: "all things have a beginning and an end." Besides a poignant tribute to his grandparents and parents, his January 11 entry reflects: "now we turn the page." "The Palm is not dead, nor closed, the Palm is us, the Viglietti family in every place we go, not just those four walls that we have hosted and protected for all these years, but our hearts, our passions and our characters…"

He brought the spirit, talent and warmth of Palma to Rome. But Alassio is poorer for the loss. At one point earlier in his blog he spoke both of guarding the house and sometimes being caged by it. Rome would be a new stage on which he would prevail.

Over the years, I saw small signs of rebellion and some despair: an earring; briefly, a Mohegan haircut; more permanently, an extensive tattoo covering one arm. Losing the second Michelin star really hurt him. With his own restaurant at an impasse, he dabbled with designing menus for others. But he was too much of an idealist to work for long with someone else, especially when they were perceived as cutting corners or not living up to their commitments.

A few years ago, Silvio wrote a little book about the early days of the restaurant. Now there is a second small book, a memoir, which I am laboring to read. Much is in Ligurian/Genoese dialect. The book is titled: "*Ma se ghe pensu*", a very telling phrase. It is a famous Genoese song written in 1925. The rough translation is: "But if I think about it." The song is the story of an old Ligurian man homesick for Genoa after living much of his life in Latin America. He wants to go home to Genoa. His son tells him: "don't even think about it." But he does, and he goes home to the city he loves.

Silvio has never left Alassio, although for the past twenty years his son took the restaurant in an avant garde direction, cooking from time to time as a guest chef throughout Europe. The Michelin Stars brought prestige and respect, but not great wealth or security.

There wasn't much more that could be said. Massimo, in his fifties, was leaving home. Italy was in deep flux, battered by economic and political ambiguity. I admired his courage and sensed some sadness. I asked would he be there for a few minutes. I would get the *Wine Spectators*. He said yes, and I dashed back to our apartment. I walked quickly, both ways, and clasped half a dozen thick magazines, our perennial little gift to someone who had brought us so many enjoyable evenings. I rang the bell again, and Massimo stepped out. In a gesture that I had seen so many times, and seemed inherited, he took the magazines and gave a slight gracious nod, not quite a bow. This time, I said: "Salve and arrivederci" as he quietly closed the door. Someday, I suspect, Massimo will come home to Alassio.

It took two years, but Massimo earned a new Michelin Star in Rome.

Some twenty miles away, another fine chef named Massimo, struggled with his demons.

His 68-year-old, second generation restaurant, Lanterna Blu, was buffeted by the same economic malaise engulfing Italy and the miserable rainy weather that had closed roads, derailed trains and gave people another series of excuses not to dine out this winter. Instead of going away, this Massimo had returned home. After cooking in the U.S. and Germany for many years, his father had encouraged him to tie his fortunes to the tony new marina in Porto Maurizio. Or perhaps he knew his dad, well into his 70s by then, couldn't go on for much longer alone.

The Marina's promise proved a mirage, mired in missing money and poor timing. Italy's and Europe's financial problems continue to trim the number of well-heeled diners. Another fine restaurant, that had inexplicably lost its Michelin star, was on the ropes. Massimo Fiorillo experimented with being open fewer days, incorporating entertainment and painting exhibitions and preparing a wonderful, but limited menu. He battled the tight-fisted banks and the capricious taxing authorities, the former unwilling to budge on rent, mortgages or loans.

Without a car, we make it a point to come for lunch in Porto Maurizio on a Saturday or Sunday, when the train schedule made the trip feasible. On the first Sunday, we factored in a longer trip due to a train derailment in Andora. A charter bus took passengers several miles between stations, bypassing the gouged ledge where a derailed train sat forlornly askew. It was the victim of boulders and rubble from a landslide. Fortunately, there were few and minor injuries.

It was a sunny warm day, and a third of the tables were full. Our waitress cheerfully recounted a packed house the night before. Besides a wonderful meal, and a little banter with Massimo, the highlight was a warm greeting from Tonino, his Father. Still trim and cheerful, he spoke briefly about the political problems in both our countries. When we told Massimo that we would love to return the next weekend, Tonino smiled and said: "I will sing for you!"

Among our most treasured possessions are two of Tonino's CDs of Neopolitan bel canto songs with him singing and playing his mandolin. He still has a lovely tenor voice. In the restaurant, on a wall near the entrance, is a charming black and white photo of a young, handsome and smiling thin waiter carrying a tray. Reminiscent of a young Frank Sinatra, the picture was that of Tonino more than sixty years ago.

The week went by, and we looked forward to returning on another sunny day after a week of rain. We would take the 1110 regionale, as we had done a dozen times. We stood on the train platform for twenty or thirty minutes, assuming the train was late, as it often is. But no, they had cancelled that train, and the written schedule didn't reflect the change. The next train wouldn't be for another hour and a half.

Angry and frustrated, we walked up the street, deciding to take the whole trip by bus. It would be two busses, with a change in Andora. Then an Imperia Province bus would take us to Porto Maurizio. The schedules were not well coordinated.

In fifteen or twenty minutes the next bus came along. The trip went as expected until we arrived at the far end of Laigueglia. The bus turned to resume the coastal road and suddenly stopped. Two regional police sat on a wood barrier. Next to it was their patrol car, also blocking the road. Falling rocks on the Via Aurelia the night before had closed the road around Capo Mele. It was very close and below where the train had derailed.

The most striking thing for us was how the police and our bus driver were so matter of fact and unperturbed. Within a few minutes, a small car drove up with a bus company official. He conferred with our bus driver, and then with us and the few other Sunday passengers. A small mini-bus was being dispatched, and would take us over Colla Micheri, an even steeper and narrower road inland, then down and around to the last stop on the line in Andora. It would be a half an hour or so before the bus arrived.

There is no taxi stand in the tiny village of Laigueglia. A faded sign had an illegible phone number. A kindly newspaper stand proprietor gave me a card with the number-for the taxi company. It was the one back in Alassio. But for Tonino's promise to sing for us, we would have abandoned our plans. I called Massimo and told him we still wanted to come, but the road was closed, and I didn't know how long it would take. His response was swift and kind: "it is a beautiful and sunny day in Porto Maurizio. Whatever time you arrive, I will cook for you." "Then, we are on our way!"

The little bus pulled up, and we inched our way over the small mountain. We have driven the road, and it takes your full attention in a car much less a bus. We passed a few bicycles and thankfully no cars on the barely one lane passage. Besides the bus driver and us, there was an elderly lady and a young foreign man, a Tunisian or Bangladeshi, who still had to get somewhere that afternoon.

Eventually, we reached the Andora stop. A half an hour or so later, the San Remo bus appeared, and we continued along the coastal road. Three more foreign young men boarded the bus with us, and in the next town two young Australian back-packers.

In Porto Maurizio, the road becomes one way and heads to the upper town. We didn't know the stops and guessed where to get off the bus. Then descending on nearly a hundred stone steps, we reached the sloping street that led to the train station. From there, it was a short and familiar walk the last two blocks to Lanterna Blu. The trip, which normally takes about 40 minutes, had lasted nearly 4 hours.

It took nearly a week to reopen the road and a good 6 weeks to restore the railway line. I can't say Americans would have done things that much faster. The crumbling of hundred-year-old infrastructure is not just an Italian problem.

Massimo greeted us with handshakes and kisses. A young Russian couple was finishing their meal at nearly two thirty in the afternoon. Four plates of antipasti were quickly placed on our table with marinated shrimp, magnificent whole anchovies that had never suffered the indignity of a can, beautiful buffalo mozzarella and juicy small tomatoes, and a definitive version of Ligurian stockfish.

I won't go into all the details of the meal, although Massimo surprised us in the end with guinea fowl in a white truffle cream sauce, with the "last of the season's truffles." Even more importantly, as the other diners cleared out, Tonino appeared trim in jeans and a chambray shirt. Massimo went to the piano and accompanied his Dad who sang a beautiful Neopolitan love song for us. We wouldn't have missed it for the world. I thought of Hemingway and Chaplin listening to a much younger Tonino at the Cafe Roma in Alassio in the fifties.

We discretely asked how the battle was going. Massimo was angry and exasperated. On Friday night, the place was packed. Approaching Saturday evening, there were no reservations and the phone rang about eight thirty, with a very young voice inquiring about bringing his girl friend over. Massimo told him they were closed for a private party. He wasn't in the mood to cater to an absent minded twenty something couple in an otherwise empty restaurant.

Short, cocky and athletic, he has a volcanic personality and the moves of a featherweight boxer. With a Neapolitan Father and Sicilian Mother, there is plenty of passion. Most of the energy and aggression are channeled productively into creative cooking, the piano, collecting art and biting humor. But I wouldn't want to be around in and argument with him. Some of that kinetic force could easily be transferred to his fists.

The local bank demanded higher rent payments than the restaurant could support. He couldn't get a loan from a French or Italian bank to buy and reopen a closed restaurant in Valbonne where his girl friend is a realtor. He said after he settled some legal matters at home, he was tempted to go back to the Caribbean or the States. In his view the Riviera, and all of Italy, were a mess. It will take years for it to recover. I told him to keep us advised. Wherever he landed, we would be there. Also, we would be back in September.

457

He asked how we were getting back to Alassio, and I smiled and said by bus. Then our cheery and attractive German waitress offered to drive us home. She was meeting a friend there. The return trip, in her mini-Chevrolet, was swift and enjoyable. We learned that she had worked for awhile in Ecuador, knew Massimo from his days running a restaurant in Germany and had now lived in Italy for a number of years. Her English was far better than our German or Italian. At least we knew Alassio better than she, and guided her to a safe parking lot. We quickly covered the parking fees. "You are good until tomorrow morning, if you need to stay that long!"

We said goodbye and she walked towards the sea pulling a cellphone out of her purse.

By now, Massimo was on the motorway to Valbonne and his Greek-American girl friend. There wasn't enough business to open for a Sunday dinner.

A few more years have gone by. Business has picked up a bit in Porto Maurizio. The restaurant in France is still a mirage. We have seen Massimo Viglietti on the street in Alassio from time to time. He comes back faithfully to see his parents. The region is still struggling, but the merchants and restauranteurs admit they had a good summer. They are tough people and know how to survive. Old black and white pictures sometimes turn up in town. They show what life was like when this was a fishing village with some hardscrabble farmers with their donkeys on the hills. Tourism may be a fickle business, but it has brought a measure of prosperity to the town and region.

In the Spring of 2018, we finally returned to Rome. Our principle objective was to dine at Enoteca Parlamento Achilli, Massimo's starred restaurant in the Centro Storico. As luck would have it, one of my favorite and most respected trial attorneys and his wife were vacationing there. They live in San Francisco. Jim and Jessica joined us for an extraordinary lunch. The restaurant is like a wine and spirits library. We sat next to a wall of premium Single Malt Scotch . Next to it was a masterful collection of Barolos and Barberescos. We savored a nine-course tasting menu of small plates. Each was a work of art. Our chef friend continues to explore the far reaches of taste, texture and form. Afterwards, Massimo gave us a tour of the incredible wine cellar in the medieval bowels of the building. The kitchen, unlike his imagination, is tiny and cramped. In the country's capital, he now has a close fraternity of exceptional chefs to work with and compete against. But ever restless, perhaps there is one more pinnacle that he might climb. If he does, we will visit him in another location.

OOO

34

Backwards and Forwards

T he years go by, and many of the memories of our trips overlap. Some are crystal clear and others meld together. In the winter 2014, there were reasons to be both gloomy and hopeful about our town. There were many empty storefronts in Alassio. Some losses were almost personal. We had been customers of congenial places that were now gone. From Anna and Egidio we learned snippets of their demise.

The young and vivacious owner of a fine florist store, Erica, moved on, to a larger city. There are other florists in town, but this was the closest and most caring. Vanilla, a delightful home furnishing and clothing store, closed and emptied in the middle of one night. The owner's wealthy husband was in serious financial straits. Rent and supplier bills went unpaid. Several of our stuffed animals came from this little shop. Another upscale and enjoyable beachfront restaurant, Branzino Laureato, closed before Christmas. It was replaced by a precarious gastropub.

We can get by, perhaps easily, without these shops. But for owners and the city, were these temporary setbacks or worse? The main street through town looks tired. The "Russian strategy" is mired in that country's pariah status and sanctions. Europe's problems, especially Italy's own, have taken their toll. Of course, everything isn't rosy and on the upswing at home.

Our friends, the Scalas, former owners of Doppoio Zero gastronomia returned to Monte Carlo and bought an apartment in Florida. Their little band box shop had been the best of its kind in town. The address has gone through several subsequent iterations, none as good or lasting.

We had coffee with Sergio just before he moved back to Monaco. He told us about their son Luca's visits to hotel schools in Switzerland. He had long dreamed of a career in professional basketball, encouraged by coaches at several basketball camps. But Luca is not much over six feet tall. While playing college basketball in Florida, he also saw the people who were going to make it a career. It was not for him. He was growing up. With a degree from an American college and an internship in a Monte Carlo hotel, he was taking his first steps into the world of business.

Winter rains and mudslides blocked roads and train lines throughout the region. For us, it was a nuisance, but a heavy burden to commuters, pensioners and anyone needing to go from A to B and back at a certain time. Cuts in hospital budgets, bus and other public services further eroded the quality of local life. Layoffs and factory closings added to the gloom. All this meant emptier stores and restaurants.

But spring would come soon and our friends in the hospitality business hung on to guarded hopes. What else could they do? Egidio led Alassio delegations to tourism fares in Switzerland, Russia, Germany and Sweden seeking new business. The veterans knew they could not just rely on their country men. Egidio, Rita and Anna seemed weary.

Even with the economy fraying and the town looking a little worn, it still had much appeal. The hundreds of little Mom and Pop businesses may not be efficient, but there is something good about their intimacy and sincerity. They remind me of the little neighborhood stores of my childhood. The person you buy a pair of shoes from, a cup of coffee or a loaf of bread lives here and has a deep stake in the community. They must please their customer day in and day out. There are no executives hundreds of miles away plotting marketing, inventory control and cost cutting measures. The prices are higher, but the money stays in town. Still, the inexorable currents of the internet and large distant stores erode all but the most adept. I think of Alessandra and Renata's (the manager at Villa

Firenze) young children, not quite teenagers. Also, the older kids we saw in white uniforms at a dinner at the hotel school or those riding the local buses. But for the cell phones and tablets, they look and sound like kids from prior generations. Will they build their lives here or move on? Will they have much choice?

As usual, the weather always brightens as it is time to leave. Over the border, in Nice, France things seem more prosperous, vibrant, but less friendly. The restaurants were full, and there is more traffic in stores.

On our next to last night in Nice, Sergio and Luca drove over from Monte Carlo and met us for coffee. Luca was at the Hyatt in Monte Carlo and this was his one day off. That first job away from home opened his mental landscape. We hadn't seen him in a year. He still beamed with youthful enthusiasm. So far, he was enjoying the hotel, working long hours and absorbing experience like a sponge. Handsome, clean cut and at ease with his Dad and us, he would thrive on either side of the Atlantic.

The Scala's attachment to Alassio was more transitory than ours. They were originally from Piemonte. They like Florida, and might well be the next Italian family to become Americans. Both Sergio and Luca see more opportunity in the states. That is good news for us, bad for Italy. The family's jewelry business, with suppliers in Asia, can be anywhere Sergio chooses.

As we headed home, a brash new Italian Prime Minister began his term. His bold but unproven plans to rescue Italy from economic drift were commendable, but could he deliver? When we return in September we will see if things have changed.

The sea is both timeless and transient. The jigsaw puzzle of people and businesses that form our town, memories and future experiences, meld in the drifting sand, waves, sunrises and sunsets.

OOO

35

Changing Tides

E ugenio Rabolli is an ebullient and athletic looking fellow who hasn't slowed down in his early
seventies. His business card reads: "Taxi No. 1"
followed by four bullets in Italian: Serious; Courteous;
Enthusiastic; Punctual. They are all true. Elected by his
peers as President of the Alassio taxi driver's union,
you won't find him languishing at the train station
stand. He has longstanding customers, like the Mantellassis. For years he drove Rita's Mother back and
forth to or from Milan and Alassio when ill health and
a wheelchair ruled out the train. Egidio mentioned that
Eugenio owned a large garage in town for many years.
This was his second or third career.

Eugenio bounded into the lobby of the Hotel Le Grimaldi
in Nice ten minutes ahead of schedule and before 2. He gave
us a smile and greeting that politician's can only approximate. His English is as limited as our Italian, but we all do

marginally better in French. At the curb was his brand-new Renault Grand Espace. After the mugging incident in Ventimiglia a few years back, we used a French van service to Bordighera and then rode the rest of the way by local train. Last winter, rail service was interrupted by mud slides and a derailed train. The Mantellassis suggested Eugenio. He drove us to Nice for about the price of the partial trip with the French service. We were ready for another transit in September.

Not wanting to ride in silence, I teed up topics with my few words or phrases of Italian. Eugenio cheerfully launched into a charming response often underscored with sound effects, facial gestures and even hand movements, one hand on or near the wheel. We never felt at risk, as I suspect he has as many miles under his belt as a Greyhound bus driver. We glean a little of what is going on in town and in the country from roughly translated on line newspapers. Google Translate gives you the gist if not a precise rendition. I asked about the reopening of the town pier; how the new mayor was doing, whether Berlusconi was gone for good; what he thought of Prime Minister Renzi. How he liked his Renault Espace was a safer topic. The banter was cheerful and much like a parlor game in a foreign language.

As we left the motorway in Andora we learned that it was Eugenio's home town, although he had lived in Alassio for many decades. "A quiet town with a good beach" was his observation on Andora, and we agreed. There were many cookie-cutter 4-6 floor apartment complexes, neat, clean and austere, Most seemed vacant, perhaps summer second homes. Andora had always seemed bland to us. But the beach was beautiful and the hinterlands have character.

We had made very good time. So much so that Gayle didn't want us to show up before the requested check in time. We asked Eugenio to drop us off at the crossroads of Via Dante and via Torino. We said we would wait at Café San Lorenzo. He beamed with real emotion. The owner of the Café, Alberto's father, was one of his best friends, underscored briefly with clasped hands next to his heart.

It is a small town of many connections. San Lorenzo is the classiest café in town on the prettiest street. The waitresses wear a smart and conservative uniform and always provide service with a smile. We asked Eugenio to join us for a coffee, but he gracefully declined. We wheeled our bags down the short pedestrian street and piled them next to a large planter at the ocean end of the café. The owner's daughter, a gracious, attractive but tired looking lady in her forties greeted us in excellent English: "welcome back!" We ordered freshly squeezed orange juice and savored the sea view.

Within minutes, Rita rode by on her bike and stopped for a hug. We asked her how she was and she proudly showed us a scar on one knee. The first of two knee surgeries were done. Hopefully, that meant more freedom and less pain. After a few moments and a nod, she rode on, stopping at the other end of the café to have a macchiato with the owner's wife. Gayle nudged me to pay quickly. I stood up and walked to the inside register. Not quick enough! Rita had taken care of our tab.

A few minutes after four we walked into the Residence's busy lobby. Two large families, with a dozen or so bags, boxes and fidgety children were checking in. We knew the drill. Egidio was politely doing the honors. A tall young man waited by a large luggage cart to assist.

After a warm greeting, we were soon in our usual apartment on the third floor overlooking the strand. The narrow promenade below was full of an exubereant crowd, the beginning of the early evening passegiata.

Gayle unpacked and I scooted down the back stairs with a small list of needed groceries and supplies. Some were bought at Billa, the large and impersonal supermarket, and choicer items at the little gastronomia, La Piazetta. There, the welcome was personal and genuine. Across the street, I peered into the tiny windows of the little corner Polleria, the chicken rotisserie place hoping to see Renato, the silver haired owner. His wife and son smiled and gave the same cheery greeting, "Buona sera, Amerika!"

After the bags were empty and stored, we walked to Bar Impero on Via Dante for an early evening cocktail. Strange, all of our staff friends were gone. Someone new was behind the bar. The window displays had changed. They had switched

470

from Lavazza to Illy coffee, the equivalent of changing allegiance from the Yankees to the Red Sox, or vice versa.

From the on line newspapers, I knew the iconic 75 year old Bar Roma was now managed by the new owner of Café Mozart. Perhaps he was no longer involved with Bar Impero. Yes. There were a lot less people in the outside covered area. Inside was deserted. The next day, Egidio confirmed a change in management. The building owner raised the rent and the Mozart people left. Now a son and other relatives ran the café, and Egidio hinted they really weren't up to the task.

It was a warm and glorious Saturday evening. Gayle always relishes the chance to eat outside. Next door to Le Terrazze is the cheery and nautical decored Barcala Mare. Our favorite waiter, from Ecuador, greeted us and gave us the last outdoor table not already booked. Beautiful fresh anchovies and fine sea bass fillets helped to celebrate our homecoming.

Twenty and thirty somethings were in their full glory on a Saturday evening. As the bars filled and the recorded music became louder we returned to our apartment. We closed the doors and amped up the A/C and television. The sound of the waves would have to wait until the wee small hours.

The next day, Egidio confirmed that he had won his noise enforcement law suit against Rudy's Café. Standing next to his neighbor in court, he told the judge that he respected the bar trying to satisfy its customers. But he too had to protect his guest residents. Loud bands and music until 2 or 3 in the morning was not what his patrons (and his own family) appreciated. A city noise ordinance wasn't being followed. Rudy honored the court ruling. Indeed, his apartment was above Ristorante Recantu next door and equally impacted by the sound his sons were inflicting on us. I was happy to see all of the Mantellassi family, at various times, again buying some of their coffees next door.

As our first week progressed, we were curious to see what changes, if any, had happened in town over the past 7 months. Businesses come and go. Perhaps that is trivial. But we see the changing contours of the community. Two deaths and a serious illness brought great sadness.

We would not see Renato at the Polleria again. He had passed away suddenly in April after a short and severe illness. We miss this kind and hard-working gentleman. We learned he was filled with great joy and anticipation of welcoming his first grandchild this December. At least on this planet, he didn't have that opportunity. While his wife doesn't speak any English, his son does. I told him how much we respected his Father and felt privileged to know him in a small way. I will always remember his little salute when we had an espresso delivered from Bar Impero as we waited for our evening chicken; or how he would add some Gorgonzola cheese gratis to our order, especially when my wife was there. A man with a painful limp, we saw him bicycling to work and standing long hours in the tiny shop, never complaining.

Deep in the budello, we looked for the corner store with the endless supply of Italian tschotchkes and the little hunch-backed ancient man who seemed to live in the shop. The store was bordered up, from floor to ceiling with the metal blinds one might see in the Bronx or another precarious neighbor-hood. The store had always been open, often into the mid-evening. We never found out for sure, but certainly he was ill or deceased. Retirement wouldn't have been in his vocabulary. The next year, an antique store opened in that space. No more tschotzkes.

The San Lorenzo owner's daughter, our favorite waitress and first official greeter for several years at the cafe, became gravely ill. She had grown faint on a Saturday evening or Sunday and fallen down a flight of steep stairs. She was in a coma at Santa Corona Hospital in Pietra. There was only marginal improvement by the time we left four weeks later. As Anna put it, "in just a few moments, their whole world had changed." None of us are still under warranty. But this seemed an es-pecially cruel affliction for a hard working and decent family that have faced many other medical burdens. Fortunately, after many months she made almost a full recovery.

As we strolled through the town on a sunny day we ran into Silvio Viglietti, Massimo's father, walking slowly near the Café Roma. He seemed much older and frailer. He greeted us warmly and directly by name. Animated, he told us a little about his son's exploits in Rome and that he was cooking in Mougins as a guest chef that weekend. After a few minutes his energy faded. He nodded to us, turned and continued his walk. Newspaper clippings about Massimo in Rome were taped to Il Palma's door. We saw Silvio a few more times, but he seemed distant, lost in thought or reverie. One fine day he was siting on a park bench, alone, across the street from his once elegant and famous restaurant. We didn't see his elderly dog and assumed the worst.

Beyond the necrology and critical list, we looked to the health of local businesses. As usual, we went to some of our favorite restaurants, to visit with the chefs and savor their handiwork. At Babette, the lovely waterfront place in Albenga, Fabio Bonavia greeted us warmly. He had moved from the center of Albenga to a beachfront setting next to an upscale Residence. Fabio is an intense perfectionist in the kitchen and a gracious host.

On a quiet and sunny Monday afternoon, and after a fine meal, he confided that his second restaurant, La Gritta would be closing. The landlord wanted to increase the rent. With taxes of nearly 55%, hospital and public services in decline, he wasn't sure if he would stay in Italy. There were business opportunities in Singapore and Dubai that he was looking into. He said he loved his country, but its future was uncertain.

Back in Alassio, a rumor proved true. Chef and restaurant owner Gianpiero Colli was considering moving on to a new luxury hotel under construction in Monte Carlo. For 20 years, Sail Inn had been a bastion of high quality dining. Perhaps, like Massimo, the chance to perform on a larger stage and the limited local rewards might tip the scales.

By our next visit, the Monte Carlo opportunity had melted away. Gianpiero was still keeping his patrons happy at Sail Inn. Fabio soldiered on in Albenga, perhaps having second thoughts about venturing half way around the world for a new and risky start.

The warm sunny weather, decreasing crowds, and the beautiful beach are always alluring. We walked a few yards over to the narrow entrance to Bagni Selin. From the promenade, the beach concessions all looked much the same, except for different colored umbrellas. Several years back we had asked Egidio for his advice as to which beach concession to choose. While diplomatically mentioning three or four, he gently suggested Selin, "a nice family; they will take care of you-and they speak English".

It was the family of the Swedish lady we see most days at Rudy's. She once mentioned she was from Gothenburg. Along with her late Italian husband they were the proprietors of Selin. Now it is in the hands of her daughter and son in law. Grandmother often minds a starry eyed two-year-old. Her granddaughter is very pretty, with a sometimes-rambunctious temperament. She is a beachcomber in training.

How all these businesses carry on for generations is a somewhat opaque mystery. Pressure builds for Italy to become more competitive. These franchises are supposed to be put out to more competitive bidding. But the date for that change keeps receding into the future.

The price for the privilege of using a nice beach chair, umbrella and the changing booths and shower in most of these concessions is on an itemized card at the front. But it is also somewhat variable. Are foreigners charged more? Are you charged less if they like you or if it is a quiet day? The fee is often "black". It is unlikely you will get a receipt. Yet, I have never seen the Guardia Finanza on the beach.

It is a long, shallow and gentle slope to deep water. The sea is often nearly as placid as a lake. The water is fairly clean, but agricultural runoff in Albenga and a less than adequate sewage treatment system in the region raise questions. Alassio's is not and as far as I can remember never has been a "Blue Flag Beach" although its Marina has qualified for that designation.

John and Maria were in town, now both officially retired. We were all invited for dinner at the Mantellassi's apartment. After a vigorous barked greeting, all four dogs quietly settled into separate corners. As usual, Egidio was the chief narrator, orchestrating a cheerful conversation that ebbed and flowed with many delicious courses. Some had been cooked by Rita and some by him. Maria and Rita kept bantering in a mix of Spanish and Italian. John took pictures of every course. Soon, it was nearly 11 PM. Knowing our hosts had to go to work the next day, we guests bid good night.

With much depressing news in town, we headed for Moglio in the hills. As the time for the mini-bus departure approached, a dozen mostly elderly ladies appear. The cheerful driver knows them all and greeted and bantered with them like longtime friends. Some need assistance up the steep bus steps. A few times we stop at unmarked places to allow one of the ladies to depart. They smile and wave and slowly, sometimes painfully, totter towards some ancient apartment or cabin.

A few buses go on to more distant towns, Stelanello and Testico, but frankly we have never seen any passengers beyond Moglio. The bus backs in the narrow parking area next to the village trattoria. After ten minutes, usually with no returning patrons, the bus heads down the hill.

Across the street is a beautiful 120-degree view down through a steep valley. Alassio, its beaches and ocean are arrayed in postcard perfection. In the foreground is a large grassy terrace with small olive trees and metal sculptures of animals made from automobile and other recycled parts. I can't tell if it is a commercial or amateur artist's residence.

The trattoria had changed hands and we had heard good things about it. Just before one, half a dozen workers were spread out at rustic outdoor tables under a trellis. Several drank coffee or beer and two dug in to generous plates of pasta with pesto. In the U.S., they would be wearing jackets or sweatshirts with the name of their company and phone number, and perhaps an unrelated baseball cap touting a motorcycle or beer brand. The people and attire were similar.

Inside a nattily dressed gentleman nodded and said we could eat in the bar or on the terrace. On a sunny fall day, we chose outside. The coffee drinkers had left. Without our asking, our host brought a small menu in English. It proudly noted that they used local ingredients and baked their own bread. Their rabbit stew was earthy and delicious.

After lunch, instead of waiting for a bus, we ambled down the steep and winding "red cross" trail. The partially hidden steps, streets and lanes descend sharply with long metal drains to tame occasional torrents. On short stretches the trail rejoined the main road. During the early afternoon hours, there was little traffic nor signs of human life. Solid stone apartments and small houses were mute, not revealing who or what was within. We stopped briefly and silently in the empty and simple 18th century church that smelled strongly of incense. The sun grew more intense. We welcomed the intermittent shade of tall trees. Closer to town, motorcycles and small trucks were aroused from midday stupor. Ducking traffic became more of a chore. Around the last of several dozen bends, we reached the railroad track. Alassio was now fully awake.

It is just a faded resort town. We could be critical of it's and Italy's political and economic drift. Without our longstanding friends there, perhaps it would be interchangeable with many other towns. But like friends and family anywhere, it's those people who make it palpable and real. A web of caring and trust makes one feel accepted, at home, and willing to believe in the community's viability.

We are not entirely oblivious to many family and social scars and prejudices. They underpin this place like any other. Some courtesies may just be the natural response of a town wedded to the hospitality business and living too close to be mean to people. But others are genuine. We feel content and reflective here. We and our friends have grown older, sometimes sadder or mellow. As hard as we try, we may never know this place more deeply than we do now. Having gone only half native, we glimpse sensitive issues and complex personalities invisible to more transient travelers. Even with our poor language skills, the beauty or banality of most everyday exchanges are often gleaned. We think of it as our town and we have a stake.

OOO

36

A Place in the Sun

A particularly nasty winter gripped New England and elsewhere in 2015. Two-thirds of the way through the following January we flew to Nice, briefly transiting the winter cities of Boston and Paris. The intense light and festive ambiance of Nice is reliable and mesmerizing. Two days pass quickly, with walking, fine dining and window shopping.

Saturday afternoon, an Italian taxicab pulled up to our hotel on schedule. It was not Mr. Ribolli, but one of his colleagues. Eugenio was sick and had sent him in his stead. The driver had my business card with the appointed time written on it.

We knew this gentleman from past trips to or from the Alassio railroad station. He was a good decade younger than Ribolli and had a better command of English. Personable, but quiet, he drove with confidence and skill. Despite a very wet December and January, the roads were clear with no signs of major rock or mud slides. The trip was quick and comfortable.

As the taxi threaded its way into Alassio, we saw preparations for Saturday evening. Shops, cafes and restaurants had handwritten signs luring weekend strollers. Nearly every shop was plastered with large "Saldi" (sale) signs. It was the lean month after Christmas.

In Le Terrazze's lobby, a German family was checking in. There were two animated toddlers and a pyramid of luggage, small bags, strollers, etc. Egidio was in full professional mode, but raised a hand in greeting and gave us a personal smile.

When it was our turn, he insisted on helping with our luggage. On a second trip up to our apartment, he delivered two tall orchid plants, a welcome gift from Rita. There was time for a few quick questions. Most importantly we learned that Franco's daughter, from Café San Lorenzo, was making slow but significant progress in a hospital near Modena. She had recovered consciousness, recognized her family and friends, but was still having trouble with short term memory. Since she had been in a coma for several months, this was good but cautious news.

Unpacking and provisioning followed our routine. I darted through the budello to pick up a few groceries. Passing our favorite little chicken rottiseria, I looked through a little window and saw Renato's wife and son busy inside. Startled, I saw Renato standing outside the door! He was in a beautiful oil painting hung in the window. It was done by the wife of the owner of the two Barcala Restaurants. We admired her paintings, and have one of her quilts, thanks to Rita. Everyone who knew Renato respected, and many loved the hard working and gentle man. The painting captures his spirit. We can never go there without thinking of him.

In such a small town, we vote every time we choose a restaurant, shop in a store, decide to stay or go on a field trip. The Euros in our purchase help a family or people we know. There is that small business impact everywhere we go in Italy, but here it is more personal.

Thus, our first dinner was at Barcala a Mare, next door to Le Terrazze. The owner and our favorite waiter greeted us as old friends. It was simple fare, Ligurian seafaring peasant dishes, fresh anchovies, pasta with clams and a bottle of local Pigato wine. There were just a few local couples at the restaurant at this sleepiest time of year in the resort town.

Almost immediately, we knew there would be a small problem. Rudy's Café was closed for renovations. Our favorite café and sometimes watering hole, now was a construction site. For most people in Europe, their café in France and Italy, their pub in Ireland and England, is their living room and private club. While we always tried to spread some business around, we usually felt guilty having a cappuccino or gin and tonic elsewhere. Now there was a perfect excuse to experiment. Rudy had left the supervision duties to his two adult sons, a somewhat scary thought. Still, a work crew appeared every morning. In the dust and pounding, floors and walls disappeared while the ultimate contours and objective of the work seemed obscure.

The entourage of elderly ex-pat widows and wives who met each late morning had set up temporary court at Why Not, more a bar than café, just a few doors down on the beach. Behind isinglass curtains, and in a somewhat utilitarian setting, at least there was a partial view of the water. The service was courteous and they made a respectable cappuccino. One very kind waiter was someone we knew from when he worked at three other places in town.

While there were a few new stores, many more were closed or closing, "cessation de activita" in the local terminology. Like the death notices posted on bulletin boards, there was something quite sad about those empty storefronts. All the hard work, personal and commercial transactions that transpired there were gone and only an empty shell remained.

That first Sunday was the Mantellassi's wedding anniversary. We gave them a bottle of champagne and a card. On a chilly night, we walked several blocks to dine at a fine Thai restaurant. The Alassio owner, with a Thai lady chef, is a store of local knowledge and gossip. He is very fluent in English and more importantly a pleasant and good-humored host. He welcomed us warmly, as he always does.

Alternating daytrips away and minor chores in town filled our pleasant and unstressful routine. Sunny days with temperatures in the fifties encourage walks and exploring. Without a schedule, the delays and deterioration of train and bus service merit a shrug. A ten to twenty minute "retardo" is no big deal. It is almost Caribbean time.

Egidio invited us for dinner at their house on a Friday night. The dinner guests included their lady cousin who lives in France and two of their long-time friends, Maurizio and his wife, Andreana. He is a food critic and writer for the *Corriere della Sera.*

It was a convivial and enjoyable evening even though most of the conversation was in Italian. We caught the themes and occasionally nodded in understanding. Frequently, Egidio or Maurizio would offer a brief translation and look for our comment. Five medium sized courses, wine, after dinner drinks and grappa flowed generously.

Andreana and Maurizio own a handsome home/B&B in Sicily, near Ragusa, and now spend nearly eight months a year there. They seemed pleased when I mentioned we had been to the lovely but quirky Michelin two-star restaurant in Ragusa, *Duomo.* It is owned by some of their friends. We later learned that theirs is a truly stunning guest house with accommodations in four apartments. It is named *Norma,* fittingly after Bellini's opera. Maurizio, like the famous composer, is a native of Catania and he too loves opera.

Everyone else had to go to work in the morning. Somewhere around 1030 the conversation lulled. We guests stood up and excused ourselves. We took the second elevator down, thanking our hosts for another lovely evening.

For several weeks, I had exchanged e-mails with Luca Scala. He and his parents wanted to take us to dinner, either in Monte Carlo or Alassio. I reminded him that the last train east left Ventimiglia before 8 PM, and we did not have a car. He understood, and said they would come to Alassio. On a rainy Monday night, they did. Father Sergio drove us to a country trattoria/bistro in Cisano di Neva, an ancient village in the hills behind Albenga. The road was barely more than a long mountain path, but the restaurant was bright, cheery and nearly deserted in winter.

Luca was still working on an interim basis at another luxury hotel in Monte Carlo. Sergio continued his trips to China and the far east in search of pearls. The family loved their apartment in Boca Raton. The conversation covered problems with their lawsuit to recover property damage due to a water leak in their former business in Alassio, the high taxes and aggressive tactics of the Guardia Finanza, the political incompetence and deteriorating services in Italy. As much as they loved their country, they saw a potentially better life in Florida. America has benefited for centuries from bright and hard-working immigrants. These would be wonderful additions. But it is sad for Italy.

No trip to Alassio would be complete without a trek to Porto Maurizio and a meal at Lanterna Blu. On a sunny Sunday afternoon Debra and Massimo greeted us warmly. As Massimo returned to the kitchen, Debra seemed elated. "This time, I think it is going to happen!" A closed restaurant right on the town square in Valbonne was up for sale. As a real estate agent and a mature girl friend, she had done her due diligence. Massimo had conducted cooking classes in France, and many expats and French had come to Porto Maurizio to enjoy his exceptional talents. They might fulfill their dream and reopen in Valbonne. "Massimo!" the new restaurant, could be a reality in several months.

We didn't speak about Lanterna Blu, which might close, a victim of the poor economy, inflexible banks, and the paralyzed politics of the town. Massimo's Mother had already moved to Bari. Tonino, enjoying fishing, his cronies, and crafting presipios (Neapolitan creches) seemed content to stay in Porto Maurizio. A 65-year-old restaurant might soon expire. But as with Massimo Viglietti from Alassio, now in Rome, the family spirit and talent might transform another venue.

After lunch, we drank Pro Secco. We toasted their future and they, our February birthdays.

By year-end, Massimo was still in Porto Maurizio, musing about a vacation. At least business had picked up.

Over decades, we have made our observations with a big handicap. We read menus and newspaper headlines fluently. But even an every day conversation is a challenge. Dialects and slang are even more daunting. Relying on body language, context and some English on the other side, we savor the fragments we've learned as talismans of a different culture. We glimpse bonds and grudges that may go back a lifetime. Obliquely, we feel political and social forces at work. Outsiders, yes, but sympathetic ones, indulged, forgiven and confided in-up to a point. If you have read this far, you might chastise us for not learning Italian. As with any procrastinators, we have plenty of dubious excuses.

We choose to be here and care about this place. Our regular trips are and were more than vacations. While not the place of our birth or nationality, it is the place of our heart. That is worth something. Like the British who lived here for a century, and are now nearly gone, we add something to the mix, the fabric and soul of the town. But unlike the British, we have no colony nor group to retreat to nor would we if a cluster of Americans turned up.

The grass is greener, or more tellingly the sea is bluer here. It would be a waste of time and self defeating to analyze affection too deeply. We count the weeks and days until each return. The spell is not broken. Our love adds a tiny luster and contribution that helps the community.

In the fall of 2016, the local merchants said they had the best summer season in several years. Some new businesses had opened and were still alive. A long and dangerously parched summer and fall was followed by punishing wind, excessive rain and mud slides, especially in the hills. Vast quantities of broken trees washed up on the beaches. The debris was carried by overflowing streams and rivers to the sea. The hard work of removal followed, a necessity to preserve the trademark pristine littoral. Like farmers, the resort merchants are at the mercy of the weather,

The latest scheme or business venture for twenty somethings are wine bars. At least three new ones have opened that we know of. Each has some charm and offers up some decent nibbles along with the expected wine by the glass or bottle. All three have survived for a couple of years. That still leaves a lot of empty storefronts. A few more restaurants and haberdashers have closed.

We count the days until our next winter visit. Our little Italian town is comforting and calm, if still not quite home. If not paradise, it's a decent consolation prize. I have no complaints worth listening to. Growing old, almost gracefully, with the one you love is our treasure. It beats any alternative I know of.

We haven't bought one-way tickets and moved to Italy. Every country is a matrix of cultures, traditions, history, written and unwritten rules, government and citizens. We would always be foreigners in a foreign land. Unlike the U.S., there is little tradition of hyphenated Italians. Belonging to an expatriate community has little appeal for us. The art of being a good guest is not overstaying your welcome. More than tourists, and with no strong family ties remaining at home, we could become permanent residents. Maybe we will in a burst of enthusiasm.

Italians make do with a government that is dysfunctional at best, indifferent to to their plight at worst.That seems to be the case on our side of the ocean too. Our friends feel and seem powerless to change their system for the better. Many have a mostly good life in spite of those failings. Many Italians are suffering. Refugees from the Middle East and Africa have even more precarious lives. There seems little we could do to make a major difference. I like to think every expenditure we make, whether it is a coffee, a meal or a purchased present, is a small vote for our friends and their way of life.

For now, we are content to be transients and in limbo. With all the problems we have in America, it is still our country. Our ancestors made many sacrifices to get here and I pledged to defend it for 25 years in uniform. Without agreeing with everything they said and did, I have great empathy for Thomas Paine and Garry Davis and the idea that "the world is my country." Surely, it is not unreasonable to have more than one home on this tiny blue marble in the infinity of space.

When our ancestors came to America, there was no turning back. For many, their lives were in peril. For others, their prospects were dim. Despite prejudices, our country had a track record of letting people in. People from all over the world built and still do uplift our country. We are not ready to give that country up.

37

Italian Medicine
101

Our fall and winter trips to Alassio continue, blurring together without the need or discipline of a regular journal. By late September, 2017 there were both signs of a slight improvement in the local economy and more individual business casualties. A blistering hot summer with little or no rain was a boon to the tourist industry and a burden to local agriculture. Some small stores were closed or closing for good. Restauranteurs and hoteliers begrudgingly admitted they had another good summer season. Now, everyone gives you a tax receipt when you leave their premises. More money went into government coffers. The annual and somewhat fuzzy date of October 1st, when the beach cabanas are supposed to be hauled away arrived. A few warm days and the regulation was honored in the breach. A few folks still wanted to lie on

a beach chair and go for a swim. There was money to
be made.

Restaurants and shops set their own extended closing times
as visitors and business seeped away. A few would close until
a few days before Christmas. Others would take two to four
weeks for their own vacations and/or do maintenance. We
must factor in unexpected closings as we figure who is open
for a given meal.

On a quiet Tuesday afternoon in early October, we hit an
unexpected bump in the road. Quite literally. My wife tripped
on a hidden stair at a modest outdoor restaurant. She fell quickly and hard full weight on her right shoulder on unforgiving
cement or tile. I stood behind her helpless and stunned. After a few minutes she was able to get up to a kneeling position, clutching her right arm in great pain. The waitress, and
a manager, brought an ice pack and then an anaesthetic spray.
Several long and scary minutes passed. The manager asked if
they should call an ambulance. Gayle said no, gathering her
strength. After another long minute or two, she was able to
gingerly get up to a standing position. In some ways, women
are tougher than men. We didn't stay for lunch. As we walked
back to our apartment, Gayle cradled her arm in a "Napoleon
Position" and we both contemplated a scary turn of events.

She toughed it out for a few days, hoping the arm and
shoulder would get better. The upper arm was black and blue,

and she had to hold it tight against her side. It was sore, but thankfully not a source of constant pain. She slept on her back and getting dressed or undressed was a tedious two-person project. That week, we weren't doing our usual touring and gastronoming routine. Several nights, I would bring in soup or simple prepared food from the supermarket or a café.

It was Saturday morning before she reluctantly agreed to my repeated pleas that we seek some medical help. We had kept the accident from our hosts, even during an evening restaurant outing with our friends. But they seemed to sense something was wrong.

Saturday is the busiest day at the Residence, with many guests going and coming. On top of that, Egidio was off on a golfing trip to Ireland with some friends. That made the hotelier burden even greater on Anna and Rita. I went down to the beauty shop at about 9 and briefly told Anna what had happened. She immediately turned to Rita and Angela and there was a fussilade of animated Italian. I mentioned to Anna we would be happy to go to the ambulatory clinic three or four blocks away or anywhere else they suggested to see a doctor. Anna wrinkled her nose, and said that depended on who was there on a Saturday. Rita immediately made a phone call. In a few moments Anna advised me that their personal family physician would visit our room soon! It had been more than 50 years since I heard of Doctors making house calls! I thanked them and went up to our room to brief Gayle.

In little more than half an hour, there was a knock on the door. Anna was there with doctor Pietro Ribolli, a kindly and calm general practitioner who we later learned had been their family doctor for nearly 40 years. Dr. Ribolli spoke little or no English. He gently and thoroughly examined Gayle's shoulder and arm, not forcing her to move out of her comfort zone. With Anna translating, he recommended we go for X-rays at Albenga Hospital "just in case..." -and he wrote out a request for same to deliver to the Radiology Department. I asked Anna if we could pay the doctor and she said no, that had been taken care of. Of course, Rita's doing.

We thanked the good doctor and he left. Anna insisted on going with us by taxi to Albenga. She wanted to make sure there was someone there who spoke English. I knew how busy they were getting rooms cleaned and checking out guests. I told her we could go on her own, but she had made up her mind.

The cab driver was one of the friendly young men who had picked us up and dropped us off in Nice when Eugenio Ribolli was tied up. I asked Anna, is Dr. Ribolli related to Eugenio? She smiled. "He is his brother!" Two very kind men we could count on.

A Ligurian Odyssey

In nearly 50 years of travel together, we have never needed more than a brief stop at a pharmacy. We knew, peripherally that the very ancient hospital in Albenga had been replaced by a new one a few miles back from the old quarter. The reputation of both were mixed, the latest complaints were understaffing and financial stress. In the current scheme of things, it was a satellite for the larger hospital a few towns further east in Pietra Ligure. Santa Corona in Pietra, we understood, was respected for its orthopedic surgery department.

Almost to the agricultural outskirts of town, the taxi drove into the new hospital property through a mechanical wanded gate and up into a narrow and partially covered driveway for the "Pronto Soccorso" (Emergency Services). It was eerily deserted. Behind the entrance was a large modern hospital building, dreary and quiet with no outside signs of life. The synthetic tiled floor, industrial furniture, the handful of staff in light colored smocks, confirmed we were in a medical environment. A lady behind a glass teller like window spoke a little English. She gave me a clipboard with a simple one-page form to fill out and took a photo of Gayle's Passport. Anna took leave and asked us to keep her posted. The lady gave us a preprinted form with a number on it and told us when the number was called we would be next.

Despite stories that I had heard, no one was pressing us for insurance, cash or a credit card. They now had our home address and our address in Italy and not much else.

We were ushered through a door by a nurse or medical assistant and told to sit in a nearly empty but clean looking hallway. Further down the passage I saw two or three other prospective patients. In less than fifteen minutes a nurse or aide asked us to follow her into an examining room. A young doctor sitting at a desk and a nurse, didn't bother to stand up or introduce themselves. They looked at Dr. Ribolli's note and asked us a few questions. The Doctor made a cursory inspection of Gayle's arm. They told us to wait in the hall to be called in for X-Rays. In about ten minutes, Gayle was ushered into the X-Ray room. She returned shortly thereafter to the hallway and the generic chairs. A few minutes later the X-Ray Technician came back out into the hallway and in a cheerful voice said: "It is broken!".

We were ushered back into the examining room and they advised they were calling for an ambulance car to take us to Santa Corona. They again asked her if she was in any pain, and she said no. They put Gayle's arm in a small fabric sling and we returned to the corridor.

There are ambulances and there are ambulances. A pudgy and somewhat disheveled middle-aged man arrived some twenty minutes later. He wore work pants and a pinkish orange teashirt with the Albenga Croce Rosso insignia. The Ambulance Service in Ligurian towns is a volunteee service and they have both what we would call ambulances and taxi like vehicles for those in less acute distress. He was in command of the latter. Kind and cheerful, he spoke about as much English as we do Italian. But we were less impressed with his driving skills. He chose not to buckle his seat belt and tailgated other cars on the Autostrada at 120 kilometers an hour all the way to Santa Corona. Still, he got us there without further injury.

We have ridden past Santa Corona for decades on the train and bus on trips through Pietra Ligure. The older buildings on its campus go back to its early days as a place where the nuns and doctors treated tuberculosis and other diseases of the poor. As to the newer orthopedic and oncology specialties, I had read stories of good and bad medical outcomes there in on-line newspapers. Now, we drove up along the western edge and to the ER Entrance. We followed the ambulance driver, with his clipboard into a very busy but almost hushed place of suffering.

In the middle of the packed intake room, there was a tiny office with two open doors, large glass windows and a sign saying: Triage. A nurse or administrator sat at a desk and was frequently interrupted by nurses, aides, patients, parents, ambulance drivers and phone calls. Our driver stood just outside, waiting his turn to deliver his clipboard of records from Albenga and motioned for us to take bench seats in the throng. He nodded to us and then left.

In five or ten minutes, we were called in. The hospital employee, perhaps a nurse, continued to multi-task. She

499

fielded questions from people who barged in, and answered the phone. She gave us a new clipboard with another short form to complete. After listening to our story, she said in English we were currently sixth to be seen, implicitly subject to more pressing cases coming in. We saw our Albenga clipboard lined up in one of two rows on her desk. Through the glass, we saw the clipboards shuffled like playing cards.

Over the years we have heard that Italian Medicine has fairly high standards. The Public Service does a decent and professional job while under great financial stress and at a modest price to the recipients. Those who want to go to the head of the line, see any doctor they would choose, and can afford it, buy private insurance. They may see the same Doctors, or better credentialed specialists, in private hospitals or even in the public ones through an informal system we can only vaguely understand. Up until that Fall, it was academic.

We spent four and a half hours in the strangely quiet but packed waiting room. It was as comfortable as an airport waiting lounge that is too small for that day's flights. Every half hour or so, a stretcher would be wheeled in or other patients were deposited from other ambulance crews. Young and old seemed calm and resigned to wait until they were called. I telephoned Anna and told her we were at Santa Corona and there was a fracture. She again offered to help in anyway they could. I reminded her Gayle was not in pain, and we would wait our turn.

Eventually, a handsome male nurse or orderly came and walked us further down a corridor, through a glass paneled door and to a cluster of chairs adjacent to half a dozen examining rooms. Several patients on stretchers were there ahead of us and waiting for further attention. Another half hour or so passed. We were then brought into an examining room. A short and pudgy doctor in a white coat, who we subsequently learned was an orthopedic surgeon was seated at a desk and looking at Gayle's X-Rays. He briefly looked in our direction without getting up. Apparently, he spoke little English. The orderly and a nurse did. Without introducing himself, he pointed to a spot on the X-Ray of her shoulder. He then glanced at a book, perhaps an Italian/English Dictionary. In tentative English, he looked in our direction and said: "you need a screw" and pantomined the message raising his right arm up to the left.

I looked at my wife, and instantly read her mind. I said "we would prefer to have treatment in the U.S." I told them we were scheduled to go home on the 17th, ten days later. The nurse and doctor conferred briefly and said you should go home sooner. I asked if it was safe for her to travel by commercial air. They said yes, but with a sling. The nurse said: "they won't let you get on a plane with a cast." I told the nurse, who I trusted more than the doctor, we don't want to do anything reckless, but we really would prefer our own doctors-who speak our language. She said she understood, and would probably do the same. The doctor wrote a prescription for Clexane, to be administered for

30 days to prevent blood clots. The nurse explained that Gayle or I would have to inject the tube of medicine preferably in some excess folds of the stomach or in the back of her good shoulder at the same time every day. The nurse administered the first shot in Gayle's upper arm.

The male nurse pulled a long cloth and Velcro sling from a plastic wrapper. He said to Gayle: "take off your dress." He wanted to put the sling inside her blouse. Gayle said: "I can't raise my arm to do that!" He said "I will put it on the outside, but at home you should do it close to the skin." He looked at me and said: "Watch. This is how you do this." He unwrapped the long bandage which ended in a cloth protective glove. He put the glove on Gayle's hand, wrapped the cloth around her injured arm swiftly, pulled it tight to her side, once round her waist, over the side of her neck and back down to the glove. A Velcro patch held it in place.

We asked if she could take off the sling to shower. He said, yes. The Doctor was already preoccupied doing something else. I didn't like him, and it was more than his lack of a bedside manner and our language. He got up and wandered off and I bent down a bit to read his nametag as we were ready to leave. The nurse told us to wait: "for the records". We sat down in the hallway and another half hour passed. Eventually, we were brought four or five pages of medical records in Italian and a CD of the X-Rays. We asked if someone could call us a cab to

Alassio. The nurse said she would do it, but became distracted by more pressing demands.

I called Anna to update her, but she already knew everything we did. They had called the hospital and had gotten a complete rundown. So much for patient privacy, although we would have willingly given our consent. I told her we would be heading back soon.

We went back to the outer waiting room. After a few minutes I stopped at the Triage Desk renewing the request for a cab. Two aides promised to do so immediately. The cab seemed to take forever to arrive, and we were tempted to walk the few blocks to the Train Station. I kept stepping outside the front door, where several smokers were hovering. But it was getting chilly and damp. Eventually the cab came, and we listened to Italian oldies music on the driver's radio in the half hour drive back to our town.

It was seven PM as we walked through the back streets of the Alassio budello. We stopped at the door of two of our favorite restaurants to see if they could squeeze us in for an early dinner on a busy Saturday night. The first, and smaller one, was fully booked. The other couldn't take us until 10. Both apologized profusely. But our good friends at the informal U Recantu beyond the shuttered Rudy's Café welcomed us cheerfully. We dug into bowls of sea bass filled ravioli and some much-needed white wine.

After the short walk back to our apartment, we tried to get to sleep before the Saturday revelers would make that impossible. Even with Rudy's closed, other bars would have blaring speakers and insipid music. No alarm clocks were required on Sunday. We didn't have to leave our room by 10 for cleaning, the weekday routine. I lay in bed making a mental list of cancellations, changes, insurance and doctors calls I would have to make. First and foremost, I prayed Gayle's shoulder would be repaired with minimum pain and limitations.

Because my wife was still in little or no pain, we planned on keeping her Wednesday appointment with her favorite hairdresser. Sunday morning, for penalty fees, Delta/Air France moved our return flight up four days. We called our hotel in Nice to cut our stay there from three nights to one.

I couldn't reach anyone at New England Orthopedic Surgery on Monday. It finally dawned on me, they were celebrating Colombus Day. No one was doing so in Italy! With the help of the answering service, I did get a call through to our GP and he promptly returned my call. He confirmed my inclination to contact NEO, and assured me that they would assign a very good and appropriate specialist.

The next day we secured the earliest appointment we could with NEOS in Spirngfield. Santa Corona had three Orthopedic Surgeons, NEOS had 18, three specializing in shoulder injuries. Over a long international call, we were only granted an appointment with a Physician's Assistant. He turned out to be smart, caring and competent. When we met him, he reviewed the old X-Rays and new ones taken there with one of the specialist Doctors. Their conclusion: surgery was "neither necessary nor appropriate." They also were puzzled by the prescription for Clexane and didn't think it was needed or wise.

Through Google I looked up the doctor we met in Pietra. At one ime, in another city, he had been convicted of certifying an accident that didn't happen. Perhaps he had paid his debt to society. He was on the payroll of a respected hospital. But I was not impressed.

After three months of physical therapy, both at home and in the clinic, my wife regained most but not all of her range and motion. She is almost as good as new, reasonable wear and tear excepted. We are both mindful of thinning bones and the perils of seniority. But we are not about to sit at home in rocking chairs.

I won't get into a debate as to which medical advice was better. We obviously preferred the non-surgical route. The whole experience caused some reflection. We still love Alassio, most of Italy and France and places further afield. We have many friends in those venues. No matter how many months or years we spend in country, they won't be our countries. At this late age, we will never master the language, dialects, slangs and fully understand the intricate mesh of relationships, friendships and resentments that build up in any small town over decades, sometimes generations. Nor do we have to. As "stranieri" we would never have the standing or full comprehension to challenge or change practices or transactions we thought were just plain wrong.

There have been many intriguing glimpses or clues of the "full picture". As sympathetic and mostly neutral outsiders, we have no direct stake in those burdens of family, citizenship and business that are a hidden web. There is an exemption from taking sides and perhaps forgiveness for inadvertent social mistakes.

Besides the main national language, every local place has their dialects and traditions. Each profession, doctors, lawyers, military, police, criminals, etc. have their own vocabulary, slang, turn of phrase. How do you decipher them from the outside? At least in our country, we can push back, challenge, or demand clarity when something doesn't feel right. Only then would we decide to accept or reject a statement from someone briefly in authority over us. That is hard or impossible to do as a foreigner.

Since the accident, we have had two more long, enjoyable and perhaps less eventful stays in Alassio. We are about to embark on a third. There are more chapters that will or could be written in our journal. But we might as well share this work in progress before it gets any mustier. Perhaps someone else is waiting or ready to discover our town.

OOO

Acknowledgments

Thanks go to the people of Alassio for their genuine hospitality. I have not intended to say anything disparaging about anyone. Any factual mistakes are unintentional and are mine.

Thanks to Professor Jaed Coffin for his broad, objective but kind advice. He encouraged me to cut-away much, if not all that is extraneous.

Thanks to my wife, Gayle, who made it all worthwhile.

OOO